INTERNATIONAL RESEARCH IN THE BUSINESS DISCIPLINES

Volume 1 • 1993

THE DILEMMA OF GLOBALIZATION:
EMERGING STRATEGIC CONCERNS
IN INTERNATIONAL BUSINESS

INTERNATIONAL RESEARCH IN THE BUSINESS DISCIPLINES

THE DILEMMA OF GLOBALIZATION:
EMERGING STRATEGIC CONCERNS
IN INTERNATIONAL BUSINESS

Senior Editor: CARL L. SWANSON
Department of Management
College of Business Administration
University of North Texas

Series Editors: ABBASS ALKHAFAJI
Department of Management and Marketing
Slippery Rock University

MIKE H. RYAN
Department of Management
College of Business Administration
University of North Texas

VOLUME 1 • 1993

 JAI PRESS INC.

Greenwich, Connecticut   *London, England*

CONTENTS

PART III.   MULTI-COUNTRY STUDIES

PART IV.   GLOBAL FOCUS STUDIES

Contents

LIST OF CONTRIBUTORS

Abbass F. Alkhafaji

Slippery Rock University
Slippery Rock, Pennsylvania

Cynthia Bentson

Bentson Associates
Seattle, Washington

Michael Beyerlein

University of North Texas
Denton, Texas

David M. Boje

Loyola Marymount University
Los Angeles, California

Manucher Farhang

Lulea University of Technology
Lulea, Sweden

Merle E. Frey

Rockhurst College
Kansas City, Missouri

Farhad F. Ghannadian

Mercer University
Atlanta, Georgia

Abdalla Hayajneh

Grambling State University
Grambling, Louisiana

Kamalesh Kumar

Arkansas State University
Jonesboro, Arkansas

Jooh Lee

Glassboro State College
Glassboro, New Jersey

Bo Lemar

Lulea University of Technology
Lulea, Sweden

William M. Metheny	Eastern Montana College Billings, Montana
Dilip Mirchandani	Glassboro State College Glassboro, New Jersey
Hormoz Movassaghi	Ithaca College Ithaca, New York
Joao S. Neves	Trenton State College Trenton, New Jersey
Sarath A. Nonis	Arkansas State University Jonesboro, Arkansas
Joseph Putti	National University of Singapore Singapore
Alfred P. Quinton	Trenton State College Trenton, New Jersey
Mike H. Ryan	University of North Texas Denton, Texas
Esmail Salehi-Sangari	Lulea University of Technology Lulea, Sweden
M. M. Shahid Siddiqi	Seton Hall University South Orange, New Jersey
Kulwant Singh	National university of Singapore Singapore
Dan Stage	Loyola Marymount University Los Angeles, California
William A. Stoever	Seton Hall University South orange, New Jersey
Carl L. Swanson	University of North Texas Denton, Texas

Igwe E. Udeh   Grambling State University
                         Grambling, Louisiana

Charles M. Vance   Loyola Marymount University
                         Los Angeles, California

Charles Yauger   Arkansas State University
                         Jonesboro, Arkansas

INTRODUCTION TO THE SERIES

The inherent nature of the world is change. And, nowhere has there been more frequent change than in the arena of business. No area of business operations has remained unaffected by the rapid transformation of the economic environment into a global economy. Consequently, the questions which face the operation of businesses now and into the future evoke issues not even considered a few years ago. Management research, in its effort to address these and other developing issues, has been forced to change as well. As in most fields, the transition from relatively simple ideas to those of ever increasing complexity tends to reflect the nature of their subjects. However, according to some critics of management education and academically based research the response has been too slow. Increasingly, the search for relevant business ideas has moved from the academic community back into the practitioners'. This movement away from what has been traditionally a source of new ideas has prompted many calls for changes in the academic education of managers.

> Because of the increased dispersion of technological and managerial innovation among countries and the need for firms to match global best practice, management training must embody deeper exposure to international issues. We believe that future managers must be skilled in all the following: (1) operating in an international economic, political, legal, social, and information era; (2) operating in a number of national environments and social structures; (3) managing international flows of goods, people, technology, information and financial resources and the institutions that facilitate or regulate these flows; and (4) learning across borders, by which we mean identifying, analyzing, and adapting the world's best management practices wherever they happen to be found (Dertouzos et al. 1989, p. 161).

Each of these areas also has significant implications for the research process and focus of those who educate potential managers. First, the sheer volume of information has created practical difficulties in everyone's efforts to keep up with what is going on. One might worry that the old Ph.D. adage, that as one learns more and more about less and less the real danger is knowing everything about nothing, may contain more truth than most of us might like. Thus, the academic tendency toward greater research specialization may ultimately backfire. This could be particularly tragic in as much as the real demands of industry for broader understanding of global trends, activity, and change suggest that research breadth, that is, cross-disciplinary activity, represents a better long-term value for business.

Second, as more information enters the marketplace of ideas the need for a variety of forums increases. It is possible to question the value of an endless number of publications. This is particularly true if no one reads them. However, the reality is that no single publication can be all things, nor is it likely to reach all those that might benefit from its content. The same holds for most forums in which new ideas are discussed.

Consequently, when the idea of developing a series was conceived based on research presented at the newly organized International Academy of Business Disciplines it was believed that a proximate solution was possible. A large body of new material was available. Part of this material addressed questions, issues or subjects likely to be of interest to a larger community of scholars and practitioners. By selecting from this wealth of information it would be possible to broaden the research base by making available selected papers on specific topics. Thus, the first volume was assembled with the idea of showcasing work on international management under the auspices of the International Academy of Business Disciplines.

The International Academy of Business Disciplines (IABD) was established four years ago as a worldwide, non-profit organization to foster education in the international business disciplines. The objectives of IABD were to stimulate learning and understanding of international management and to exchange information, ideas, and research results around the world drawing upon scholars, many of whom teach and do research at other than U.S. academic institutions. In addition, the Academy embarked on an ambitious goal of seeking to bridge the gap between theory and practice. It sought to increase the individual's awareness of business problems and opportunities in the international marketplace. The Academy's hope was not only to advance knowledge in the international arena but to unify and extend this knowledge by ultimately creating integrated theories that would apply across cross-cultural boundaries.

The inherent problem of publication lag time is a persistent obstacle. Therefore, the editors propose to implement a faster form of submissions for future volumes. Hopefully, we will be able to reduce the time needed for actual production by utilizing many of the same computer techniques available for magazines. Eventually, we expect article submissions to be accompanied by computer versions of each manuscript. Then as a manuscript moves through the review process it can be sequenced into the final manuscript as soon it is accepted. The same process also provides for rapid revisions or inclusions of the author's most recent data. Essentially, we do not intend to be limited by the time it takes to shuffle paper. Therefore, by the time the research is presented a book suitable for wider dissemination will also be available. Each subsequent volume will be a window on current management research as it is developing. Ultimately, we hope that the readers find each volume helps provide insight into current issues, stimulates an interest in new questions, and creates a bridge between the theory and practice of management.

In this first volume, the editors have chosen to permit a variety of reference formats. In the interest of time, each author's article retains the note and/or reference format originally used in their article. Some adaptations were made to facilitate note structures; however, such changes were minimal. If this variety of reference formats proves troublesome to the reader, the editors apologize for the inconvenience. We intend to adopt a uniform approach to notes and references for future volumes. Additionally, the editors took the liberty of making minor editorial changes in some articles to provide a measure of uniform structure throughout the volume. Where editorial changes were believed necessary to improve clarity they were made with the cooperation of the author(s).

REFERENCE

Dertouzos, M.L., R.K. Lester, R.M. Solow, and the MIT Commission on Industrial Productivity. 1989. *Made in America: Regaining the Productive Edge.* Cambridge, MA: MIT Press.

INTRODUCTION TO VOLUME 1

The aim of this volume is to introduce the reader to the complexity and variety of strategies and techniques needed to operate in a global world. An international management strategy cannot be successfully formulated without a full grasp of the different environmental variables confronting any firm doing business outside of its home country. The multinational corporation (MNC) is fast becoming the major single factor in the growth of global trade and investment. The greater the number of countries in which a corporation operates, the more "multinational" it becomes. The dilemma of globalization for undergraduate and graduate students and for managers with corporate profit responsibility is the emerging strategic concerns unique to operating in an international environment.

This book introduces students and managers of business to the exciting and rewarding field of international management. Its purpose is to provide them with some understanding of certain fundamental concepts of management when examined against a "foreign" or non-U.S. context. The book presents some examples of the logic, methodology, and application confronting firms doing business overseas. A group of experts with international perspectives concerning their specialty have contributed to this volume and shared some of their insights. This volume, where appropriate, has attempted to present as many real-world examples as the individual studies would permit.

This volume is designed for the manager with "hands on" responsibility as well as for undergraduate and graduate students. The volume can be used as a reading or supplement to courses in international business. The book can also be of significant importance to managers doing business overseas. Researchers involved in the study of international business should also find this volume useful as a reference for future research activities.

We hope that this first volume in a continuing annual series will satisfy the growing need for more studies in international management. Positive reaction to this first offering will definitely encourage us to carry on the task of publishing relevant articles in a book in future years.

Since it is important to gain new understanding of the increasing significance of international management, the features of this volume are designed to:

1. provide managerial applications;
2. provide real-world examples that add relevance to the analysis presented;
3. be relatively easy to understand by minimizing or explaining complicated terminology; and,
4. present experts' points of view.

The book consists of fifteen original studies in international business, many of them written by academics who teach outside of the United States. Some of these studies were presented at the 1991 Conference of the International Academy of Business Disciplines (IABD). The IABD has and continues to play an instrumental role in creating an environment that promotes learning, teaching, research, and the practice of management, marketing, and other business disciplines, and their contribution to the volume is acknowledged.

The fourteen studies are divided into four sections as follows:

I. Introduction
II. Two-Country Studies
III. Multi-Country Studies
IV. Global Focus Studies

No book is the product of one or two individuals and this volume is no exception. Many people have contributed to writing, revising, and improving this text and the editors take this opportunity to express our thanks to all of them. Our special thanks go to those who submitted their research for inclusion in this volume. The editors also extend their appreciation to our colleagues at the University of North Texas and Slippery Rock University for their support and cooperation.

PART I

INTRODUCTION

INTRODUCTION TO PART I

The paper found in Part I by Dr. Alkhafaji is a stage setting piece intended to evoke the types of questions a changing international environment demands. Beginning with a somewhat historical perspective it points out most of the factors that are now equated with a global economic arena. It then addresses a number of critical areas before focusing on general solutions.

Few will quarrel with either the author's identification of specific problem areas or with the general means he suggests are needed to improve things. However, the complex nature of the difficulties associated with topics such as: competitiveness, quality manufacturing, education, and energy policy is very clear. As each potential solution is applied to business there are particularly strong demands for appropriate time and resources. Unfortunately, both time and the resources concomitant with specific approaches are in short supply within the United States. They are also in increasingly short supply abroad.

Nations in the midst of restructuring, such as the former Soviet Union, lack the needed capital for extensive change. Other nations, such as Germany, are currently absorbed in their own internal difficulties for the foreseeable future. Even Japan may experience greater economic and competitive dislocation in the face of a declining birth rate and increased labor costs. The only certainty is that there is no certainty.

International Research in the Business Disciplines, Volume 1, pages 3-4.
Copyright © 1993 by JAI Press Inc.
All rights of reproduction in any form reserved.
ISBN: 1-55938-538-3

Fundamental work remains to be done in how changes in the global business environment will occur. Consistent with our experience to date in other areas one must also ask how and under what circumstances such changes should be implemented. No less important is the realization that most, if not all, of these factors require the attention and efforts of the entire global community.

WHAT A SMALL WORLD AFTER ALL

Abbass F. Alkhafaji

INTRODUCTION

In our rapidly changing world the necessity of countries to produce, expand, develop, and advance has become overwhelming. International competition for goods and services has gone far beyond national boundaries. The international dimensions of business have not always been a significant part of American managerial thought. Even though American goods and services were in demand all over the world in the past, it was not because U.S. managers were so highly dedicated to international business or trade. The demand for U.S. products was because the words, "Made in USA" stood for excellence in quality and duration. American business and industry by and large have had no real interest or need to compete in international markets. The United States was rich in natural resources and this abundance provided an unparalleled degree of independence and self-sufficiency. The country also had the world's largest consumer market, and led the world in technology and management.

Such a combination of factors enabled this country to become one of the most productive of all industrialized nations. Increasing productivity led to high standards of living, and the U.S. economy became one of the most

International Research in the Business Disciplines, Volume 1, pages 5-18.
Copyright © 1993 by JAI Press Inc.
All rights of reproduction in any form reserved.
ISBN: 1-55938-538-3

developed in the history of nations. It is not surprising, therefore, that American managers were not concerned with the rest of the business world. Business was being concentrated at home, and not well developed abroad.

GLOBAL MARKETING PLACES SHRINKING

International competition has caused the world to become a global market. Through the extensive use of computers and communication, the world is becoming closely knit. In the last three decades there has been a rapid growth of international business and the proliferation of multinational organizations. Although a number of companies have been engaged in this area for nearly a century, the explosive growth in size and quantity of international companies is a recent phenomenon. Today's multinational corporations are different from those of the past. Technological progress, such as telecommunication advancement, transportation, and computerization, have made it possible for management of a Multinational Corporation (MNC) to exercise a much closer central control. In the past, the management of a subsidiary was generally in a localized (decentralized) style. Today, centralized control of management is possible in spite of the distance between a corporation's headquarters and its subsidiaries. The MNC has evolved into a major force in world economy, taking advantage of technology advancement and geographic diversification.

When business activities are extended in an international sense, new challenges and practices are presented to management. Management must first understand the decision to pursue the scope of business activities internationally; and, second, management must carefully examine the interaction of variables which constitute international strategic management. Although the size of our planet has not changed, it appears to be shrinking in terms of the available space and other natural resources in relation to the world population. While statistics do not exist prior to the nineteenth century, it is assumed that natural resources, especially food, were in adequate supply for residents of the planet in previous centuries.

Within the last 200 years, the world has undergone a change that has divided it into the developed versus the underdeveloped nations. This change has occurred primarily because of population growth and the Industrial Revolution. The increased population has taxed the availability of the planet's resources to an alarming degree in some countries today, while the Industrial Revolution has resulted in a depletion of resources because of a lack of foresight and planning, as well as a disregard for a global perspective Myrdel 1961, p. 1150).

Today's global perspective is a result of the need for interdependence between the world's nations, brought about in part because of growing shortages of resources and the technological explosion. Japan is an example today of the critical need for nations to depend on other nations. While that island nation has virtually none of the natural resources needed for production, it has become one of the most powerful economies in the world—producing approximately ten percent of the world's goods and services. Japan has accomplished this through dependence on many other countries to supply the enormous quantities of raw materials needed.

Interaction between nations at the level of ordinary citizens was almost nonexistent as late as the last century. Most interaction was a result of military intervention and conquest. Advances in technology, especially in the areas of travel, transportation, and communications has changed this. The development of rail and air travel and instantaneous worldwide communication have brought the peoples of the world closer in a physical sense. Better understanding of each other has helped to dissipate the mysteries of other cultures and societies. These have influenced international business, making it a most significant, ever-growing, and predominant aspect of the modern world.

THE CHALLENGES TO THE U.S. ECONOMY

The United States is no longer the dominant country in productivity, management, and technology. American industries are losing ground in the international market. The United States has fallen in manufacturing and automobile manufactured for the last fifteen years. Americans were painfully introduced to the growing interdependence and resulting problems in 1973 when the oil embargo resulted in a petroleum shortage, forcing the price of gasoline to more than double. With abundant natural resources, the United States came the closest to being a totally self-sufficient society. In the 1960s, the United States did not need to import any oil for domestic use. But the U.S. transportation system, with its "gas-guzzling" dinosaurs, had become one of the most inefficient in the world. Extravagance was the order of the day, as the American consumer used gasoline with abandon, and larger engines consuming more fuel with no thought of efficiency was a major selling point (Alkhafaji 1990, pp. 3-7).

The shocking realization of this newly created dependence gave rise to a whole new relationship between America and other countries, with a new set of political and economic elements. The United States emerged from World War II as the most militarily powerful and economically developed nation in the world. This forced it to assume the leadership of the free world. Gone was the prewar era of colonialism seen among industrialized European countries. The Soviet Union followed its own course designed to prove that communism was a viable economic system. In Europe Great Britain reigned supreme, and it was said that the sun never set on the British Empire.

World War II changed the situation drastically. The USSR found itself aligned with the Allies. Great Britain emerged from the war totally drained, in resources as well as will. Its colonies demanded and obtained their freedom. The United States reluctantly assumed the leadership of the free world and soon was locked in a cold war with the Soviets. In control of Eastern Europe, the Russians were threatening further expansion of their dominance. The remainder of Europe and the rest of the free world looked to the United States for protection and assistance in economic development (Alkhafaji 1990, pp. 3-7).

Promising to eradicate poverty, redistribute wealth, and provide the basic necessities of life to everyone created strong inducements for the people of newly independent countries. The U.S. countered with economic aid through the Marshall Plan and later through massive foreign aid programs. The almost total demolition faced by the European industrial base and the vacuum this created was quickly filled by a combination of factors, including the U.S. government pouring billions in aid into these countries followed by the entry of U.S. companies with technology and finances. Since the basic infrastructure was intact, economic recovery was swift. The dominance of U.S. companies on the European scene was the beginning of American businesses becoming multinational. Underdeveloped countries lacked the prerequisites of industrialization and had to begin from scratch.

Foreign aid programs experienced problems from the earliest days mainly because of U.S. ignorance of the environment of these underdeveloped countries, and resulted in encountering barriers of sociological—cultural or other elements. While the hundreds of billions of foreign aid dollars over the last several decades has become a political issue many times, it has gotten U.S. companies involved in hundreds of projects throughout the world, contributing to the international thrust. The United States, until the late 1960s, was the most economically powerful country in the world, and its supremacy in technology and management was unsurpassed and unchallenged. Its abundance of natural resources and its technological and management abilities are seen as the main factors contributing to U.S. economic dominance. In addition, its facilities were undamaged during World War II and massive facilities built to supply the war effort were converted to peace-time production. These factors, including the abundant resources, production capabilities, high productivity, level consumption patterns, and enormous buying powers, allowed U.S. business to become indifferent toward international trade. Refusal to recognize markets for their products other than domestically is seen in the auto industry's refusal to produce U.S.-built cars with a right side steering and driving controls option for exports abroad. This attitude permeated producers of consumer items, household appliances, tools, and machines. Instructions were printed only in English.

The U.S. economic dominance led in the 1960s and early 1970s to consumption patterns bordering on squander and waste. Mass transit systems were not developed and the few efficient ones in existence were often dismantled.

The oil embargo in 1973 and resulting skyrocketing of gasoline and other petroleum prices brought the reality of dependence on others to the American consumer for the first time. Assessment and reassessment, spurred by the oil shortage, led to the perception that international business could be an effective element. Other significant changes were taking place both within the United States and in the international environment during the 1960s and 1970s. Japan has made phenomenal economic leaps, challenging U.S. economic supremacy—now second in the world to only the United States the Pacific Basin countries have come a long way and the unification of Europe poses additional challenges.

In the United States, the 1960s ushered in a new era—unfamiliar foreign names like Sony and Hitachi appeared in stores with very attractive price tags. Wary consumers were impressed by the quality and price. Beginning with televisions and spreading throughout the automotive industry and other production segments, the Japanese influence grew. However, it was not until the invasion translated itself into massive layoffs and plant closings that the alarm was sounded. Industries such as steel were unable to compete with Mitsubishi, for example, who brought better quality steel all the way from Japan to the United States and sold it $20 a ton less than domestic mills such as U.S. Steel and Bethlehem whose product was inferior in quality due to the use of equipment and processes that were over two decades old (Alkhafaji 1990, pp. 3-7).

According to Krajewski and Ritzman (1990), during the period between 1948 and 1973 the average annual income in productivity was 2.5 percent, but during the period of 1974 to 1989 it was less than 1 percent. This annual trend has been the cause of real concern for U.S. economists. The annual percentage of change in production of the United States has fallen behind most of the developed countries, such as Japan, Italy, France, Germany, Britain, and Canada. One of the main reasons for productivity decline is the loss in global market share. The United States contains only 5 percent of the world population but produces 22 percent of the worlds goods. This figure, impressive as it may seem, is very misleading. In 1950 the United States produced 52 percent of the worlds goods and in 1970 30 percent (Krajewski and Ritzman 1990, p. 8). If this current declining trend continues Japan will overtake the United States as the economic leader of the world in this coming decade.

By the late 1970s the situation reached crisis proportions with unemployment, inflation, and interest rates all reaching double digits. By 1980 the economic malaise was complete and the standard of living began to be pushed downward. Perhaps the most significant change within the United States was the declining productivity. After leading the world in productivity for decades, the United States found its productivity not only dropped against previous years at home but also lagged in relation to many other countries of the world. Aging machines and outdated processes were only part of the problem. Management policies based on short-term return on investment, reduced R&D, the inability to motivate workers, and the conflict between human needs and the complex, dehumanized, machine-dominated industries that "turned off" workers were all factors contributing to the problems. Government fiscal and monetary policies discouraged modernization, while unions continued to push for higher wages in the face of declining productivity.

The productivity decline resulted in pricing American products out of world markets. Meanwhile the American influence in improved production processes and the introduction of the concept of quality bolstered Japan to a post-World War II high industrially and economically. The secret of Japan's phenomenal success is, of course, its productivity. Other Pacific Basin countries, including Hong Kong, South Korea, Taiwan and Singapore are now able to produce goods of higher quality at much lower cost that the United States and are competing fiercely in U.S. markets.

THE DEFICIT

During the 1980s the U.S. had an unfavorable annual rate of about $200 billion (Ashegian and Ebrahimi 1990, pp. 2-3). The deficit, as of January of 1991 is projected to be in the area of $168.8 billion, or $231.4 billion if the savings and loan bailout is included. The most obvious factor affecting the budget deficit currently is the impact of economic recession along with the huge amount of debt (Wessel and Birnbaum 1990). The U.S. national debt is more than $3 trillion, and in 1992 the United States will spend $210 billion in interest on debt alone. Nations that were considered less developed (LDCS) have a much stronger trade position than the United States. Some of these countries, such as Brazil, Taiwan, South Korea, Hong Kong, and Singapore have increased their role in the international market. Those countries are among the top 20 exporters of manufactured goods while in 1965 none of the LDCs were included in the top 30 exporters. The increasing importance of LDCs in the international market has decreased the power of the developed countries in dominating these markets.

Federal spending has increased considerably on five expenditure categories. Increases based on a percentage change from 1989 to 1990 of these five categories include interest payments (10.7%), medicare (13.5%), federal salaries (18.9%), health and human services (19.1%), and unemployment insurance (24%). The major proportion of federal outlays are mostly on medicare and interest on the national debt. The most obvious factor affecting the budget deficit currently is the impact of economic recession. Along with recession comes inflation, which inevitably creates a negative demand in the economy and results in increasingly tighter monetary policies to compensate for decreasing demand. By issuing tighter monetary policies to control inflation, a higher demand for credit by the U.S. government is needed to finance debt. Although interest on national debt is multiplying at an alarming rate, government spending is increasing in spite of this fact (Koretz 1990).

The effect of increasing interest rates on international trade created a cyclic phenomenon in which devaluation of the U.S. dollar eventually caused other countries to follow suit, displaying that the deficit in the United States impacts the international economy as well. The proof of this consequence was evidenced with the stock market crash in 1987 which complemented the collapse of the European and Asian markets (Asheghian and Ebrahimi 1990, pp. 2-3). Dealing with a problem of this magnitude is far from simplistic. Extinguishing the budget deficit has baffled government administration and economists as well. By devising solutions in order to solve one problem with the deficit, almost inevitably another problem begins to fester. Solving the deficit problem has fallen short of a solution since the administration and Congress have no real plan to eliminate the deficit. One main concern has been protecting Social Security benefits, since the government has been focusing on the retirement fund in order to ease the debt, especially in interest, by dipping into the fund in order to finance its debt. With this government action in mind, a proposal was instituted to give back $62 billion of Social Security benefits over the next two years. The chances of this proposal passing is dim, but a similar method may be promising (Nasar 1990).

Since the United States has been decreasing in its trading position compared with countries abroad, a major focus of the United States on international trade is now concentrating its efforts on exporting more goods than it is importing in order to spark economic trade, increase production, and increase incoming capital into the United States all of which contribute to decreasing the national debt Asheghian and Ebrahimi 1990, pp. 14-16). Another method of dealing with the deficit problem is that if budget cuts are proposed and interest rates decline, the interest payback on government loans abroad create a staggering impact on the U.S. ability to finance this portion of debt (Koretz 1990). Therefore, the deficit problem has a long way to go before it is resolved, if it ever can be resolved. Budget cutbacks, as explained, impact many variables, especially during an economic recession, increasing the dilemma for the United States in finding an appropriate solution.

The U.S. balance of trade further reveals the problems faced by foreign competition. American business and industry have finally begun to realize that if they want to maintain economic supremacy, they must consider the international dimension of business just as vital as the domestic business. As the global marketplace becomes more entrenched the differences between international and domestic business markets become less visible. Clearly increased international business and participation in the global market becomes increasingly vital for the United States to maintain a dominant economic position and maintain its leadership in technology and management in the world.

HOW WILL AN INCREASE IN OIL
PRICES AFFECT BUSINESSES?

An increase in oil prices is a concern to a majority of American managers because of the increases in business expenses associated with the higher oil prices. A rise in oil prices, such as that which occurred after Iraq invaded Kuwait, creates a serious problem for managers, who must try to balance the increased cost incurred to his business with the increased costs he must pass on to his customers. Transportation companies, such as airline and trucking firms, would most likely be the hardest hit, since their profits are directly proportional to the cost of fuel. Their increased cost for fuel would initially be difficult to recover, considering the fact that they will be forced to increase charges to their customers. Even a manager of a simple business would be affected by higher oil prices, since it would create higher costs for items to be transported to their place of business (Buderi, Riemer, and Rossant 1991).

CHALLENGES IN EUROPE 1992

On December 31, 1992, the economic environment of Europe will probably be a lot different than it is today. This is primarily due to changes in the economic relations between many of the European countries. The creation of a single market among the 320 million people in the twelve member states of the European systems will represent "the United States of Europe." Then, later, the likely creattion of several new capitalist countries in Europe will thereby, among other things, bring about a larger market. In 1992 it is the EC's objective to have created a single market among its member states. This means mainly to breakdown (by EC laws) the trade barriers that the member countries currently have. Also the liberalization of capital movements and the harmonization of VAT and excise duties. The European Community will then enjoy an economy of scale and further escalate the global competition. However, realistically it is very doubtful that the single market really will be in function and effective by 1992. This is mainly due to the complexity of such a single market, both culturally and economically (Rentoul 1988). One must not make the mistake of identifying this market with a federal market consisting of non-sovereign states, like the United States. There exists a trade-off between the homogeneity of the market and the complexity/variability of the factors required to service that market. Most homogeneous are, naturally, the local markets (because they have the lowest complexity); a market like the single EC market will be located somewhere below the homogeneity of a mature federal market like the United States, and above the homogeneity of a geographical entity (like Southeast Asia), which is pretty low (Delors 1989).

However, it is obvious that the single market (when effective) will create many opportunities for the businesses within it, that are prepared for the market, because they now have access to sell their products, skills, and services in markets that before were protected by many barriers. American business (and their managers) therefore, face an expanded array of challenges in trying to succeed in the European market and the markets outside Europe where European companies are present. The U.S. multinational companies exported to the EC a total of about $86 billion and imported about $75 billion in 1988 (U.S. Department of Commerce 1989). The opportunities are not limited to goods. Markets for financial services are even more important in the long term as the U.S. moves toward the service sector in domestic and international services. This indicates the importance of Europe to U.S. international trade.

Before the single market the Europeans are facing the challenges always present when competing in a foreign country (i.e., involved in international business): the environmental variables, political/legal, economic, socio-cultural, geographic/demographic, and technological. But with the creation of a single market the businesses within the market have a very strong competitive advantage solely because of the fact that their access to the member countries now will be more or less unrestrained. This is the advantage that American companies will lack; therefore, for example, they will have a much harder time in competition with a German firm operating in Italy or a French company operating in the Netherlands. Also, the European companies will have a much easier time in terms of merging and acquisitions. They will be stronger financially. These are all what could be called advantages created by EC laws. But in addition to this, European companies also have an advantage when competing in Europe with American companies because the European countries also act together in socio-cultural relations. One must remember that the EC is much more than just an economic community, the countries work together and cooperate their efforts on many different aspects. This gives European companies a much better understanding of the markets in their fellow member countries. In fact, many EC countries prepare their business communities for the single market. These advantages are what we could call socio-cultural advantages, or, more broadly, "Local Knowledge Advantages" (Cooney 1990).

THE REFORM OF THE EASTERN BLOC

We are entering an unprecedented era of global economic competition and global opportunities. The reform of the Eastern Bloc has crafted "a new era" for the Western and Eastern countries. With Eastern Europe's political walls crumbling, its economic walls surely must topple soon. This prospect means grand opportunities—and hidden snares—for Western corporations and investors seeking to cash in on the twin revolutions. This in turn gives many industries the opportunity to expand their business to the eastern bloc. The United States must be concerned with International Business Machines and Digital Equipment, that will be strongly positioned to take advantage of changes in Eastern Europe. Mr. Roches, a long-time Eurowatcher and investor, has many ideas and predictions on the Eastern Bloc. Mr. Roches's focus is mainly on the long-term effects of Western European business. He thinks that, "We are going to see an increasing political, social, and economic integration of Eastern Europe into Western Europe" (Rustin 1990).

Mr. Roche's sees more western auto manufacturers establishing more plants in the East because there are favorable labor situations, which will enable them to export cheaper cars back to the West. Hungary, Poland, Czechoslovakia, Yugoslavia, and East Germany are leading in creating positive environments for doing business.

A PANACEA FOR REDUCING THE PROBLEM OF COMPETITIVENESS

There are many things the United States can do to become competitive again. The answer to America's productivity problems is not to simply copy other successful countries' experiences. Rather, the United States, like any other company, should utilize its strong aspects and minimize its weak points in its struggle to be competitive in the global market. Some of the factors that need to considered are presented below:

Improve The Quality Of The Education System

In order to support the dynamic changes in the international market the United States needs to revive its Education system by eliminating its weaknesses and capitalizing on its strengths. This reform has already begun with the publication of the government report *A Nation at Risk* in 1983. Since then, a few states have launched major reforms, about fifteen states now require high school students to take four years of English, as proposed in the national report of 1983. Although these results are not an overwhelming reform movement, it is a beginning, and there are many instances similar to these across the country.

In recent years, international business, competitive management, and other related areas of international interactions in this multiplicity of contexts have become an integral part of curriculum in business schools across the nations. Although courses in international trade and its peripheral areas, as well as comparative international economics, have been offered for a long time in U.S. universities, the interest was mainly academic. The level of emphasis in the internationalization of the business curriculum is a recent phenomenon. The variety and the depth and breadth of courses in this field has increased. In addition there are now majors and areas of concentrations available at both undergraduate and graduate levels in almost all schools of Business courses. The American Assembly of the Collegiate Schools of Business (AACSB) has called for the "internationalization" of business curricula. The AACSB requires that all of the schools that it accredits require students to complete at least one course in international business. The future of business is evidently an international one, and today's business students cannot afford to ignore this fact.

In the 1990s and beyond, the successful business person will treat the entire world as their domain for securing both supply and demand. In such a globalized market, a purely domestic company will simply not be competitive.

Improve The Quality Of Products

To compete successfully in domestic or international markets, U.S. companies need to demonstrate that their products meet or exceed the high customer expectations in a world market and do so consistently. The quality of any product or service must begin with innovation. Bring the old concept of "made in America to mean acceptance" back. This means that American companies must be willing to make larger investments in research and development as well as their readiness to adopt the technology needed. Without this investment, innovation and new technology will deteriorate, leaving the company unable to compete with international rivals. The multinational companies of other countries such as Japan and Europe have proven to be willing to make the long-term investment into research and development. Currently, some U.S. industries are making this investment, and the payoffs are evident in their successful competition.

Improving Management/Labor Relationships

It is imperative that U.S. industries make a sincere and substantial effort to improve the relationship between management and labor. Ways to accomplish this could be to give employees responsibility along with accompanying work to allow improvement in job performance, or present ownership stakes or profit-sharing programs. Eventually, U.S. companies will modernize their management style if for no other reason than to improve their company's productivity and competitiveness.

Promote Alternative Energy Resources

The United States realizes that it can no longer rely so much on oil as an energy source. The U.S. government has to establish an efficient energy policy, taking into consideration the environment and convenience outlining possible energy alternatives to oil. In the late 1970s former Presidents Gerald Ford and Jimmy Carter supported an energy policy. However when President Ronald Reagan assumed office that policy disappeared. One alternative to wean the United States from crude oil is to promote natural gas. There are several advantages to natural gas. First, experts believe that there are more natural gas deposits in the earth than oil deposits and they are distributed more or less evenly around the world. Second, natural gas is the cleanest-burning fossil fuel known to man, and in these days environmental awareness is a must.

A complete change from oil to natural gas would not happen overnight. The people would first have to learn how to decrease oil consumption. This could be accomplished in two ways. First, if the auto manufacturers were forced into building more gas-efficient cars, oil consumption would decrease. Another way to discourage oil consumption would be an annual tax on gasoline over a period of many years.

Emphasis On International Technology And Productivity

With expanding international markets, MNCs have witnessed the importance of technological innovation that will lead to increased productivity. In the past, the demand for U.S. products was because the words "Made in USA" stood for excellence in quality and duration. American businesses and industries have discovered that in order to compete successfully in the international market they have to improve productivity as well as the transfer of technology. The technology and competition in certain industries, such as the automobile industry have been getting tougher with foreign countries attempting to obtain a large percentage of the market. In order for U.S. companies to compete successfully in the international market they have to develop superior technology. In 1987, the combined earnings of General Motors, Ford, and Chrysler fell almost twenty percent. The Japanese were building cars $800 to $1000 cheaper than the Americans. General Motors, in turn, has updated their plants so that they are now perceived as having the most technologically advanced manufacturing system in the industry. When General Motors developed and used robots they began to build cars cheaper and with a higher level of quality.

For the future, U.S. automobile manufacturers are preparing for the use of computerized chips that will be used in producing cars. Chrysler has taken the lead by developing air bags. Technology and productivity improvement, therefore, is the answer to the tough, internationally competitive market.

Overcoming Trade Barriers

This concern for quality must follow the product from innovation to product design to production. The next step in the process of becoming competitive is entering foreign markets where trade barriers have been established. It is obvious that excessive government regulations and barriers will hinder international trade. An important factor to be considered in dealing with the barriers evident in foreign markets is to form a joint venture in which both partners could benefit through access to each others' markets. There should not be a reluctance to use advice from experts along with R&D groups to investigate potential markets as well as partners.

Overcoming Political/Governmental Obstacles

Exchange rates are important factors to be considered when dealing with international trade. Fluctuated exchange rates make doing business in other countries very difficult and even more risky. A possible solution to such a problem is to adopt fixed exchange rates, or quasi-fixed exchange rates as used in the European Monetary System. The most feasible solution is to implement a series of solutions aimed at stabilizing exchange rates. Other goals might include passing out export subsidies and establishing some minimal level of access for imports in highly protected markets.

CONCLUSION

International competition has caused the world to become a global market. Technological progress such as telecommunications advancement, transportation, and computerization, have made it possible for management of a MNC to exercise much closer central control. The United States is no longer the dominant country in productivity, management, and technology. American industries are losing ground in the international market. The United States has fallen in manufacturing and auto making for the last fifteen years. Americans were painfully introduced to the growing interdependence and resulting problems in 1973 when the oil embargo resulted in a petroleum shortage forcing the price of gasoline to more than double.

The United States has begun to fight back in an attempt to regain lost market share and a reputation as a quality producer. As experts attempt to resolve the problems of the falling U.S. productivity rate and present feasible solutions the following factors need to be kept in mind. First, the education standards of the United States need to go through a considerable change that would allow equal competition with other foreign industrial nations. Certainly, the study of international business is necessary to the business student. It is nearly impossible for a business to operate in a purely domestic market today. The international economy is interconnected. The crash of the stock markets, "Black Monday," in 1987, wiped out over $500 billion in wealth in a few short hours. Also, in those short hours, the European and Asian markets fell sharply in response to the crash.

Second, U.S. management needs to provide long-term goals that will allow them to identify needs and opportunities available in the international market. There are bound to be big changes in the world economy, not the least of which is the EC in 1992. With a strong knowledge base in international business, American business managers as well as students will be well equipped for the new world market. If such a trend continues then the United States would be able to regain its position of leadership in the world market.

Third, no longer can the organization function just to maximize profits, it must also consider the environment and its occupants. The managers of today have to know and understand how their actions can be helpful or harmful to the organization. Actions must be carried out in a way that is beneficial to the employee as well as to the public as a whole. Management needs to make a sincere effort to develop a cooperative attitude with labor that is based upon a team marketplace. Not only through fair collective bargaining, but also by giving employees a say in corporate governance as well as ownership or profit-sharing involvement. Employee ownership is a fast developing new concept in corporate governance. In 1989 there were 10,000 employee-owned U.S. firms, up from 1,000 in 1976. Many people believe that U.S. companies are beginning to show evidence of strength in the world economy, and if this trend continues the United States will have the chance to regain its place as a quality producer in many industries.

REFERENCES

Alkhafaji, A.F. 1990. *International Management Challenge.* Acton: Coply Publishing.

Asheghian, P., and B. Ebrahimi. 1990. *International Business.* New York: Harper and Row.

Buderi, R., B. Riemer, and J. Rossant. "Is It Time to Call up the Oil Reserves?" *Business Week* (January 28), p. 35.

Cooney, S. 1990. "Europe 1992: The Opportunity and The Challenge For U.S. Economic Interests" *SAIS Review.*

Delors, J. 1989. "Europe on The Way To 1992." *International Affairs* (November).

Koretz, G. 1990. "The Deficit Plays a Scary Game of Catch-Me-If-You-Can." *Business Week* (August 13), p. 23.

Krajewski, L.J., and L. Ritzman. 1990. *Operations Management Strategy and Analysis.* New York: Addison-Wesley.

Myrdel, G. 1961. *Asian Drama: An Inquiry into the Poverty of Nations,* Vol. 2. New York: The Twentieth Century Fund.

Nasar, S. 1990. "Fantasy and Facts About the Budget Deficit." *U.S. News and World Report* (February 5), p. 61.

Rentoul, A. 1988. "Mergers and Acquisitions in the Light of 1992—Ensuring Strategic Good Sense Underpins Corporate Ambitions." *European Management Journal* 6(4).

Rustin, R.E. 1990. "Europe's Political, Economic Makeovers Offer Opportunities and Pose Snares, for Investors." *Wall Street Journal* (February 1), p. B2.

U.S. Department of Commerce. 1989. Washington, DC: U.S. Government Printing Office.

Wessel, D., and J.H. Birnbaum. 1990. "Politics and Policy: White House Warns of $100 Billion Cut in Spending if Budget Negotiations Fail." *The Wall Street Journal* (July 17), p. A12:1.

PART II

TWO-COUNTRY STUDIES

INTRODUCTION TO PART II

All four papers in Part II have three characteristics in common. First, all of them involve a two country comparison of business practices and one of the countries is always the United States. Second, all of the authors have employed research techniques and/or conceptual models with a strong United States orientation in studying the differences and similarities between the United States and their chosen country. Most of the authors did a portion of their graduate academic studies in United States business schools where they were trained to do academic research employing techniques and conceptual models developed in the United States or Canada. Whether they remained in the United States to teach or returned to their native lands, they retained an interest in doing research that was not always United States focused. Instead, they expanded their academic research into the international arena and thus they provide, in this book, a rich mosaic of studies that examine United States ideas against a non-United States international background.

Third, all of the authors have as their objective, often specifically stated in their study, a need to determine whether a change from the United States environment to another national environment results in differing conclusions when United States developed techniques and concepts are applied in a non-United States context. In essence, all of the authors pose the question of whether the research that dominates the academic journals so prolifically published in North America is germane only to the United States experience,

International Research in the Business Disciplines, Volume 1, pages 21-23.
Copyright © 1993 by JAI Press Inc.
All rights of reproduction in any form reserved.
ISBN: 1-55938-538-3

or does it have international application? This latter characteristic is the key one dominating this section and sounds its central theme in the first volume of *International Research in the Business Disciplines.* Thus, Part II asks the continuing question: Are United States oriented research ideas parochial to the United States or do they have broader international application?

For all international managers, regardless of their country location, a primary concern of strategic management and industrial organizational economics is the relationship between strategy and performance. But, as the authors of our first article in this section note, "Much of the research in this area has been conducted and is generalized to the United States context only." Thus, Drs. Lee and Mirchandani pose a central research question: "Which strategic variables have the greatest impact on firm financial performance in *both* (editors' emphasis) Korea and the United States?" A step-wise regression analysis is performed, using eleven factors and data gathered from 100 manufacturing firms from each of the two countries under study—Korea and the United States. The results are not surprising, namely, that "a different set of strategic variables appears to be crucial in each of the two countries." Thus, while United States models proved to be helpful in developing research questions and in conducting the actual research, the research results are likely to differ from country to country.

The second author, Dr. Ghannadian, compares the United States and Japan and focuses on the "causal relationship between stock returns and foreign exchange rates." His empirical analysis examines "the information efficiency of the foreign exchange markets in response to innovations in the stock market" for the United States versus Japan. This study is most informative "in light of the around-the-clock global security trading" by showing that there are different causal relationships between the stock returns and the foreign exchange rates depending upon the country under study. Dr. Ghannadian suggests that there is greater stochastic dependence for Japan and more stochastic independence for the United States. Thus, "in the United States, foreign exchange rates are more influenced by news and random unpredictable events," while "in Japan, the stock market returns strongly lead the foreign exchange markets."

The third study applies Minzberg's topology describing the various roles played by managers within an organizational structure to a narrowly focused industry outside of the North American experience—the maritime merchants of Eastern Nigeria. In identifying significant differences in managerial roles as defined within the context of United States business firms versus Nigerian firms, the authors, Drs. Udeh and Hayajneh, demonstrate a need for United States expatriate managers to redefine their managerial roles when operating in what may be an unfriendly national business environment.

The fourth study, by one of the editors, Dr. Swanson, again focuses on two countries, the United States and Japan. Probably no two national cultures are more dissimilar than are these. This study is concerned with employment problems created when the host country codifies its cultural concepts of human relationships into legal mandates. The cultural/legal result is to frustrate the ability of the expatriate firm (Japanese) to incorporate its organizational culture based upon its home country culture (Japan) into its foreign operations (the United States). The synergistic compromises that are required to successfully operate an overseas firm when the cultures of the home and host countries are not compatible demonstrate the growing practical need for international managers to develop new techniques and concepts that are truly international in thought and application.

STRATEGIC DETERMINANTS OF
FIRM PERFORMANCE:
A COMPARISON OF U.S AND KOREAN
MANUFACTURING FIRMS

Jooh Lee and Dilip Mirchandani

INTRODUCTION

A primary concern of strategic management and industrial organizational economics is the relationship between strategy and performance (see Beard and Dess 1981; Christenson and Montgomery 1981; Hambrick 1982; Hirschey 1982; Hitt and Ireland 1985; Jose, Nichols, and Stevens 1986; Rugman 1983; Sharader, Taylor, and Dalton 1984; Varadarajan and Ramananujam 1987). Such studies have emphasized the relative importance of different strategic variables in determining business performance. However, much of this research has been conducted and is generalizable to the U.S. context only. Since economic market structure as well as its corresponding strategic elements vary across countries (Adams 1976; Bhaatt and Miller 1984; Ravenscraft 1983; Wright 1984), it is questionable whether the conventional relationship between

International Research in the Business Disciplines, Volume 1, pages 25-35.
Copyright © 1993 by JAI Press Inc.
All rights of reproduction in any form reserved.
ISBN: 1-55938-538-3

strategy and performance using U.S. firms (or other industrialized countries' firms) is of value and equally applicable to other economic contexts. Consequently, the organizational strategy-performance linkages demonstrated by previous studies need to be examined, in different economic contexts, across countries.

In spite of a growing interest in a comparative study, until recently very little empirical work has been conducted on the cross-national comparison of strategy-performance relationships. Although previous studies (Adams 1976; Jones, Laudadio, and Percy 1977; Kono 1984; Schneeweis 1983) provided a fair amount of support for the close linkage between strategy and financial profitability in industrialized countries, such as the United States, United Kingdom, Canada, and Japan, the relative impact of strategic factors on performance remains untested in other countries, particularly in newly industrialized countries.

Therefore, the objective of the present study is exploratory in nature. The central research question is: which strategic variables have the greatest impact on firm financial performance in Korea and the United States? Such a question is important because it identifies the key strategic elements that lead to success in two different economic contexts and it addresses the pertinent question of whether the general relationships between strategy and performance previously posited by various studies, mainly based on U.S. firms, are equally applicable to firms of other countries with different business environments. Such information will also be useful to managers in deciding the appropriateness of a competitive strategy in a given economic context.

REVIEW OF THEORY

There are a number of strategic elements that define the competitive posture a firm adopts in the market. Inclusion of all such variables would be cumbersome, so this study focuses on a selected set of strategic variables based upon the importance of these variables in past empirical endeavors. Diversification strategy (DIVSF) refers to the distribution of a firm's activities in different industries. Diversification strategy is a distinct aspect of corporate strategy. The firm's decision to enter different lines of business is at the heart of diversification issues. Grant, Jammine, and Thomas (1988) and Ramanujam and Varadarajan (1989) provide extensive reviews of studies relating to diversification strategy. In genaral, there is clear theoretical and empirical evidence that diversification strategy influences firm performance in a significant way. There is some controversy, however, about the direction of the effect. There are sound theoretical reasons to favor both related (low) and unrelated (high) diversification.

The previously mentioned aspect of diversification refers to product diversity. There is also an aspect of diversification that refers to multi-national diversity (EXPOR). This crucial aspect of diversification strategy is the international dimension which is particularly relevant in the present context of globalization. Until recently, however, little attention has been paid to this issue. The empirical evidence indicates a strong positive link between international or multinational diversification and profitability (see Geringer, Beamish, and DaCosta 1989; Grant, Jammine, and Thomas 1988; Kim, Hwang, and Burgers 1989).

Firm size (FSIZE) is one of the most acknowledged determinants of a firm's profits in terms of their effect on competitive market power in a given industry (Beard and Dess 1981). Most empirical research (Collins and Preston 1969; Hall and Weiss 1967; Ravenscraft 1983; Scherer 1980) has shown that a positive relationship exists between company size and profitability. In fact, large corporate size often results in market powers that can be used to extract favorable terms on the firm's costs of raw material and capital. Firm size also helps in achieving economies of scale due to the large quantities involved. The positive relationship between firm size and profitability has been supported by previous research (Hall and Weiss 1967; Scherer 1980). More recently, however, Amato and Wilder (1985) found that there is no relationship between firm size and profitability with respect to the return on assets (ROA).

Strategy and industrial economics research suggest that a firm's closeness to its customers and its ability to differentiate itself are required for effective financial performance. For a corporation to achieve a substantial competitive advantage, it must invest heavily in its advertising activities (ADVIN). The pioneering research by Comanor and Wilson (1967) shows that advertising is associated positively with profitability. In fact, for industries where products are diverse, investment in advertising can be highly profitable. Today, a great deal of evidence (Adams 1976; Ravenscraft 1983; Porter 1979; Scherer 1980) indicates that an increase in advertising expenditure leads to higher profits.

Capital intensity (CAPIN) is a another component of business strategy. It represents a firm's long-term commitment to building its technological base and upgrading its productive capacity. Therefore, a positive association between capital expenditure and corporate profitability is likely. This positive view of the relationships between capital expenditure and corporate performance has been well supported in several studies (Comanor and Wilson 1967; Ravenscraft 1983). In contrast to the positive relationship of capital intensity with performance, some studies found negative associations (Adams 1976; Hatten and Schendel 1977). Similarly, plant and equipment utilization (PL&EQ) captures the extent to which capital is being used efficiently while labor productivity (LAPRD) captures the efficiency in using labor as a factor of production.

Debt leverage (DEBTR) captures the financial risk as measured by the debt-to-equity ratio. Several studies have found a negative association between debt leverage and firm profitability (Arditti 1967p; Gale 1972; Hall and Weiss 1967). The higher debt loads tend to depress profits due to the higher financial burden of servicing the debt. The increased risk of such firms also tends to raise their cost of capital. However, it can be argued that to the extent the cost of a firm's capital is less than the returns earned by the firm, debt can have a positive impact on profitability. Similarly, investment activity (INVST) is another aspect of financing operations. The operations aspect of the firm is captured by four important variables: Inventory management (INVEN), credit activity (CREDT), labor productivity (LAPRD), and plant and equipment utilization (PL&EQ). Most operations strategy variables reflect aspects of efficient operations for firm performance. A dramatic increase in firm performance can be achieved by improving inventory management (Johnston 1982; Hambrick and Schecter 1983) also asserted that receivable collection, inventory management, labor productivity, and plant and equipment newness are major avenues toward improved profits.

Table 1.

	Variable Definitions
Strategy Variables	
Diversification (DIVSFi)	Ratio of sales volume of the major product to the total sales volume of ith firm.
Firm Asset Size (FSIZEi)	Natural logarithm value of Assets (1/ln Assets)
Advertising Inten. (ADVINi)	Advertising expenditure percentage of Total sales.
Capital Intensity (CAPINi)	(Total assets)/(Total sales)
Credit Activity (CREDTi)	Collection period (= Receivable account $\times$ 365 / Total sales)
Foreign Trade (EXPORi)	(Export volume)/(Total sales)
Debt	
Leverage (DEBTRi)	(Total Debt)/(Stockholder's Equity)
Inventory Management (INVENi)	(Total Inventory)/(Total sales)
Labor Productivity (LAPRDi)	Ln(Total Sales/No. of Employees)
Investment Activity(INVSTi)	(Investment)/(Total Sales)
Plant and Equipment	(Plant and Equipment)/
Utilization(PL&EQi)	(Total Sales)
Performance Variables	
Return on Equity (ROE)	Ratio of the net profit before tax to the stockholder's equity
Return on Investment (ROI)	Ratio of the net profit before tax and interest to the sum of long-term debt and shareholder's equity.
Return on Assets (ROA)	Ratio of the net profit before tax to the total assets.
Return on Sales (ROS)	Ratio of the net profit before tax to the total sales.
Composite Measure of Business Performance (CMBPi)	Unweighted average value of various performance measures (ROE,ROI,ROA,ROS)

SAMPLE AND METHOD

The research sample consists of 100 manufacturing firms from each of the two countries-Korea and the United States. The sample characteristics with respect to size and industry type are displayed in Table 2. The variables are measured according to the definitions in Table 1 and encompass five-year averages for

Table 2.   Sample Characteristics ($n = 100$)

	United States	Korea
Average Sales Volume (millions)		
Under $ 300	12	35
$ 301 - $ 500	21	26
$ 501 - $ 700	18	9
$ 701 - $1000	38	18
Over $1000	11	12
Industry Types		
Fishing and Mining	4	—
Food and Beverage	6	13
Textiles and Apparel	4	13
Lumber and Wood Product	3	3
Paper and Allied Product	6	2
Chemicals and Allied Products	11	13
Rubber and Misc. Plastics	5	5
Stone, Clay and Glass Product	4	4
Primary Metal Product	8	8
Machinery and Equipment	10	4
Electric and Electronic Product	10	10
Transportation Equipment	6	7
Instrument and Related Product	6	4
Construction and Related Product	3	10
Misc. Manufacturing Product	4	4

Table 3.   Stepwise Regression Analysis: Multiple Correlation
Coefficient and Statistical Significance (U.S.)

Steps No.	*Variables Entered*	*Multiple*		*Change in R^2*	*Adjusted R^2*	*F-ratio*
		R	*R^2*			
1	CAPIN	−0.382	0.146	0.146	0.137	16.771*
2	PL&EQ	−0.489	0.240	0.094	0.204	13.659*
3	CREDT	0.554	0.307	0.067	0.237	10.326*
4	ADVIN	0.589	0.347	0.040	0.306	7.875*

Note: * $p < 0.05$

the period 1981-1985. Data were collected from *Compustat* and *10-K Reports* (U.S.) and *Annual Corporation Reports of Listed comanies* and *Advertising Report* (Korea). The dependent variable (in Table 3) is the composite measure of business performance (CMBP) which is an unweighted average of ROE, ROI, ROA, and ROS.

The model is:

Firm Financial Performance = f(DIVSF, EXPOR, FSIZE, ADVIN, CAPIN, PL&EQ, LAPRD, DEBTR, INVST, INVEN, and CREDT)

Step-wise regression analysis is performed in order to identify the strategy variables that have the greatest influence on firm performance. A separate analysis is conducted for each country and the results are shown in Table 3.

RESULTS AND DISCUSSION

The results of statistical analysis are displayed in Tables 4 and 5. The means, deviations, and intercorrelations for the U.S. and Korean samples are displayed in Tables 4 and 5 respectively. It is important to note that, in general, the variance inflation factors (VIF) do not indicate serious collinearity problems. It is interesting to note the major differences in the strategic profile of the firms in the United States and Korea. First, the average firm size is larger in the United States when compared to Korea (14.5 compared to 11.8) which is as expected since Korea is a much smaller market and is at an earlier stage of economic development. Second, the advertising intensity of U.S. firms appears to be much higher than Korean firms, perhaps reflecting greater competition.

Third, the credit collection period for the United States is much lower than that in Korea. Fourth, the Korean firms have a much higher percentage of foreign sales compared to U.S. firms. This is also consistent with the notion that Pacific Rim economies grow, to a significant degree, by actively developing foreign markets. Finally, the debt ratio for Korean firms is more than three times that of U.S. firms. Once again this finding is confirmation of the fact that Korean firms, like Japanese firms, rely very heavily on debt financing, in contrast to U.S. trends which favor equity financing.

Table 3 shows the strategic variables that have the greatest impact on firm performance. For U.S. firms the most important variables that influence performance are capital intensity and plant and equipment utilization (both of which appear to have a negative impact), while credit collection period and advertising intensity appear to have a positive impact. The negative impact of CAPIN and PL&EQ is consistent with the findings of Amato and Wilder (1985) and Hatten and Schendel (1977), while the positive impact of ADVIN

Variable

Table 4. Mean, Standard Deviation, and Intercorrelations for Variables (United States)

	1	2	3	4	5	6	7	8	9	10	11	12
1. CMBP	1.00											
2. DIVSF	.18*	1.00										
3. FSIZE	-.02	.08	1.00									
4. ADVIN	.03	.12	.05	1.00								
5. CREDT	-.12	-.19*	.15	.14	1.00							
6. CAPIN	-.38***	.13	.08	-.12	-.08	1.00						
7. EXPOR	.05	.05	.25**	.22*	.29**	-.12	1.00					
8. DEBTR	.21*	-.00	.02	-.20*	-.23*	.46***	-.19*	1.00				
9. INVEN	-.12	-.07	.03	.08	.40***	-.15	.24**	-.25**	1.00			
10. LAPRD	-.10	-.08	.03	-.07	-.05	-.07	.00	.58***	-.14	1.00		
11. INVST	.30***	.15	.32***	.10	.12	.45***	.25***	.02	.09	-.05	1.00	
12. PL&EQ	-.18*	-.01	.15	.01	.04	.22*	-.07	-.00	-.16*	-.08	-.04	1.00
Means	9.9	59.5	14.5	3.6	55.4	88.9	15.3	66.8	16.9	12.2	7.6	33.2
Std. Dev.	5.2	21.6	3.8	3.5	21.9	99.9	15.4	60.7	8.1	9.1	9.5	29.0
VIF	1.2	1.2	1.6	1.3	1.7	4.0	1.6	3.9	1.4	2.6	3.1	1.4

Notes: * $p < 0.05$
          ** $p < 0.01$
          *** $p < 0.001$

Diversification (DIVSF), Firm size (FSIZE), Advertising intensity (ADVIN), Credit activity (CREDT), Foreign trade by export (EXPOR), Capital intensity (CAPIN), Debt leverage (DEBTR), Inventory management (INVEN), Labor productivity (LAPRF), Investment activity (INVST), Plant & Equipment utilization (PL&EQ).

Table 5. Mean, Standard Deviation, and Intercorrelations for Variables (Korea)

Variable

	1	2	3	4	5	6	7	8	9	10	11	12
1. CMBP	1.00											
2. DIVSF	.21*	1.00										
3. FSIZE	.13	-.09	1.00									
4. ADVIN	.05	.10	-.39***	1.00								
5. CREDT	-.05	.05	-.07*	.07	1.00							
6. CAPIN	-.23**	.09	.03	-.05	.56***	1.00						
7. EXPOR	.28**	-.15	.48***	-.53***	-.16	-.10	1.00					
8. DEBTR	.22*	-.24**	.45***	-.24**	-.13	.01	.44***	1.00				
9. INVEN	-.14	-.05	-.07	.04**	.16	.25	.07	.02	1.00			
10. LAPRD	.02	-.01	.42***	-.35***	-.24**	-.28**	.30***	.43***	-.30***	1.00		
11. INVST	-.20*	-.02	.26**	-.05	.19*	.44***	.04	-.11	.07	-.11	1.00	
12. PL&EQ	-.22*	.08	.03	-.11	.11	.73***	-.14	.03	-.05	-.18	.32***	1.00
Means	9.1	62.9	11.8	1.6	98.6	91.3	36.9	232.1	15.9	11.2	4.6	30.9
Std. Dev.	4.9	16.3	1.1	2.1	46.9	40.7	29.3	190.6	8.9	0.9	4.1	29.0
VIF	1.2	2.1	4.8	7.4	2.0	1.9	1.9	2.8	1.9	2.1	1.9	20.9

Notes: $*$ $p < 0.05$
          $**$ $p < 0.01$
         $***$ $p < 0.001$

Diversification (DIVSF), Firm size (FSIZE), Advertising intensity (ADVIN), Credit activity (CREDT), Foreign trade by export (EXPOR), Capital intensity (CAPIN), Debt leverage (DEBTR), Inventory management (INVEN), Labor productivity (LAPRD), Investment activity (INVST), Plant & Equipment utilization (PL&EQ).

Table 6.   Stepwise Regression Analysis: Multiple Correlation
Coefficient and Statistical Significance (Korea)

Steps No.	Variables Entered	Multiple		Change in R^2	Adjusted R^2	F-ratio
		R	R^2			
1	EXPOR	0.245	0.060	0.060	0.051	6.281***
2	INVEN	−0.316	0.099	0.039	0.081	5.370**
3	DIVSF	0.380	0.144	0.045	0.125	4.876**
4	DEBTR	0.412	0.170	0.026	0.154	3.678**
5	LAPRD	0.430	0.185	0.015	0.178	2.456*

Notes: * $p < 0.05$;
          ** $p < 0.01$;
          *** $p < 0.001$

Diversification (DIVSF), Advertising intensity (ADVIN), Credit activity (CREDT), Foreign trade by export (EXPOR), Capital intensity (CAPIN), Debt leverage (DEBTR), Inventory management (INVEN), Labor productivity (LAPRF), Plant & Equipment utilization (PL&EQ).

is also supported by many findings (Block 1974; Ravenscraft 1983; Porter 1979). The positive impact of CREDT is perhaps due to the favorable terms offered to customers in terms of credit periods or due to interest earnings on customer financing. The said variables explain approximately 30 percent of the variance in firm performance.

In the case of Korean firms (Table 6), foreign sales, diversification, debt leverage, and labor productivity are all significant explanatory variables showing a positive association with performance. Product diversity and international diversification are the hallmark of Korean conglomerates and allows such firms to extract synergies and enlarge markets based on similar technologies. Debt leverage, in the Korean context, provides a stable source of long-term financing at relatively low cost. Korea also enjoys a factor-based advantage with respect to labor, and hence LABRD shows a positive impact. Inventory management shows a negative impact, which is to be expected since an increased inventory/sales ratio indicates poor utilization of capital. The overall explanatory power of these variables is weaker than that of the United States (18% compared to 30%).

CONCLUSION

The comparison of strategy-performance links across countries such as the United States and Korea serves as a useful extension of knowledge and is crucial in the present-day context of globalization. It is interesting to note that a different set of strategic variables appears to be crucial in each of the two countries. However, the premise that strategic factors are important determinants of firm performance is applicable to the Korean context even though the size effects appears to be weaker when compared to the United States.

A final note of this study concerns the limited, but growing, interest in a cross-national comparison of the strategy and performance linkage across countries with different business environments. Nevertheless, these results need to suggest that more room remains both for the specification of additional explanatory strategy variables and for better performance measurement. Future research is essential in extending the generalizability of the basic tenets of strategic management to other economic contexts.

REFERENCES

Adams, W.J. 1976. "Inernational Differences in Corporate Profitability." *Economica* 43:256-276.

Amato, L., and R.P. Wilder. 1985. "The Effects of Firm Size on Profit Rates in U.S. Manufacturing." *Journal of Southern Economics* 52(1):181-190.

Arditti, F. 1967. "Risk and the Required Return on Equity." *Journal of Finance* 22:19-36.

Ayanian, R. 1975. "Advertising and Rate of Return." *The Journal of Labor and Economics* 18(2):479-493.

Beard, D., and G. Dess. 1981. "Corporate-Level Strategy, Business-Level Strategy and Firm Performance." *Academy of Management Journal* 24:663-688.

Bhaatt, B.J., and E.L. Miller. 1984. "Industrial Relations in Foreign and Local Firms in Asia." *Management International Review* 24:62-75.

Block, H. 1974. "Advertising and Profitability: An Appraisal." *Journal of Political Economy* 82(2):267-286.

Christensen, H., and C. Montgomery. 1981. "Corporate Economic Performance: Diversification Strategy versus Market Structure." *Strategic Management Journal* 2:327-343.

Collins, N., and L. Preston. 1969. "Price-cost Margins and Industry Structure." *The Review of Economics and Statistics* 51:271-280.

Comanor, W.S., and T.A. Wilson. 1967. "Advertising, Market Structure and Performance." *The Review of Economics and Statistics* 49(4):423-440.

Gale, B. 1972. "Market Share and Rate of Return." *The Review of Economics and Statistics* 54:412-423.

Geringer, M.J., B.W. Beamish, and R.C. DaCosta. 1989. "Diversification Strategy and Internationalization: Implications for MNE Performance." *Strategic Management Journal* 10:109-119.

Grant, R.M., A.P. Jammine, and H. Thomas. 1988. "Diversity, Diversification, and Productivity Among British Manufacturing Companies, 1972-1984." *Academy of Management Journal* 31:771-801.

Hall, M., and L. Weiss. 1967. "Firm Size and Profitability." *The Review of Economics and Statistics* 49:319-331.

Hambrick, D.C. 1982. "Operationalizing the Concept of Business-level Strategy in Research." *Academy of Management Review* 5:567-575.

Hambrick, D.C., and S.M. Schecter. 1983. "Turnaround Strategies for Mature Industrial-Product Business Units." *Academy of Management Journal* 26:231-248.

Hatten, K.J., and D.E. Schendel. 1977. "Heterogeneity within an Industry: Firm Conduct in the U.S. Brewing Industry." *The Journal of Industrial Economics* 24(4):97-113.

Hirschey, M. 1982. "Intangible Capital Assets of Advertising and R&D Expenditure." *The Journal of Industrial Economy* 30(4):375-390.

Hitt, M., and R.D. Ireland. 1985. "Corporate Distinctive Competence, Strategy, Industry, and Performance." *Strategic Management Journal* 5(3):273-293.

Jones, J.C., L. Laudadio, and M. Percy. 1977. "Profitability and Market Structure: Across Section Comparison of Canadian and American Manufacturing Industry." *The Journal of Industrial Economics* 25:195-211.

Johnston, R. 1972. "The Inventory Management Can Increase Profitability Dramatically." *National Public Accountant* 6:21-23.

Jose, M.L., L.M. Nichols, and J.L. Stevens. 1986. "Contributions of Diversification, Promotion, and R&D to the Value of Multi-Product Firms: A Tobin's *q* Approach." *Financial Management* 15(Winter): 33-42.

Kim, C.W., P. Hwang, and W.O. Burgers. 1989) "Global Diversification Strategy and Corporate Profit Performance." *Strategic Management Journal* 10:45-57.

Kono, T. 1984. "Long Range Planning of U.K. and Japanese Corporation." *Long Range Planning* 17:58-66.

Porter, M.E. 1979. "The Structure within Industries and Companies' Performance." *The Review of Economics and Statistics* 61:214-227.

Ramanujam, V., and P. Varadarajan. 1989. "Research on Corporate Diversification: A Synthesis." *Strategic Management Journal* 10:523-551.

Ravenscraft, D.J. 1983. "Structure-Profit Relationships at the Line of Business and Industry Level." *The Review of Economics and Statistics* 65(1):22-31.

Rugman, A.M. 1983. "The Comparative Performance of U.S. and European Multinational Enterprises: 1970-1979." *Management International Review* 23:4-14.

Scherer, F.M. 1980. *Industrial Market Structure and Economic Performance,* 2nd ed. Chicago: Rand McNally.

Shepherd, W.G. 1972. "The Elements of Market Structure." *The Review of Economics and Statistics* 54(1):25-37.

Schneeweis, T. 1983. "Determinants of Profitability Perspective." *International Management Review* 23(1):15-21.

Sharader, C.B., L. Taylor, and D.R. Dalton. 1984. "Strategic Planning and Organizational Performance." *Journal of Management* 10:149-171.

Varadarajan, P., and V. Ramanujam. 1987. "Diversification and Performance: A Reexamination Using a Two-Dimensional Conceptualization of Diversity in Firms." *Academy of Management Journal* 30:380-397.

Wright, P. 1984. "MNC-Third World Business Unit: Performance Application of Strategic Element." *Strategic Management Journal* 5:231-240.

THE RELATIONSHIP OF
FOREIGN EXCHANGE AND
THE STOCK MARKET:
EVIDENCE FROM JAPAN AND THE UNITED STATES

Farhad F. Ghannadian

INTRODUCTION

While the bull market was moving the Japanese (Tokyo) stock exchange to an all time high of 60 times P/E ratio, Wall Street was delighted with a 20 times P/E ratio for the S&P 500. This was prior to the October 1987 crash. Before the crash the total value of the Tokyo stock exchange of 1500 stocks was greater (in dollars) than the total value of 2250 stocks listed in the New York Stock exchange (Burnstein 1988).

It is important to note that Japan has eight stock exchanges, of which Tokyo and Osaka are the most important. The Japanese government requires a 10 percent withholding tax on dividends as well as interest. There are many similarities between the Japanese stock exchanges and the U.S. stock exchanges. For example, the Tokyo Stock Exchange has two catagories of

International Research in the Business Disciplines, Volume 1, pages 37-47.
Copyright © 1993 by JAI Press Inc.
All rights of reproduction in any form reserved.
ISBN: 1-55938-538-3

listings; the first is very similar to the requirements of the NYSE and the second similar to the AMEX. The market is extremely liquid with high trading volume. The average price of a share is usually under ten dollars. Some of these shares are also traded in the United States in the form of American Depository Receipts (ADRs). It is also important to note that the Japanese stock market has had a correlation of 0.07 to 0.84 to the U.S. stock market in the past decade.

Both the U.S. and Japanese stock markets have witnessed fluctuations in the past several years due to changes in the fundamental economies of the two countries, and changes stemming from their exchange rates. Various studies have pointed to the direction of causality between fundamental variables. Fama and Schwert (1977) studied the stock returns and inflation, Rogalski and Vinso (1977) study stock returns and the money supply, Ghannadian and Schneider (1988) study the relationship of economic growth and financial development. Very little conclusive evidence exists on the effect of foreign exchange volatility on stock returns. In the volatile world of exchange rates, little understanding exists on how depreciation or appreciation of a currency affects the value and earnings of a stock. It is generally understood that exchange rate changes directly affect economic factors which are reflected in stock prices. The major question is whether there is a causal relationship between the two. Lessard and Solnik (1976) conclude that even with international influence on stock returns, domestic effects are much stronger. Adler and Simon's (1986) research on currency movements and stock market indexes suggested a weak correlation between these markets.

This paper investigates the causal relationship between foreign exchange rates and the stock returns of the two countries: Japan and the United States. The establishment or the nonexistence of a relationship between these two markets has many policy ramifications. One of the most important is the fate of future negotiations on trade or the stability of the value of the dollar.

A MODEL OF EXCHANGE RATES
FOR THE UNITED STATES AND JAPAN

The determination of a model that investigates the factors that determine the exchange rates is crucial in investigating volatility in the market. Assuming that the United States and Japan are the only two countries in the world, we can develop a model of exchange rates to illustrate their effects on their respective equity markets. Equations (1) and (2) illustrate this model for the United States and Japan, respectively.

$$EX_{U.S.} = (M_J - M_{U.S}) - e(i_J - i_{U.S.}) - s(GNP_J - GNP_{U.S.}) + V \qquad (1)$$

$$EX_J = (M_{U.S.} - M_J) - e(i_{U.S.} - i_J) - s(GNP_{U.S.} - GNP_J) + V \qquad (2)$$

where:

> EX = nominal exchange rate in units of foreign currency per unit of domestic currency.
> M = nominal money supply for Japan and the U.S.
> i = interest rate in nominal terms.
> GNP = real income.
> s = income elasticity of real money demand.
> e = interest elasticity of real money balances.
> V = shift factor that affects exchange rates of factors not mentioned.

The model clearly illustrates that a country's exchange rate will appreciate (EX will decline) if a country's money supply growth decelerates, domestic nominal interest rates increase, real GNP accelerates relative to the foreign country (Japan for Equation (1) and United States for Equation (2)). Also exogenous shocks can influence the nominal exchange rate independent of the three factors described. Policymakers and monetary authorities have complete control of policies which affect domestic interest rates and output. Whether the policies will work largely depends on their influence on the V factor which is not controlable, and largely on the relative changes of the variables prescribed.

Equations (1) and (2) can be modified to include price level changes for it to become real. Therefore, if $-(P_J - P_{U.S.})$ is added to Equation (1), and $-(P_{U.S.} - P_J)$ is added to Equation (2) the equations become real exchange rates. However, most empirical work has shown that nominal exchange rates and real exchange rates move in close unity in the short run (Mussa and Black 1986). Monetary policy will only be effective in affecting real exchange rates if the price level and nominal exchange rate differential adjust at different speeds. Even then, the change in the real exchange rate will be temporary, and the real exchange rate will in the long run return to its former level.

Movements in the exchange rate could be due to nominal changes like the fact that domestic money supply is rising faster in the United States versus Japan. This could also be attributed to real factors that originate outside of the monetary sector of the economy. These could be supply side changes that could cause fundamental changes in the economy and a rise in domestic real GNP.

It is very difficult to isolate real and nominal changes since only nominal exchange rate changes can be observed in world financial markets. Theoretically, if exchange rates are only a monetary variable and reflect the relative prices of two countries, then the exchange rate should have no impact on stock returns. Assuming the purchasing power parity is valid, then exchange rates adjust solely on price level changes and stock returns should remain unchanged. Disparities in the purchasing power parity has been noticed by Frenkel (1981), Adler and Dumas (1983), and Dornbusch (1988). These disparaties cause departures from the original equilibrium either due to differential speeds of adjustment in goods and asset markets (transitory) or in response to permanent changes in equilibrium relative prices.

Inflexibilities in wages and prices, monetary and exchange rate changes bring about transitory deviations in price ratios. Economic growth and structural factors change relative prices of traded goods versus price of home goods. Finally, changes in the trade pattern bring about changes in the terms of trade.

Solnik's (1984) study of the relationship of the stock returns and exchange rates is of great interest. Solnik looking at nine countries found significant but small, the effect of depreciation of domestic currency on stock returns. The methodology employed by Solnik was multivariate regression technique. The following section will focus on the different methodology employed and the empirical analysis.

EMPIRICAL STUDY

The empirical analysis aims to examine the information efficiency of the foreign exchange markets in response to innovations in the stock market for the United States versus Japan. If the notion that the stock markets are efficient is accepted, then all available information is reflected in the current stock prices. The stock markets under the efficiency criterion will be able to anticipate future exchange rate movements based on present available information. If the stock market is not efficient, but rational, the stock prices will adjust with a lagged effect. This is based on the asset market apoproach of foreign exchange rate determination which views exchange rates that are purely influenced by future events.

Methodology

Granger and Newbold (1986) points out the shortcomings of the word "causal." Most philosophers would say a cause occurs before an effect. However, most academicians have accepted "Granger causality" as a seperate phenomenon based on Granger's (1980) definition. According to his definition, if, through the use of past information on exchange rates stock price changes could be more accurately predicted than otherwise then changes in the exchange rate Granger cause changes in the stock prices.

Haugh (1976) improved the initial procedure of the Granger test by introducing a filtering process to create a white noise stationary series. Then the two white noise series are used to check for stochastic dependence by running cross correlations. Utilizing an autoregressive moving average process (ARMA):

$$Z_t = \Phi \; 1 \; z_{t-1} \ldots + \Theta p \; z_{t-p} + a_t - \Theta \; 1 \; a_t\text{-}1 - \ldots \Theta_q a_{t-q} + c \tag{3}$$

where Θ and Φ are polynomials of degree p and q in the lags. Z is the changes in exchange rates, a is a white noise series, and c is a constant term. Through an iterative system the residual series a_t is found for stock returns and changes in the foreign exchange rates.

In this study a cross-correlation function is plotted for every pair of variables; one variable is assumed to be input (independent) and the other is assumed to be output (dependent). All variables are prewhitened prior to calculating the cross-correlation functions. The first is to show if any relationship exists between the variables. The second is to show the exact lag or lead specification of the relationship. Cross correlations between two residual series is calculated next denoted as r_b. The cross correlations should be statistically insignificant if stock returns and changes in foreign exchange are statistically insignificant. To test significance of the group of cross correlations an S statistics is described by:

$$S = N^2 \sum_{k=m}^{n} (N - b)^{-1} r_{b^-}{}^2 \tag{4}$$

where:

$S =$ distributed chi-square
$N =$ number of observations
$m =$ number of future lags
$n =$ number of past lags

Temporal relationships between foreign exchange rates and the stock prices to show undirectional causality would require:

$$\text{Foreign Exchange} \rightarrow \text{Stock Prices} \tag{5}$$

Foreign exchange rates will lead stock returns if past lags of foreign exchange and stock prices were significant, but past lags of stock prices and foreign exchange were not significant. Equation (5) illustrates the requirement for foreign exchange to cause stock prices. If both past lags are significant, then there is a feedback relationship. This comes directly from the Granger and Newbold (1986) definition of causality. They make two major assumptions. The first is that in causality testing the future values cannot cause the past, and only the past can cause the present or future. Their second assumption is that causality can only be discussed for a group of stochastic processes, not deterministic processes.

Data

The data were based on the month-end indices of the Tokyo stock exchange obtained from various issues of the *Economist*, and the calculated monthly return on the S&P 500 reported in the *Wall Street Journal* for a period of 60 months from January 1982 to December 1987. Foreign Exchange rates were based on Special Drawing Rights (SDR) values per unit of the local currency obtained from various issues of the International Financial Statistics of the IMF.

Results

Both the stock returns and foreign exchange rate movements were filtered into white noise for the United States and Japan. The Box-Jenkins univariate three-step approach (identification, estimation, and diagnosis) is carried out. A twelve-lag estimated auto correlation S of stock returns is presented in Table 1. A Q statistic was utilized to test if a group of the estimated auto correlations were significant.

Table 1.   Autocorrelation of Stock Returns Versus Exchange Rate Series

	United States		Japan	
S	*Stock*	*Exchange*	*Stock*	*Exchange*
1	0.14	0.12	0.20	−0.01
2	0.05	−0.06	−0.13	−0.01
3	0.04	0.04	−0.06	0.03
4	−0.07	−0.14	−0.07	−0.08
5	0.11	−0.09	−0.05	0.04
6	0.13	−0.05	0.17	−0.11
7	0.09	0.15	−0.16	0.03
8	−0.04	−0.02	−0.20	0.04
9	0.21	0.04	−0.23	−0.14
10	0.15	−0.06	0.01	0.03
11	−0.19	−0.05	−0.02	−0.10
12	−0.20	0.09	−0.03	0.13
Q	9.22	6.65	5.36	4.19

$$Q = N\,(r_1^2 + r_2^2 + \ldots r_b^2) \tag{6}$$

where r_b is the estimated auto correlation coefficient for lag b. Table 1 shows that there is no serial correlation in the stock return series and none of the Q statistics is significant at the five percent level. This is also true of the exchange rates where none of the Q statistics are statistically significant.

Table 2 estimates cross correlations of the United States and Japanese stock returns and their foreign exchange rate movements up to twelve future lags and twelve past lags. The estimated cross correlations between exchange rates and stock returns (lagged) are insignificant for the case of United States. However, for Japan the results are different. The future lag (0.36) and the past lag (−0.38) of the eight period are significant. These significant past and future lags represent a temporal relationship which in Granger causality terms could mean bidirectional causality. For the United States future period eleven shows some significance (−0.24), but the contemperaneous cross correlations for the United States (−0.08) is much smaller than for Japan (0.28).

The next step would be to check for stochastic independence between changes in foreign exchange rates and stock returns. Table 3 reports the S statistics described earlier. The S statistics reported for both changes in the exchange rate and stock returns with a lag, and stock returns with exchange rate lagged were notsignificant at the five percent or ten percent level for the United States. In other words, there is a strong indication of stochastic independence. This means that in the United States, forecasting the stock market is not going to help predict future changes in the exchange rate, and forecasting exchange rates will not aid and improve the forecast on the stock

Table 2. Cross-Correlations of Foreign Exchange Movements Versus Stock Market Returns[a]

Lags	0	1	2	3	4	5	6
United States							
0 to 6	−0.08	0.01	0.05	0.06	−0.04	−0.05	−0.18
7 to 12		−0.05	−0.02	−0.07	0.05	−0.12	−0.03
−1 to −6		−0.04	0.01	−0.02	−0.07	−0.04	−0.07
−7 to −12			−0.07	0.11	0.03	0.06	−0.24
Japan							
0 to 6	−0.28	−0.01	−0.3	0.12	0.07	−0.06	0.17
7 to 12		0.07	−0.38	−0.03	0.06	0.04	0.08
−1 to −6		0.35	−0.08	0.08	−0.21	0.22	0.13
−7 to −12		0.01	0.03	0.13	−0.17	−0.20	0.08

Note: [a]lags of 1 to 12 are for past 12 quarters and lags −1 through −12 are 12 periods in the future.

market. The results for the United States confirm the efficient market hypothesis and the random walk theory, that changes in the foreign exchange rates and stock prices are to a great extent unpredictable. Also Wolff (1988) and Frenkel and Mussa's (1980) work in this area support the hypothesis that innovations in the equity markets are not able to improve forecasts in the foreign exchange rates.

In the case of Japan, as can be seen from Table 3, the Japanese equity markets were affected and also influenced exchange rates. Table 3 shows that causality does flow from stock returns to changes in the foreign exchange at the five percent level. In other words, the equity markets in Tokyo fully anticipate future fluctuatons in the exchange rates. Also at the the ten percent level the direction of causality runs from exchange rate to stock returns. This shows that bidirectional causality or feedback exists between changes in the foreign exchange rate and stock returns in the Japanese market. However, since the flow from lagged stock returns to foreign exchange is stronger than the reverse, it could allude to the fact that the foreign exchange market moves slower than required under the efficiency criterion to consider economic data than the stock market.

This form of causality testing is comparable to econometric exogeneity testing. By performing this type of test, the researcher can justify correctly why the variable in the equation was assumed to be endogenous or exogenous. The endogeneity and exogeneity of variables that determine foreign exchange are extremely important in econometric forecasting models used by businesses, investors, and researchers.

Table 3. The Chi-square Test: Causality between Foreign Exchange Rate Movements and Stock Market Returns

Future Lags	Past Lags	United States	Japan
A. Foreign Exchange vs. Lagged Stock Returns			
−6	4	1.48	17.91*
−6	0	1.12	18.65*
−5	8	4.76	28.80*
−4	1	1.83	17.22*
−3	0	0.71	11.16*
−1	12	4.92	24.21*
B. Stock Returns vs. lagged Exchange Rate			
−6	4	4.01	15.02
−6	0	3.92	7.64
−5	8	8.93	24.13**
−4	1	1.71	12.49
−3	0	0.86	6.17
−1	12	7.84	22.89**

Notes: * Significance at $p < .05$.
            ** Significance at $p < .01$.

POLICY IMPLICATIONS

The United States and Japan are two vastly different countries. The United States is abundant in capital, land, and skilled work force. Japan has limited natural resources and is in need of food and raw materials. Yet with it's limitations Japan has utilized its energies in exporting manufactured goods to the rest of the world. According to the *World Development Report* (1989) Japan's international reserves went from $4,876 million in 1970 to $92,702 million by 1987. This is roughly a twenty-fold increase.

Japan's Trade surplus with the United States and the emerging unified Europe in 1993 will initially have to involve negotiations with Japan to open up it's markets and allow the yen to fluctuate more freely. Negotiations on the stability of the yen or other trade agreements will have differential effects on the markets in the respective countries. Since the empirical study showed stochastic dependence for Japan, and stochastic independence for the United States, it is reasonable to expect a gradual change in the value of the yen and the Tokyo Stock Exchange once an agreement is made. In the United States, since the agreement is anticipated the market will gradually creep to the equilibrium point prior to the announcement.

This relationship takes on added importance in light of around-the-clock global security trading. International transactions take place through a sophisticated computer network called SEAQ the NASDAQ system in the United States. With the time differences between the United States and Japan, a 24-hour market is virtually created. An investor could utilize the NYSE from 9:30 A.M. to 4:00 P.M. Eastern time, the Tokyo Stock Exchange from 7 P.M. to 1 A.M., and the London Stock Exchange from 4 A.M. to 10:30 A.M. There are possible arbitrage and profitable trade strategies that can be developed from the fact that the exchanges react with different speed to information. For instance, in the aftermath of the Wall Street's Black Monday crash on October 19, 1987, known as Black Tuesday in Japan's stock markets, the possibility of selling currencies would have been profitable only in Japan and not in the United States.

FUTURE RESEARCH

The present study was limited to two countries. Future research should focus on fifteen to twenty countries. This would verify the test of dependence versus independence of the stock market and the exchange rate markets on a global basis. Also factors that influence the competitive position of an individual exporting firm through changes in the real exchange rates would be of great interest.

Many economists believe that real economic growth is the major influence on the stock market. By monitoring a large number of economic, social, and political variables it is possible to develop an indirect causal model on foreign exchange from domestic factors. Other international measures may appropriately explain returns of stocks like the world stock index, or world industial index.

CONCLUSION

The United States and Japan are two of the world's greatest trading powers. The value of the dollar and the yen, the New York Stock Exchange and Tokyo Stock Exchange are watched by all investors around the world. This study focused on the causal relationship between stock returns and foreign exchange rates for the two countries. By examining this phenomenon, the information efficiency of the stock markets and the foreign exchange markets were examined. The findings show that in the United States, foreign exchange rates are influenced by news and random, unpredictable events. In the case of Japan, the S statistics, the hypothesis that that there is a causal relationship from stock returns to foreign exhange rate changes, cannot be rejected at the five percent level of significance. In Japan the stock market returns lead foreign exchange markets strongly, and lag foreign exchange markets to some degree. The implications of this finding are that the stock market fully anticipates future changes in the foreign exchange market.

REFERENCES

Adler, M., and B. Dumas. 1983. "International Portfolio Choice and Corporation Finance: A Synthesis." *Journal of Finance* 38(June):925-984.

Adler, M., and D. Simon. 1986. "Exchange Risk Surprises in International Portfolios." *Journal of Portfolio Management* (Winter).

Burnstein, D. 1988. *Yen! Japan's New Financial Empire and Its Threat to America.* New York: Simon and Schuster.

Dornbusch, R. 1988. *Exchange Rates and Inflation,* Cambridge, MA: MIT Press.

Fama, E., and W.G. Schwert. 1977. "Asset Returns and Inflation." *Journal of Financial Economics* (November):115-146.

Frenkel, J. 1981. "The Collapse of Purchasing Power Parity during the Seventies." *European Economic Review* 16.

Frenkel, J., and M. Mussa. 1980. "The Efficiency of Foreign Exchange Markets and Measures of Turbulence." *American Economic Review* (May):374-381.

Ghannadian, F., and H. Schneider. 1988. "Financial Development versus Economic Development: The Case of Turkey, Portugal and Greece." *Journal of Economic Development* (June):39-50.

Granger, C.W. 1980. "Testing for Causality: A Personal Viewpoint." *Journal of Economic Dynamics and Control* (June).

Granger, C.W., and P. Newbold. 1986. *Forecasting Economic Time Series,* 2nd ed. New York:Academic Press.

Haugh, L.D. 1976. "Checking the Independence of Two Covariance Stationary Time Series: A Univariate Residual Cross-Correlation Approach." *Journal of American Statistical Association* (June):378-385.

Lessard, D., and B. Solnik. "World, Country and Industry Relationships in Equity Returns." *Financial Analyst Journal* (January/February).

Mussa, M., and S.W. Black. 1986. "Nominal Exchange Rate Regimes and the Behavior of Real Exchange Rates: Evidence and Implications/Real Exchange Rates and Deviations from Purchasing Power Parity under Floating Exchange Rates: A Comment." *Carnegie-Rochester Conference Series on Public Policy* (Netherlands) 25(Autumn):117-220.

Rogalski, R.J., and J.D. Vinso. 1977. "Stock Returns, Money Supply and the Direction of Causality." *Journal of Finance* (June):1017-1030.

Solnik, B. 1989. "Stock Prices and Monetary Variables: The International Evidence." *Financial Analyst Journal* (March/April):69-73.

Wolff, C. 1988. "Exchange Rates, Innovations, and Forecasting." *Journal of International Money and Finance:* 49-61.

World Development Report. 1989. New York: World Bank.

ASSESSING OUTCOMES OF AUTONOMOUS WORK GROUPS:

AN INTERNATIONAL PERSPECTIVE

Abdalla F. Hayajneh and Igwe E. Udeh

INTRODUCTION

The sociotechnical systems approach to organizational analysis and design emphasizes autonomous work groups as a form of work design (Katz and Kahn 1978; Susman 1976). In general, it appears that more organizations have implemented work designs with autonomous work groups on their shop floors than have implemented job characteristics approaches oriented to individuals (Rousseau 1977). Several researches have realized that the use of autonomous work groups increased in a number of industrialized countries (Pasmore et al. 1983) Concurrent with this trend, empirical evidence concerning the effects of autonomous work groups on employees' attitudes and behavior has not displayed a corresponding advance in developing countries. The present study helps to remedy this deficiency and to shed light on the outcomes of such groups in developing nations.

International Research in the Business Disciplines, Volume 1, pages 49-62.
Copyright © 1993 by JAI Press Inc.
All rights of reproduction in any form reserved.
ISBN: 1-55938-538-3

In January 1990, Hayajneh and his associates (Hayajneh et al. 1990) have conducted the first empirical study concerning the implementation of autonomous work groups in two developing countries: Jordan and Saudi Arabia. The findings of that study indicated that the implementation of autonomous work groups in the participating organizations in both countries affected employees' intrinsic job motivation, job satisfaction (intrinsic and extrinsic facets), and employees' life satisfaction; it was also found that the implementation of autonomous work groups affected employees' turnover and organizational production. The present study is an extension of the first one; it explores further effects of autonomous work groups on other individual and organizational variables in certain organizations in Jordan and Egypt.

RESEARCH OBJECTIVE

The major objective of this study is to examine and analyze further effects of autonomous work groups on employees' attitudes and behavior. More specifically, this study empirically tests the proposition that this form of work design increases employee happiness, work involvement, and organizational commitment. These variables are the focus of this study.

Based on the aforementioned proposition, the following hypotheses were formulated:

Hypothesis 1: There is a significant difference in employees' happiness between autonomous and traditional work groups.

Hypothesis 2: There is a significant difference in employees' work involvement between autonomous and traditional work groups.

Hypothesis 3: There is a significant difference in employees' organizational commitment, between autonomous and traditional work groups.

LITERATURE REVIEW

Scientific management of labor, known as Taylorism, was developed in the United States during the period of rapid industrial growth, 1800-1910. Although Taylorism created greater efficiency, it made production jobs boring. The better-educated work force available at present time is increasingly more reluctant to work at such jobs. New technology and flexible manufacturing require that workers do less but think more. Consequently, many companies have moved beyond Taylorism (Katz and Kahn 1978).

Some companies were forced to make radical changes, such as "high performance work-design systems" (Kelly 1978). Other companies have adopted one of the four primary work-design techniques: job rotation, job enlargement, job enrichment, and autonomous group working (Buchanan 1987). However, companies concerned in a work-design technique that helps to organize work in a new way, expand the scope of the job, train workers to become versatile, and involve employees in decision making related to their jobs, have adopted sociotechnical approaches in which autonomous work groups share much of the decision-making process (Huczynski 1985). Likewise, Gracia and Haggith (1989) indicated that some other organizations are adopting patterns of management that include employee involvement programs, team-building interventions, autonomous work groups, and quality circles. While many of these organizational developments (ODs), like autonomous work groups, are successful in helping organizations adapt and grow, many of them, like OD interventions, fail to meet the expectations of OD experts. Similarly, Gowdy (1987) indicated that a major issue facing human service organizations today is the prevalence of poor quality of working life (QWL). Inadequate QWL has led to a variety of negative results, including: (1) physical and psychological problems for workers; (2) absenteeism; (3) labor turnover; (4) loss of workers' potential contributions; (5) poor work-management relations; and (6) demands for workplace innovation. Although Gowdy (1987) has recommended several strategies to improve and enhance QWL, he has emphasized autonomous work groups as the best approach.

Van Houten (1987) examined the nature of the Swedish production system that incorporated autonomous work groups beginning in the 1970s. He concluded that the effect of an innovation such as autonomous work groups cannot be understood without consideration of the following: (1) the characteristics of the production system which may embrace both humanization and rationalization; (2) the task environment which may compel managers to design innovations based on competition and market factors; and (3) economic shifts in the political climate. As a result, Pava (1986) has demonstrated the need for redesigning sociotechnical systems design in order to generate concepts and methods for the 1990s that can yield a "best match" between an organization and its technology. It should be noted that advanced technology is a crucial element for organizational effectiveness.

It is likely that technology does not affect the autonomous work groups to a great extent. Taylor (1990), for example, surveyed all clerical workers of an automated and an unautomated division of a large social service agency in the work place. He found that automation strongly affected management expectations and control. It had some impact upon intrinsic job satisfaction and worker solidarity but minimal impact upon autonomy with respect to office automation. Blackwell (1988) pointed out that some researchers found that the introduction of personal computers initiated the second era in information systems, the era of integration. The "technology-autonomous work group" is the most important component of the second era of computing. This era is still in the future for organizations which have major investments in centralized office automation.

Finally, Hackman and Lawler (1971) and Hackman and Oldham (1976) have noticed that the properties of autonomous work groups correspond or match the features of the job characteristics approach to job design. The properties of the job characteristics approach are skill variety, task identity, task significance, autonomy, and feedback. On this basis, Rousseau (1977), Cummings (1987), and Denison (1982) argued for a synthesis of the aforementioned approaches. Hackman (1983) went further and proposed that autonomous work groups are more powerful than job characteristics approach. The rationale for this suggestion is that autonomous work groups can undertake much larger pieces of work than can individuals, and so allow more substantial manipulation of work characteristics. Thus, Wall, Kemp, Jackson, and Clegg (1986) concluded that previous studies have determined the basic characteristics of autonomous work groups relatively clearly tying them to job theory in general and to the sociotechnical literature in particular. The authors also indicated that the major difference between the two approaches is not related to the content but to the level of analysis and application. With respect to autonomous groups, job characteristics are a property of group work, but not of individual jobs. However, this difference was not in the predicted effects of these approaches to work design.

Sociotechnical theorists such as Davis (1966) and Kelly (1978) have directly or indirectly described the reason and the effects of autonomous work groups in terms of individual psychological reactions. The underlying assumptions have been that this way of organizing work is intrinsically motivating and enriches employees' satisfaction. These reactions have led to improved group performance and reduced labor turnover. These assumptions were supported by Hayajneh, Maghrabi, and Firoz (1990) who found that the implementation of autonomous work groups affected employees' job satisfaction, life satisfaction, turnover, and organization production.

Some scholars suggest that there are further effects of autonomous work groups on other variables. According to Wall, Kemp, Jackson, and Clegg (1986), the implication of autonomous work groups can affect employees' happiness, work involvement, and organizational commitment.

SUMMARY OF TERMS

Working definitions of concepts used in this study are presented. Warr, Cook, and Wall (1979) define the following terms:

1. *Happiness* is "the degree to which a person reports that he or she is currently happy."

2. *Work involvement* is viewed as "the degree to which a person wants to be engaged in work."

Cook and Wall (1980) state that "the concept of *Organizational Commitment* refers to a person's affective reactions to characteristics of his or her employing organization. It is concerned with feelings of attachment to the goals and values of the organization for its own sake rather than for its instrumental value."

Gulowsen (1972) defines *autonomous work groups* as "the workers who maintain a high degree of self-determination by work groups in the management of their day-to-day work." Typically this includes collective control over the pace of work, distribution of tasks, organization of breaks, and collective participation in the recruitment and training of new members.

Emery (1980) indicated that direct supervision is often unnecessary. Kerr, Hill, and Broedling (1986) also pointed out that the first line of supervisory position's current status will be affected substantially by societal trends. The anticipated increase of autonomous work groups will lead to less employment of them, and their functions and activities will change drastically.

To achieve such self-management, Wall, Kemp, Jackson, and Clegg (1986) require three common characteristics in the organization of work for autonomous work groups: (1) employees with functionally interrelated tasks who collectively are responsible for end products; (2) individuals who have a variety of skills may undertake all or a large portion of the groups' tasks; and (3) feedback of evaluation in terms of performance of the whole group.

With respect to the traditional work groups, they are managed in a traditional fashion, or they are managed by supervisors. The position of the supervisor here does exist. All functions are typically carried out by supervisors who maintain responsibility on the shop floor (Helfgott 1987). The investigation in this study is conducted by researchers independent of the participating firms and the consultants who together designed and implemented the work design of autonomous work groups.

METHODS

Methods include participating organizations, data collection, and statistical analysis. Each method has been carried out according to the following procedure:

Participating Organizations

This study has been conducted within certain manufacturing organizations in Jordan and Egypt. The participating organizations in both countries included autonomous and traditional work groups. In the last few years, senior management of some organizations in both countries decided to try a new method of working by implementing autonomous work groups. This choice reflected a commitment to increasing responsibility on the shop floor and an understanding of modern principles of social science governing work design. Consultants worked alongside managers and engineers throughout the planning process. The outcome of this collaboration is that these companies have designed certain jobs on the shop floor to support a well-developed form of autonomous work groups.

The purpose of these organizations is to provide shop-floor employees with substantial autonomy in carrying out day-to-day production along with a high level of involvement in operational decision making. In practice, production employees work in groups of three to five or five to eight people, all of whom are expected to carry out each of five types of jobs involved in the production process. Group members are collectively responsible for assigning jobs among themselves to achieve production targets, meet quality standards, solve problems, record production data, organize breaks, order and collect materials, deliver finished goods to stores, consult engineers for training new recruits, and participate in selecting new employees.

Moreover, individuals in each group have considerable control over the amount of variety which they experience by rotating their tasks. Each production group is responsible for one production line. Group members interact informally throughout the working day, but they make the most important decisions at formal weekly group meetings. Since nearly all the functions typically carried out by supervisors are the responsibility of shop-floor employees, the position of supervisor does not exist. Groups report directly to a support manager whose duty is to provide the necessary support and advice for the development of both social and technical skills within the work groups. Support managers are responsible for providing the facilities and the conditions within which groups can operate in a semiautonomous fashion. However, managers maintain disciplinary procedures for running an effective production facility. Thus, this method of working meets all the major criteria of an autonomous group work.

Data Collection

Data concerning employees' attitudes and behavior have been obtained by survey questionnaires. The questionnaire also included information about certain demographic variables (gender, age, and length of service). A part of the translated questionnaires (Arabic Language) was administered by some faculty members in Jordanian University in Jordan in certain Jordanian organizations in July 1990. The other part was administered by the other faculty members in Cairo University, Egypt in the participating organizations in Egypt in July 1990. Sixty complete and usable questionnaires were returned for each group (autonomous and traditional) in each country. Confidentiality was assured with concern to individuals and organizations, and questionnaire completion during work time was requested.

Scales to measure employees' happiness, work involvement, and organizational commitment were developed by Warr, Cook, and Wall (1979) response formats ranging from strongly disagree or dissatisfied to strongly agree or satisfied. The computed alpha of the overall scores for the three measurement scales are above .80 in both countries.

To assure that the translation from English to Arabic did not distort the meaning, the following procedure was followed. Thirty questionnaires in both languages were given to 30 employees whose knowledge of the English language is good in both countries. The correlation between the answers to both languages was .99 in each country. To assure the reliability of this research instrument, the split-half procedure was used and alpha was above .80 in both countries.

Statistical Analysis

Statistical analysis in this study utilized the statistical package for social sciences (SPSS-X) to compute means, frequencies, percentages, *t*-tests, and one-way analysis of variance (ANOVA). The level of significance was set at .05. These tests were used to test the significance of mean differences in terms of employees' happiness, work involvement, and organizational commitment, between autonomous and traditional work groups in certain Jordanian and Egyptian organizations. Due to the space frame, *t*-tests will be reported.

RESULTS

The results of this study are based on data from a total of 240 employees in both countries. There were 60 employees for each autonomous and traditional work group in each country. While the Egyptian sample included 52 (86%) men and 8 (14%) women, the Jordanian sample included 55 (92%) men and 5 (8%) women for autonomous and traditional work groups, respectively. The average age of the Jordanian sample was 34.7 years, and the average age of the Egyptian samples was 35.2 years. The average length of service differed between the two samples; it averaged 3.5 and 5.2 years for the Jordanian and the Egyptian samples, respectively.

Results are presented in three parts. The first part concerns autonomous and traditional work groups in certain Jordanian organizations. The second one concerns their counterparts in Egypt. Finally, the results concerning autonomous work groups in both countries are compared and contrasted.

Table 1 presents a comparison between the results of autonomous work groups and traditional work groups in certain Jordanian organizations. The *t*-test in Table 1 does not show that there is significant difference concerning employees' happiness between autonomous work groups and traditional work groups in the participating Jordanian organizations. However, the *t*-test shows that there are significant difference between autonomous and traditional work groups in work involvement and organizational commitment. Analysis of variance of the mean scores in Table 1 support these results.

Table 2 presents another comparison between the results of the autonomous and traditional work groups in the participating organizations. The *t*-test in Table 2 reveals that there is no significant difference between autonomous and traditional work groups in employees' happiness. However, the *t*-test reveals significant differences between autonomous and traditional work groups in work involvement, and organizational commitment. Analysis of variance of the mean scores in Table 2 support these results.

Table 1.   Comparison Between Autonomous and
Conventional Work Groups in Jordan

		Mean Score and SD			
Variables	Number of Items	Autonomous Work Groups (N = 60)	Conventional Work Groups (N = 60)	T	P
Employees' Happiness	3	26.14 (2.45)	20.16 (2.13)	1.32	.74
Work Involvement	6	26.60 (3.71)	16.88 (2.84)	18.04	.03*
Organizational Commitment	9	28.46 (2.63)	15.64 (2.03)	19.34	.04*

Notes: * $p < .05$
          Standard Deviation (SD) is reported in parentheses.

Table 2.   Comparison Between Autonomous and
Conventional Work Groups in Egypt

		Mean Score and SD			
Variables	Number of Items	Autonomous Work Groups (N = 60)	Conventional Work Groups (N = 60)	T	P
Employees' Happiness	3	20.60 (2.16)	18.22 (2.42)	1.22	.82
Work Involvement	6	23.02 (3.12)	14.84 (2.60)	16.16	.03*
Organizational Commitment	9	26.33 (3.60)	16.46 (2.90)	14.42	.04*

Notes: * $p < .05$
          Standard Deviation (SD) is reported in parentheses.

Table 3.   Comparison Between Autonomous and
Work Groups in Egypt and Jordan

		Mean Score and SD			
Variables	*Number of Items*	*Autonomous Work Groups (N = 60)*	*Conventional Work Groups (N = 60)*	*T*	*P*
Employees'	3	20.60	26.14	1.98	.10*
Happiness		(3.15)	(4.72)		
Work	6	23.02	26.60	1.22	.84
Involvement		(2.42)	(2.12)		
Organizational	9	26.33	28.46	1.53	.73
Commitment		(4.82)	(5.16)		

Notes: * $p < .05$
Standard Deviation (SD) is reported in parentheses.

Table 3 presents a comparison between the autonomous work groups in both countries. The *t*-test in Table 3 shows that there is a significant difference in employees' happiness between the two autonomous work groups in both countries. However, there are no significant differences in work involvement and organizational commitment between the two autonomous work groups in both countries. Analysis of variance of the mean scores in Table 3 support these results.

It is obvious now that data analysis in Tables 1 and 2 have answered the three research questions with respect to the sample employees in Jordan and Egypt respectively.

DISCUSSION AND IMPLICATIONS

This empirical study has revealed that autonomous work groups have specific rather than wide-range effects on employees' attitudes and behaviors in both countries. Although autonomous work groups as a work design substantially enhanced work involvement and organizational commitment, it did not affect employees' happiness in both countries. The striking aspects of these results is their restricted range of effects on individual attitudes compared with the range predicted from the literature review. A plausible reason for the specific affects is that the work design of autonomous work groups did not differ sufficiently from that of traditional practice. Another explanation for the restricted range of effects on employees' attitudes is that the rigorous research design eliminated causal interpretations that weaker designs would have supported (Kemp et al. 1985; Wall et al. 1986). Even within this study, it is easy to see how this could have happened with a different research design. Data analysis supports this fact. While data analysis in Tables 1 and 2 indicates that autonomous work groups in Jordan and Egypt have reported higher levels of work involvement and organizational commitment than their counterparts in traditionally designed jobs, there has been no significant difference in employees' happiness between the two groups in both countries.

Data analysis in Table 3 shows that there is a significant difference ($p < .10$) in employees' happiness between the two autonomous work groups in Egypt and Jordan. Autonomous work groups in Jordan are happier more than their counterparts in Egypt. This difference may be justified in terms of economic conditions. Although both countries are poor, Jordan has not the same relative degree of poverty. On the other hand, the mean scores of work involvement and organizational commitment of autonomous work groups in Jordan are higher than those of their counterparts in Egypt. A plausible reason is that the Egyptian government still maintains a stronger social system than that of Jordan. This notion is supported by the evidence of a large public sector in Egypt when compared to that of Jordan. Consequently, this may have led to the variation of mean scores in work involvement and organizational commitment between the two autonomous work groups in the two countries.

With respect to implications of the results in this study, there are several practical ones. The results show that autonomous group work is a viable proposition and is appreciated by those who experience it. In addition, it may have clear economic benefits which stem from the logic of the groups themselves. With decision making delegated to the shop floors, the need for supervisors declines or vanishes, indirect labor costs decrease, and productivity benefits can accrue. Given organizational designs, resources, and managerial structures, task performance could also be improved (Hayajneh et al. 1990). It should also be clear that such work systems have their costs although they are difficult to quantify because they mainly include managerial time and effort. In addition, these practical implications need to be quantified.

However, it should not be forgotten that the results obtained were from specific Egyptian and Jordanian organizations which have the advantage of allowing the implementation of specific radical and well-developed forms of autonomous work groups. But by the same token this specific job design limits generalizability. It is reasonable to assume that in established organizations the threat that autonomous work groups pose for the nature and the continued existence of supervisory jobs might reduce or outweigh their potential practical benefits. Similarly, the emphasis on employees having several skills may cut across agreed demarcation lines and customs and practices of work, especially in unionized organizations. In established organizations, people may resist such job design or change. Thus, in such context, the process of change may be as important as its content (Wall et al. 1986).

Employees in autonomous work groups have reported higher levels of happiness, work involvement, and organizational commitment than their counterparts in traditionally designed jobs. However, this job design might produce several side effects which are recommended for future research. Based on the findings form the interview programs in previous studies (Kemp et al. 1983; Wall et al. 1986), one might infer that managers of autonomous work groups in the participating organizations in both countries might probably have faced stress, as well as interpersonal and interfunctional conflict. These reactions are likely due to the difficulties involved in the implementation and management of an untried system of autonomous group working.

One explanation for this projection is that rate of dismissals will go up following any major recruitment program since a proportion of employees will not fit easily into the new system in their organizations. It is also expected that a number of disciplinary dismissals will occur as a direct consequence of autonomous work groups. Line managers will also be aware that they had dismissed employees who, under traditional conditions, would not have been required to leave. They might attribute their taking a hard line in part to the pressure on them to produce and to develop the new system of job design. However, they still relate the side effect of autonomous work grouping as the main reason. The absence of supervisors may tempt some employees to step out of line or abuse their freedom, which will not be immediately detected. Under traditional job designs, supervisors take early action and probably protect employees from managers. In autonomous work groups, misdemeanors will typically be more advanced when they are known and warrant use of formal warning procedures. In other words, management will rely more on formal procedures and sanctions than will the managers of traditionally designed jobs do.

The supporting managers are expected to feel the greatest level of pressure both in terms of production output required, and in terms of the difficulties involved in communicating, interviewing, disciplining, and providing the resources and conditions necessary for autonomous work groups to work together effectively and efficiently. The difficulty will be exacerbated because it will not be possible to promote personnel within the organization via supervisory positions. Hence, new job incumbents will need time to be socialized into the organization and to experience problems of managing autonomous work groups. On the other hand, autonomous group members might not like to discipline members who consistently break group norms and report such problems to their support managers.

But in pointing to such side effects, we should not lose sight of the advantages of autonomous work groups. The advantages of autonomous work groups were sufficient to ensure that the group members and mangers supported them, and this trend will continue for the foreseeable future. The results of this study indicated that shop floor employees actively enjoyed such job design and its attendant responsibilities. They are expected to be happy not to have supervisors breathing down their necks, and also appreciate the way in which management treated them as mature adults.

SUMMARY

The results of this study provided evidence that the effects of autonomous work groups are strong, but restricted to work involvement and organizational commitment in the developing countries of Egypt and Jordan. Contrary to our prediction, autonomous work groups have no clear effects on employees' happiness in these countries. Interpreted with a strict line of causal inference, the results of this study showed that autonomous work groups in both countries had specific rather than a wide-ranging effects on employees' attitudes and behavior compared with the range predicted from the literature. Possible explanations for this are: the form of the work design of autonomous work groups does not differ sufficiently from the traditional practice; the results are idiosyncratic; and, the rigorous research design eliminated causal interpretations which weaker designs could have supported. However, one might argue that these explanations are implausible ones.

The comparison between the results concerning autonomous work groups in both countries revealed that the sampled Jordanian employees are happier than their counterparts in Egypt and their mean scores of work involvement and organizational commitment are also higher than those of their counterparts in Egypt. A plausible explanation for this is that the economic and social systems in both countries are different. In general, the economy in Jordan is relatively better than that of Egypt and the size of the public sector in Egypt is bigger than that of Jordan.

The results of this study have practical implications. They showed that autonomous work groups are a viable proposition appreciated by those who have experienced such job design. Furthermore, the implementation of autonomous work groups might have vital economic advantages. However, the implementation of autonomous work groups might be associated with side effects which have been recommended for future research. An example is the managers' stress. The pressures on managers to produce, develop, and manage under this new job design required to the implementation of autonomous work groups is likely to be a main reason for their expected stress.

REFERENCES

Blackwell, G. 1988. "Office Systems Entering a New Era." *Computing Canada* 14: 48-57.
Buchanan, D. 1987. "Job Enrichment is Dead: Long Live High Performance Work Design." *Personnel Management* 19: 40-43.

Cook, J., and T. Wall. 1980. "New Work Attitude Measures of Trust, Organizational Commitment, and Personal Need Non-Fulfillment." *Journal of Occupational Psychology* 53:39-52.

Cummings, T.G. 1987. "Self-Regulating Work Groups: A Socio-Technical Synthesis." *Academy of Management Review* 3:625-634.

Davis, L.E. 1966. "The Design of Jobs." *Industrial Relations* 6:21-45.

Dension, D.R. 1982. "Sociotechnical Design and Self-Managing Work Groups: The Impact on Control." *Journal of Occupational Behavior* 3:289-313.

Emery, F.E. 1980. "Designing Socio-Technical Systems in Greenfield Sites." *Journal of Occupational Behavior* 1:19-27.

Garcia, J.E., and C. Haggith. 1989. "OD Interventions that Work." *Personnel Administrator* 34:90-94.

Gowdy, E.A. 1987. "The Application of Quality of Work Life Research to Human Service Management." *Administration in Social Work* 11:3-4.

Gulowsen, J. 1972. "A Measure of Work Group Autonomy." Pp. 374-390 in *Design of Jobs,* edited by L.E. David and J.C. Taylor. Harmondsworth, UK: Penguin.

Hackman, J.R. 1977. "Work Designing." Pp. 93-162 in *Improving Life at Work,* edited by J.R. Hackman and J.L. Suttle. Santa Monica, CA: Goodyear.

————. 1983. "The Design of Work Teams." Pp. 70-94 in *Handbook of Organization Behavior,* edited by J. Lorsch. Englewood Cliffs, NJ: Prentice-Hall.

Hackman, J.R., and E.E. Lawler. 1971. "Employee Reactions to Job Characteristics." *Journal of Applied Psychology* 55:259-286.

Hackman, J.R., and G.R. Oldham. 1976. "Motivation Through the Design of Work: Test of Theory." *Organizational Behavior and Human Performance* 15:250-279.

Hayajneh, A., A. Maghrabi, and N. Firoz. 1990. "Assessed Outcomes of Autonomous Work Groups: International Perspective." *Self-Managed Team Proceedings* 1:295-301.

Helfgott, R.B. 1987. "Moving Beyond Taylorism." *International Journal of Technology Management* 2:3-5.

Huczynski, A.A. 1985. "Designing High Commitment: High Performance Organizations." *Technovation* 3:111-118.

Katz, D., and R.L. Kahn. 1978. *The Social Psychology of Organizations,* 2nd ed. New York: Wiley.

Kelly, J.E. 1978. "A Re-appraisal of Sociotechnical Systems Theory." *Human Relations* 31:1069-1099.

Kemp, N., T. Wall, C. Clegg, and J. Cordery. 1983. "Autonomous Work Groups in a Greenfield Site: A Comparative Study." *Journal of Occupational Psychology* 56:271-288.

Kerr, S., K. Hill, and L. Broedling. 1986. "The First-Line Supervisor: Phasing Out or Here to Stay?" *Academy of Management Review* 11:103-117.

Pasmore, W., C. Francis, J. Haldeman, and A. Shani. 1983. "Sociotechnical Systems: A North American Reflection on the Empirical Studies of the Seventies." *Human Relations* 35:1179-1204.

Pava, C. 1986. "Redesigning Sociotechnical Systems Design: Concepts and Methods for the 1990s." *Journal of Applied Behavioral Science* 22:201-221.

Rousseau, D.M. 1977. "Technological Differences in Job Characteristics, Employee Satisfaction and Motivation: A Synthesis of Job Design Research and Socio-Technical Systems Theory." *Organizational Behavior and Human Performance* 19:18-42.

SPSS, Inc. 1986. *SPSS-X: User's guide,* 2nd ed. Chicago, IL: Marketing Department, SPSS, Inc.

Susman, G.I. 1976. *Autonomy at Work.* New York: Praeger.

Taylor, W. 1990. "Autonomy and Social Integration: A Study of Office Clerical Workers." Unpublished doctoral dissertation, The American University, Washington, DC.

Van Houten, D.R. 1987. "The Political Economy and Technical Control of Work Humanization in Sweden During the 1970s and 1980s." *Work Occupations* 14:493-513.

Wall, T.D., N.J. Kemp, P.R. Jackson, and C.W. Clegg. 1986. "Outcomes of Autonomous Work
    Groups: A Long-Term Field Experiment." *Academy of Management Journal* 14:483-513.
Warr, P.B., J.D. Cook, and T.D. Wall. 1979. "Scales for the Measurement of Some Work Attitudes
    and Aspects of Psychological Well-Being." *Journal of Occupational Psychology* 52:129-
    148.

THE CULTURAL IMPACT OF U.S. EMPLOYMENT DISCRIMINATION LAWS ON FOREIGN MULTINATIONAL CORPORATIONS:

THE CASE OF JAPANESE FIRMS DOING BUSINESS IN THE UNITED STATES

Carl L. Swanson

INTRODUCTION

As national economies become more global, what were formerly domestic business enterprises operating in a familiar home country culture are now multinational business corporations (MNCs) operating in host country cultures alien to their own. Understandably, these MNCs want to continue to achieve the superior performance and maintain the competitiveness they enjoyed in their home country as they go international. But too often, they also want to use familiar home country labor/management techniques in their overseas

International Research in the Business Disciplines, Volume 1, pages 63-71.
Copyright © 1993 by JAI Press Inc.
All rights of reproduction in any form reserved.
ISBN: 1-55938-538-3

operations. It is not surprising, therefore, that these MNCs, in transferring their national management culture overseas, are often confronted with differing sociocultural attitudes—attitudes that have often been translated into legal requirements or restraints by the host country. The objective of this study is to explore a microcosm of this problem by focusing on the difficulties experienced by foreign multinational corporations when doing business in the United States and to do so from the perspective of the U.S. employment discrimination laws. U.S. laws dealing with employment discrimination strongly reflect American sociocultural attitudes on the kind of management culture and the type of labor/management techniques that can and cannot be used by business firms operating in the United States. Thus, we can explore within the confines of a narrowly defined area transnational problems arising from the exportation of culture-based management values into what may be a hostile environment.

Since foreign MNCs are doing business in the United States under international treaties between the United States and their home country, this paper will first scrutinize the growing body of law dealing with the relationship between treaty rights given to MNCs and the statutory obligations imposed upon them when doing business in the United States. This scrutinization will allow us to gain new insight into the tension between treaty rights and statutory obligations when viewed in the context of conflicting cultures.

The study will conclude by exploring some of the cultural barriers that make it difficult for some MNCs, particularly Japanese firms, to comply with U.S. employment discrimination laws. Thus, we may gain some understanding of how sensitive or insensitive the Japanese have been to the sociocultural concerns of the United States regarding employment discrimination.nation and how successful they have been in the past and may be in the future in transferring their management culture to the United States.

TENSION BETWEEN FCN TREATIES AND U.S. EMPLOYMENT LAWS

Treaties of Friendship, Commerce & Navigation (FCN Treaties) gained momentum after World War II when the foreign policy of the United States aggressively pursued an objective of encouraging American investment abroad by fostering the principle of equality of treatment between the nationals of the potential host country and United States business citizens. These FCN treaties provided for "national treatment" rather than "most-favored-nation treatment." Under the former, the alien was entitled to freely carry on his/her chosen business under conditions of non-discrimination and to enjoy the same legal opportunities to succeed and prosper on his/her merits as was allowed citizens of the host country. When signatory nations were unwilling to grant "national treatment," investment in the host country was permitted under the "most-favored-nation treatment" by ensuring no less favorable treatment for the United States firm than that under which the most privileged foreign company operated (Walker 1956).

For firms wishing to do business in the United States, these FCN Treaties granted two rights that are pertinent to this study: (1) the right of MNCs to incorporate and do business in the United States, and (2) the right of MNCs to use expatriate personnel in their U.S. operations. Exercise of these rights, however, raised two important legal issues—issues that created a tension between FCN Treaty rights permitting foreign MNCs to do business in the United States and the legal mandates imposed on employment practices in the United States under the U.S. employment discrimination laws.[1] The first issue was whether foreign MNCs are exempt from U.S. employment discrimination laws. The second issue involved the extent to which expatriate personnel could be employed by a foreign MNC when U.S. employment laws forbid employment discrimination based on nationality.

Issue One: Are Foreign MNCs Exempt from U.S Employment Discrimination Laws?

The first major challenge involving a key application of FCN Treaty rights was raised by a Japanese firm who contended that the United States-Japan FCN Treaty giving Japan the right to establish a corporation in the United States also exempted the Japanese firm from compliance with United States employment laws. The Supreme Court was unanimous in a 1982 decision which staated that a company incorporated in the United States, even though it was a wholly owned foreign subsidiary, was a United States company under United States laws and subject, like any other United States company, to United States employment laws. The purpose of the treaty was to ensure that Japan did not suffer discrimination in doing business in the United States based "on their alienage" (*Sumitomo Shoji America, Inc.* v. *Avagliano* 1982). Under the "national treatment" reasoning, the Japanese firm was not being treated any differently than U.S. firms. To the contrary, the Japanese firm was being treated the same as a U.S. firm. The answer to the first question was a resounding NO.

The key to the Sumitomo decision can be found in the fact that the wholly owned Japanese subsidiary was a U.S. corporation. This is not to suggest that all foreign organizations are subject to U.S. employment laws. Immunity from domestic laws can be granted to international organizations by treaty. Thus, the World Bank enjoys immunity under the International Organizations Immunity Act from the employment laws of the United States. The U.S. Court of Appeals, District of Columbia Circuit, noted that opening the Bank's operations to the laws of the more than 140 nations in which it does business would render the ability of the Bank to operate as an international organization, created by the joint action of several states, "nearly impossible" (*Mendaro* v. *The World Bank* 1983).

Issue Two: To What Extent Can Expatriate Personnel Be Employed By A Foreign MNC?

This second issue is still being tested, although some important parameters have been established by the U.S. courts. To give effect to both the treaty obligations of the United States and the expressed will of Congress regarding employment discrimination, the United States Court of Appeals for the Third Circuit acknowledged that the FCN Treaties give the foreign firm the right to employ alien executive personnel of its own choosing in executive positions. The issue before that court involved the replacement by Korean Air Lines of older American managers with younger Korean personnel—the American suing on the basis of age discrimination.

The Third Circuit drew a careful distinction between national origin discrimi-nation and citizenship discrimination. As the court interpreted the history of U.S. negotiations leading to the various FCN Treaties, it held that the target of the Treaty Articles permitting foreign firms to use their home country personnel was the overturning of former U.S. domestic legislation that had discriminated against the citizens of certain nations. The purpose of these new FCN Treaty provisions regarding expatriate personnel was to secure freedom for the foreign investor to place their own citizens in key management positions (*McNamara* v. *Korean Air Lines* 1988). By contrast, the FCN Treaties did not exempt foreign firms from laws prohibiting race, national origin, or age discrimination. In essence, the right to use expatriate personnel was a limited, not an absolute right (*McNamara* v. *Korean Air Lines* 1988).

Still another U.S. appellate court held that the privilege to employ expatriate personnel was a "narrow privilege." As the court noted: "... companies . . . are permitted to discriminate in favor of their own nations or citizens for certain high level positions, but not to discriminate against others in the labor force of the host country on any other basis" (*Wickes* v. *Olympic Airways* 1984).

Under the judicial reasoning of these two appellate courts, foreign MNCs have a right to employ expatriate personnel in key management positions. But can foreign firms "flout" the labor laws of the host country by defining all of its employment positions as executive positions to be filled by expatriate personnel? The answer appears to be no. The national safeguard on the misuse of expatriate personnel is found in the granting of visas by the U.S. State Department. The U.S. State Department must grant treaty trader status before expatriates can fill an executive position of a foreign firm doing business in the United States. The court contended that the issuance of a treaty trader visa permitted the United States to limit the hiring of expatriate personnel to key positions only (*Wickes* v. *Olympic Airways* 1984).

THE UNITED STATES/JAPAN SITUATION

It is against this legal backdrop that this study explores some of the cultural barriers that make it difficult for Japanese MNCs to comply with U.S. employment discrimination laws. Unlike the citizens of other nations, Americans and Japanese are especially prone to disregard the cultures of other nations, but for different reasons.

Americans do so because the vast size of their country and the common language spoken in the United States makes it possible for many American firms to avoid real exposure to foreign ways of behaving and thinking. U.S. pride in its "melting pot" ideology hides the fact that the United States has many of the aspects of a closed and parochial culture—just as the United States can be viewed as essentially a closed economy in which foreign trade represents only a small percentage of gross national product. Furthermore, the United States is a young nation with all of the brashness of youth and the accompanying belief that they can do a better job of "inventing the wheel" than their forbears.

The Japanese, on the other hand, tend to ignore other national cultures because they are a small nation with a highly homogenous population and well-defined shared values. Minority rights represent little threat since minorities comprise only about one-half of one percent of the population (Wokutch 1990). In addition, they have a cultural history that reaches back centuries into the past. More tradition-oriented, they are willing to adopt modern technology, but are not necessarily willing to sacrifice the basic cultural values of their ancestors. Trade barriers, erected for the initial purpose of protecting their "infant" industries, have tended to maintain this closed-society mentality, historically associated with Tokugawan Japan prior to the Meiji Restoration more than a century ago. This cultural antiquity, furthermore, sustains a national perception that they have the superior culture.

Mr. John Kageyama, president of American Kotobuki Electronics, spoke of this perception in a recent article. After expressing surprise when his American workers experienced culture shock over the introduction of Japanese management techniques into a U.S. Panasonic subsidiary, he proceeded to justify the imposition of Japanese management values as a means of making it "easier for Americans to live with" his culture. In subsequent Letters to the Editor, he was accused of "outright cultural chauvinism" by imposing the Japanese way on American workers and failing to "synthesize a new corporate culture based on a fusion of the best aspects of both national cultures" (Eisler 1988).

The Case of the Japanese Firms Doing Business in the United States

The Japanese were forced to go international due to global economic realities. As a result, there has been a tremendous increase in Japanese investment in the United States over the past two decades. It has been sufficient to raise a public alarm in the United States over the desirability of permitting the Japanese to use their American trade deficit dollars to "Buy America." This investment pace has accelerated as more and more Japanese manufacturing facilities were opened in the United States to build Japanese products and avoid U.S. "protectionist" policies.

The Japanese invasion has meant more than dollars, however—it has also meant the importation of their management culture into the United States. Because of significant socio-cultural disparities between the United States and Japan, both the obstacles and challenges confronting any multinational enterprise in the area of "expatriate" management practices can be seen in the experience of Japanese firms doing business in the United States. (This is not to suggest that U.S. firms have been more successful when going overseas into cultures alien to their own.)

The cumulative effect of the introduction of Japanese values has now gained sufficient momentum that its impact in the United States has begun to be felt by a variety of groups. These groups, in turn, have begun to respond, both positively and negatively, to this importation and a legal record of their responses is emerging that is open to analysis. As noted by one law firm specializing in advising Japanese companies on labor matters: "Discrimination lawsuits are becoming a significant risk for Japanese companies operating in the United States." A Japanese government survey found that 57 percent of Japanese companies operating in the United States were worried about discrimination suits ("Japanese Firms" 1990).

A byproduct of these discrimination lawsuits has been the growing body of judicial decisions defining the relationship between FCN Treaty rights and the U.S. employment discrimination laws. What is perhaps unusual is that these decisions are emerging from the growing litigiousness of Japanese firms in resisting U.S. socio-cultural demands—a surprising tactical move considering the Japanese attitude about solving societal problems through compromise rather than through adjudicative confrontation (Tsubota 1984).

Why are 57 percent of Japanese firms doing business in the United States concerned about U. S. employment laws? At least four factors can be identified that suggest that Japanese MNCs may have difficulty in complying with the U.S. employment discrimination laws: (1) the U. S. propensity for the use of law to change sociocultural attitudes, (2) gender discrimination on the part of Japanese male managers, (3) a lack of Japanese understanding of the Western legal concept of rights, and (4) the insensitivity of Japanese managers to social concerns.

Factor One: The Use Of Law To Change Social Attitudes

One of the characteristics of American society today is the extensive use of laws to change societal attitudes and the reliance of individuals and groups on the judicial branch of the U.S. government to protect them by recognizing and enforcing constitutional rights. Americans, therefore, operate under a misconception that since U.S. legal mandates will lead to a change in employer/employee relationships in U.S. firms, it should be equally effective with foreign firms. But as the Senior Vice President of Merrill Lynch Capital Markets in Japan noted with reference to Japanese securities legislation contrasted with the U.S. approach to securities violations: "Japan is not the United States" (Twakuni 1988). In the United States, laws are effective in changing society largely because traditions, as a societal control mechanism, are viewed with suspicion by many powerful interest groups. On the other hand, the use of laws to change society and enforce such social change has the approval of U.S. society generally. In Japan, tradition, not the law, plays a dominant role in Japanese society. Thus, while the Japanese will scrupulously follow the letter of the law, the customary way of doing business is continued and inexorably works to defeat the stated purpose of the law (Twakuni 1988, p. 304).

Factor Two: Gender Discrimination In Japan

The "male chauvinistic" attitude of Japanese society can be seen in the Japanese approach to employment discrimination as evidenced in the recent passage of a Japanese Equal Employment Opportunity Law. "Achieving freedom from discrimination in employment on the basis of sex would require change so basic and far-reaching as to shake society to its very roots" ("Japan's Equal" 1989). To soften the blow on Japanese society, the 1985 law is attempting to achieve this dramatic change through evolution rather than revolution. The Act calls for voluntary compliance rather than legal coercion. Its approach is persuasive, educational, and mediative in character based upon the twin Japanese societal pillars of voluntarism and gradualism. Two reasons are given for this approach: (1) the Law is before its time, and (2) "neither Japanese women or Japanese men are entirely ready" for such a basic change ("Japan's Equal" 1989).

It is, therefore, not surprising that it took ten years for the first Japanese sex-bias case to work its way through the Japanese courts and that the first sexual harassment case to be filed in Japan was not filed until 1989 ("Women Workers" 1990). It is also not surprising that one of the first U.S. employment discrimination cases involving a Japanese firm filed in 1975 has still not been heard on the merits/facts of the case but has been fought entirely on procedural grounds (*Spiess* v. *C. Itoh & Co. (America) Inc.* 1984).

Factor Three: The Western Notion Of Rights

Complicating the managerial problem for Japanese firms is that the notion of "rights" is a Western idea. This concept does not exist in traditional Japan. Relationships are basically intuitive and unexpressed, not delineated as a "right" (Minami 1986). To discuss employer/employee relationships in terms of rights rather than obligations is alien to Japanese thinking.

This difference between rights and obligations was rather dramatically brought home to an American female employee who sued her Japanese employer on grounds of sexual harassment. As she continued her employment while her case was pending in the courts, she experienced great difficulty in understanding why she was being ostracized by the Japanese members of the firm as a disloyal employee. When her case was ultimately settled out of court, one of the conditions of the settlement was that she immediately terminate her employment effective the day the settlement was signed by the litigants.[2]

Factor Four: Lack of Social Responsibility

Professor Nobuo Noda, a noted Japanese management scholar, has observed that the three requirements of a corporation are: to produce a profit, to provide for the welfare of employees, and to be responsible to society. According to Professor Noda, it is the third factor which, until recently, has not been given sufficient attention by Japanese companies.[3] Underpinning Professor Noda's observation is an awareness that far too many Japanese firms doing business overseas tend to treat alien legal standards as vague, nonquantifiable variables that require only nominal managerial attention, particularly when they reflect sociocultural views that differ from Japan. This parochial or, at best, ethnocentric view can be seen in the position taken by some Japanese firms operating in the United States when confronted with an employment situation involving U.S. employment discrimination laws.

CONCLUSION

The United States-Japan experience discussed above suggests that the new frontier in global management is the urgent need for MNC executives to cope with the emerging realities of intercultural management. Successful performance of this management task requires careful analysis of the legal/ cultural environments of the host nations in which business is being done and concomitant adjustment of business strategies, administrative structures, and corporate cultures to achieve synergistic results that comply with the cultural/ legal demands of the host nations as well as the home country. For firms engaged in international business operations, developing synergistic responses to conflicting demands imposed by diverse national social concerns may be the single important task confronting international managers today.

NOTES

1. Examples of U.S. employment laws include Title VII of the Civil Rights Acts of 1964, as amended; the Age Discrimination in Employment Act; and so forth.

2. The author was involved in a lawsuit in 1990 as a consultant on Japanese management practices, hired by the plaintiff. As part of the court settlement and subsequent payment of consulting fees, the author was required to consent to a court order forbidding the disclosure of the identity of the parties to the litigation or discussion of the specific facts of the case.

3. For perspective on Japanese adaptation of United States business practices, see Noda (1969).

REFERENCES

Eisler, G. 1988. "Bridging Gaps." *Oregon Business* (December 12), Sec. 1, p. 21.

"Japan's Equal Employment Opportunity Law: An Alternative Approach to Social Change." 1989. *Columbia Law Review,* p. 605.

"Japanese Firms In United States Face Personnel Danger." 1990. *Wall Street Journal* (October 15), p. B1.

McNamara v. *Korean Air Lines.* 863 *F.2d* 1135, 1145 (1988).

Mendaro v. *The World Bank.* 717 *F.2d* 610, 619 (1983).

Minami, K.A. 1986. "Japanese Thought and Western Law: A Tangential View of the Japanese Bengoshi and the Japanese American Attorney" *Loyola Los Angeles International & Comparative Law Journal* 8:301.

Noda, N. 1969. *How Japan Absorbed American Management Methods.* Tokyo, Japan: Asian Productivity Organization.

Spiess v. *C. Itoh & Co. (America) Inc.* 725 *F.2d* 970 (1984).

Sumitomo Shoji America, Inc. v. *Avagliano.* 102 *S.Ct.* 2374 (1982).

Tsubota, J. 1984. "Myth & Truth on Non-Litigiousness in Japan." *The Law School Record* 30(Spring):9.

Twakuni, T. 1988. "Laws May Change But Japanese Society Does Not." *Japanese Law & Society* 6:300.

Walker, H. 1956. "Treaties for the Encouragement and Protection of Foreign Investment: Present United States Practices." *Am.J.Comp. L.* 5: 229-230.

Wickes v. *Olympic Airways.* 745 *F.2d* 363, 367 (1984).

Wokutch, R.W. 1990. "Corporate Social Responsibility Japanese Style." *Academy of Management Executive* 4(2).

"Women Workers In Japan Win Sex-Bias Case." *Wall Street Journal* (July 6-7), p. 10.

PART III

MULTI-COUNTRY STUDIES

INTRODUCTION TO PART III

The third part of this volume broadens the focus to include groups of countries. The authors are interested in questions whose dimensions transcend national boundaries but have simultaneous application in several areas. Thus, the interesting feature of the section is the authors' ability to render conclusions having application for both practitioners and academics across a broad spectrum of countries.

Our first study in Part III, by Drs. Kumar, Nonis, and Yauger, focuses on the negotiating process in the international arena. To support their contention that there is a definite need for international managers to be aware of cultural differences in attitudes, values, and norms as they negotiate in overseas markets, the authors examined differences in negotiating patterns for four major global regions: North America, Latin America, the Near East, and the Far East. Using a factor analysis of a twenty-one item survey instrument from 247 individuals, the authors' study supports earlier research that "the heart of the matter in business negotiation" does vary across cultures. Using a four-stage negotiation model, the authors find that the building relationship stage is most important for Latin American and Arab managers while the persuading stage is most crucial for North American managers. Far Eastern managers, on the other hand, tend to treat negotiation as an holistic experience and de-emphasize the division of the negotiation process into definitive stages.

International Research in the Business Disciplines, Volume 1, pages 75-77.
Copyright © 1993 by JAI Press Inc.
All rights of reproduction in any form reserved.
ISBN: 1-55938-538-3

Is there such a thing as an "Asian management style" that differs from the "U.S. management style?" Certainly, most practitioners would welcome such a conclusion as an easy and comfortable way of operating in the international arena. The next study, by Drs. Boje, Vance, and Stage, challenges the belief, which far too many of us share, that there is really an Asian management style that can be compared with a U.S. management style. Thus, the authors of this study take exception to the assumption in the previous study that managers in a given cultural region have a commonality in managerial approach that can be identified and analyzed. To support their challenge to the conventional wisdom, the authors analyzed the management styles of 736 managers in five Asian countries: Hong Kong, Malaysia, Indonesia, the Philippines, and Thailand. The authors found that, in the case of the planning and organizing functions, the rate of industrialization within a given country is the key explanation for differences in management style, while influencing and controlling are largely determined by culture. Leadership, the fifth managerial function, is a product of both the nation's industrial stage and its culture. Is there such a thing as an "Asian management style?" The authors' conclusion is No—that it is inappropriate to speak of an Asian management style.

The third study, by Drs. Putti, Singh, and Stoever, examines a question important to all managers operating overseas. How much control is retained by the parent company versus how much autonomy is granted to the overseas management and to what extent is the answer to this question determined by the nationality of the parent company? The authors selected Singapore as the host country for their study because few restrictions are imposed on the operational decisions of foreign MNCs doing business in Singapore and, yet, there is significant differences between local Singapore and foreign management practices. The authors analyzed the degree of autonomy and localization as perceived by the local managers for 78 MNCs doing business in Singapore—34 American, 28 European, and 16 Japanese. They concluded that American and European MNCs tend to treat their overseas subsidiaries as distinct legal and organizational units with separate management and to employ host country citizens in almost all managerial posts. The Japanese, on the other hand, tend to view an overseas subsidiary as an extension of the parent company, and while it appears that the overseas subsidiary is being granted considerable autonomy, in fact the overseas management is merged with the management of the parent company. This third study should be of particular value to academic researchers since the authors attempt to reconcile the conflicting conclusions of previous studies, some of which reported that Japanese subsidiaries enjoy greater autonomy than American and European subsidiaries while other studies found that Japanese subsidiaries are closely controlled by the parent.

The last paper, by Drs. Salehi-Sangari and Lemar, is a short study that focuses on the subject of marketing research. Marketing research techniques were essentially developed by firms doing business in industrialized countries where this approach is a way of life for the firms' marketing managers. How useful are these same techniques when employed in developing countries and are there some research techniques that can be successfully transferred to a national culture that may not have the necessary marketing infrastructure associated with industrialized countries? The authors conclude that mail questionnaires and/or personal interviews are the best tools when conducting research in developing countries. This study should be of particular interest to the marketing practitioner because of its brevity and the absence of some of the statistical approaches favored by academic researchers used in the previous studies in this section.

CULTURAL APPROACHES TO THE PROCESS OF BUSINESS NEGOTIATION:

UNDERSTANDING CROSS-CULTURAL DIFFERENCES IN NEGOTIATING BEHAVIORS

Kamalesh Kumar, Sarath Nonis, and Charles Yauger

INTRODUCTION

Since people from different cultures do not share similar ways of thinking, feeling, and behaving, it is not surprising that they also negotiate in very different ways. Over the past several years a large number of studies have documented differences in international negotiating styles (see Beliaev et al. 1983; Dupont 1982; Fisher 1980; Graham 1985; Insley et al 1990; Stewart and Kewon 1989; Tung 1984; Wright 1981). Most of these studies have either described the negotiating behaviors of managers from a particular country, or compared negotiating behaviors across cultures. Yet, despite the growing literature on international negotiation, very few studies have focused on cross-

International Research in the Business Disciplines, Volume 1, pages 79-89.

ISBN: 1-55938-538-3

cultural differences in negotiating behaviors as they relate to the process of business negotiation.

It has been noted that process is the single most important factor in predicting the success or failure of a business negotiation (Adler 1991). Therefore, an investigation of negotiating behaviors as they bear on the process of business negotiation across different cultures could provide a set of useful guidelines for international negotiators. It may also assist them to better prepare themselves for business negotiations with members of other cultures by making them aware of the differences at each stage of the negotiation process.

PURPOSE OF THE STUDY

The purpose of this study is to explore the differences in negotiating behaviors of managers from the North American, Latin American, Arab, and Far Eastern countries during different stages of negotiation. Next, the study examines how these behavioral differences affect the negotiation process, thereby highlighting the differences in the negotiation process across the four cultures. The study uses actual descriptions of business negotiation activities involved in each stage of the negotiation process to identify behavioral differences and to assess the effects of these differences on the business negotiation process.

THE NEGOTIATION PROCESS

As with other aspects of negotiating, the negotiation process has been noted to vary considerably across cultures (Hamett 1980; Sawyer and Guetzkow 1965; Stewart and Kewon 1989; Van Zandt 1977). Although different researchers have suggested different approaches to international negotiation (Fisher and Ury 1981; Graham and Herberger 1983), there is a general consensus about the stages through which the negotiation process normally progresses. After the preparation stage, business negotiation proceeds roughly through four stages; interpersonal relationship building, exchanging task-related information, persuading, and making concessions and agreements.

More recently, Graham (1989) and Graham and Sano (1984) have suggested a four-phase linear model of the negotiation process that offers a reasonable and plausible explanation of how cultural differences may influence the process of business negotiation. Researchers using this model have found it to be a particularly useful framework for studying the negotiation process in the international context (Hawrysh and Zaichkowsky 1990). This study uses a similar framework for examining cross-cultural differences in the negotiation process. According to this framework business negotiation is viewed as proceeding in the following stages: (1) personal relationships (all activities that establish rapport between neotiators); (2) bidding (activities related to understanding each party's needs and preferences); (3) persuasive tactics (attempts to modify one another's views); and, (4) concessions and outcomes (series of smaller agreements leading to consummation of an agreement).

SAMPLE

Respondents for this study consisted of 247 natives of North American, Far Eastern, Latin American, and Arab countries. Past studies have noted such similarities in values, attitudes, norms, and behaviors of countries included in each of the four groups which allows them to be treated as culturally homogeneous groups (Ronen and Shenkar 1985). Also, researchers of international negotiation have found considerable uniformity in the behaviors manifested by members from the countries included in each of these groups (Glenn et al. 1977). The national origin of the respondents was as follows; North American (60), Latin American (58), Far Eastern (66), Arab (63). One hundred and forty one of the respondents were male and one hundred and six were female.

These respondents were enrolled for advanced education in management in two major southwestern universities of the United States. At the time of data collection, the average length of time spent by each respondent in the United States (except for U.S. nationals), was less than two years. The average respondent was between 26 and 30 years of age, had three years of college education, and had worked for business enterprise for over five years. It has been noted that business persons negotiate differently than students (Fouraher and Siegel 1963), therefore, only those respondents who had at least three years of business experience in their native countries were included in this study.

DATA COLLECTION INSTRUMENT

A 21-item questionnaire was developed for identifying various verbal and non-verbal behaviors associated with the four stages of negotiation. Behaviors included in the questionnaire were drawn from earlier research identifying cross-cultural differences in negotiating behaviors (Adler and Graham 1989; Fisher 1980; Graham 1985; Graham 1983; Graham et al. 1988; Rackham 1982; Wright 19811). Respondents were asked to refer to their negotiating experiences in their native countries and indicate how frequently the behaviors (described by each of the 21 items) were used in the course of business negotiations in their native countries. Responses were obtained on a Likert-type scale with "very frequently," "somewhat frequently," "occasionally," "seldom," and "very infrequently," as the five response categories.

FACTOR ANALYSIS AND SCALE RELIABILITY

The 21-item instrument was factor analyzed using the principle component analysis technique with varimax rotation. Factor analysis was used to

Table 1.   Factor Loading of Negotiating Behaviors

Item		Factor Loading*			
No.	Negotiating Behaviors	1	2	3	4
11.	Indirect discussions	.68	—	—	—
12.	Getting quickly to the heart of matter	.62	—	—	—
13.	Being thorough/proceed cautiously	.64	—	—	—
14.	Insistence on trading information	.72	—	—	—
3.	Threats/warning to end negotiation	—	.66	—	—
4.	Being assertive and forthright	—	.70	—	—
6.	Speaking simultaneously/fighting for floor	—	.64	—	—
16.	Deliberate delay in counter proposal	—	.50	—	—
17.	Pretend to lack authority	—	.57	—	—
1.	Extreme initial position	—	—	.67	—
2.	Allow room for subsequent concessions	—	—	.66	—
5.	Creating/seeking favors	—	—	.64	—
7.	Normative appeal to secure concessions	—	—	.70	—
8.	Developing relationship of trust	—	—	—	.49
9.	Getting to know the people involved	—	—	—	.75
10.	Developing personal rapport	—	—	—	.65
15.	Understanding other party's situation	—	—	—	.66
18.	Establishing long-term association	—	—	—	.57

Note: * None of the items loaded >.30 on any other factor.

determine which of the behaviors related to which stage of negotiation. Table 1 provides a brief description of the negotiating behaviors included in the instrument and their factor loading. Three of the items which had loaded simultaneously (.40 or above) on more than one factor were dropped from further data analysis, leaving a total of eighteen items. All other items loaded .45 or better on one factor and .30 or less on all other factors.

As expected, a four-factor solution emerged out of the factor analysis. These four factors explained over 58 percent of the total variance. Following the four stages of negotiation, these factors were labelled as information exchange behaviors (factor 1: relating to the second stage of negotiation), persuading tactics (factor 2: relating to the third stage of negotiation), concessions and agreement (factor 3: relating to the fourth stage of negotiation, and relationship building (factor 4: relating to the first stage of negotiation).

The internal consistency of the scale, as measured by Cronbach's alpha was .76. Internal consistency of the items making up the four factors was .76, .67, .71, and .81 for factors one through factor four respectively.

ANALYSIS AND RESULTS

The differences in the negotiating behaviors of four cultural groups across four factors were analyzed using MANOVA. The overall MANOVA results showed that the four groups were significantly different in terms of the behavior shown by them during different stages of negotiation ($F = 6.64, p < .001$). Univariate

F-test results (reported in Table 2) showed that the behaviors of the four groups differed significantly during three of the four stages of negotiation: relationship building, information exchange, and persuasion. There was no significant difference in the behavior of the four groups during the concession and outcome stage of negotiation.

These findings seem to indicate that differences in negotiating behaviors also result in differences in the emphasis placed on each stage of negotiation. The question then arises as to what are those behaviors—verbal as well as non-verbal—that cause these differences. To determine this a post-hoc analysis was performed. The approach used was a series of univariate *F*-tests conducted on the eighteen individual dependent variables (negotiating behaviors) to determine which variables discriminated significantly between the four cultures at each stage of negotiation. Results of the post-hoc analysis are presented in Table 3.

Table 2. Results of Manova

Stages of Negotiation	F Ratio	Probability of F
Relationship Building	7.45	.000
Information Exchange	5.39	.000
Persuasive Tactics	9.51.	001
Concession and Agreement	1.40	.248

Table 3. Results from Post-hoc Analysis

Item No.[a]	Mean[b]				F-value
	North American	Latin American	Far Eastern	Arab	
1.	2.00	3.05	2.89	2.61	2.42*
2.	1.53	3.07	2.78	2.73	2.65*
3.	3.13	2.27	2.12	2.94	2.42*
4.	3.72	1.87	2.15	3.17	5.10**
5.	2.20	2.31	2.42	2.57	1.62
6.	2.25	3.52	2.88	3.82	4.42**
7.	2.14	2.24	2.25	2.57	0.12
8.	2.14	3.03	2.80	3.91	6.35**
9.	2.21	3.05	2.48	2.93	2.43*
10.	2.10	3.09	2.57	3.08	2.81*
11.	1.60	3.30	2.24	2.88	6.42**
12.	3.85	1.88	1.94	1.32	16.59**
13.	2.05	2.84	2.89	2.57	1.48
14.	3.39	1.84	2.25	2.31	6.24**
15.	2.79	2.62	2.89	2.59	1.29
16.	2.02	3.37	3.45	2.83	2.54*
17.	1.16	2.61	3.04	3.00	6.36**
18.	1.66	3.25	2.68	3.06	9.35**

Notes: [a]description of items is in Table 1
[b]Higher means denote more frequent use of behavior
*significant at .05 level
**significant at .01 level

DISCUSSION

Results obtained from the data analysis (both MANOVA and post-hoc analysis) show that intercultural differences in negotiating behaviors primarily affect the first three stages of the negotiation process. Results of the post-hoc analysis show that negotiating behaviors vary most markedly at the persuading stage of negotiation, followed by the relationship building and information exchange stage. Some differences in behaviors were also noted at the concession and agreement stage, but these differences did not affect the overall negotiation process involved at this stage.

Differences at the Relationship Building Stage

The relationship building stage appears to be "the heart of the matter" and the most important of all stages of the negotiation process for the Latin American managers. On the other hand, from the point of view of the American managers this stage appears to be least important. This is exhibited by the reported frequency of behaviors associated with this stage of the negotiation process. Three specific behaviors account for most of the differences noted at this stage: (1) "developing relationship of trust;" (2) "developing personal rapport," and (3) "establishing long-term association." Overall, the Latin American managers appear to be spending most of their time in developing a strong, personal, long-term relationship (with no definite business motives). This finding is similar to the negotiating behaviors noted by previous researchers about managers from Latin American countries (Graham 1985; Graham and Herberger 1983).

Arab managers also see negotiation as a means of establishing long-term relationships, with a strong emphasis on developing trust and personal rapport. A finding which confirms the observations made by previous researchers (Glenn et al. 1977). Managers from Far Eastern countries appear to take a middle of the road position—putting reasonably high emphasis on behaviors associated with this stage of the negotiation. As compared to the American managers, they place a considerably stronger emphasis on developing personal rapport and establishing long-term relationships.

Differences at the Information Exchange Stage

At the information exchange stage, major variations in the emphasis placed by managers of different cultures arise on account of differences in three important behaviors. These are: (1) "indirect talking;" (2) "getting quickly to the heart of the matter;" and, (3) "insistence on quick trading of task-related information."

American managers, in general, appear to go through this stage quickly. They do not seem to like the idea of beating around the bush and try to get to the heart of the matter quickly. Similar behaviors among American managers have also been noted by other researchers. For example, it has been noted that American managers " . . . understand that, like dollars, information must be traded," and they approach this stage of negotiation with an attitude of, "You tell me what you want, and I will tell you what I want" (Glover 1990; Graham and Herberger 1983). Such an approach to information exchange is in marked contrast to the approach taken by the Far Eastern managers who exchange information in a drawn out and indirect manner. Moreover, they are extremely thorough in securing all information and proceed very cautiously with the process. In essence, they try to patiently procure information about the other party while trying build mutual understanding.

The Arabs and the Latin American managers also appear to frequently use an indirect, "beating around the bush" approach to information exchange. While Arab managers prefer a cautious and slow exchange of information, Latin American managers take an even more "laid back" approach, not insisting on quick exchange of task-related information.

Major differences in the negotiating behaviors at this stage, therefore, appear to arise out of two factors. These are the time taken in arriving at task-related information exchange and the speed with which managers from different cultures try to exchange task-related information. American managers have an extremely matter-of-fact and quick (at times impatient) approach, Far Eastern managers employ an approach marked by thoroughness and indirect talks. The Latin American and Arab managers have a slow and cautious approach.

Differences at the Persuading Stage

The most significant differences in the negotiating behaviors of managers were noted at the persuading stage of the negotiation process. From the point of view of the American managers this stage of the negotiation process appears to be the "heart of the matter." The behavior of American managers at this stage of the negotiation process is marked by forthrightness, assertiveness, and even obstinacy. Unlike the managers of other cultures, they are interested in a quick decision. To get that decision they frequently resort to threats and warnings (to end the negotiation) and push the other party into reaching a decision. Once again, these findings are consistent with the remarks and findings of previous researchers who have noted similar "inflexibility" and "persistence-pays" behaviors among American negotiators (Woliansky 1989).

In contrast, Far Eastern managers appear to approach the persuading stage as a drawn-out process. They are willing to spend a much longer time to reach an agreement. When not sure of the offer, they frequently resort to the tactics of "pretending to lack authority" or "deliberately delaying counter offer." In general, it would not be typical to get a quick answer from the Far Eastern manager. This could be the result of the fact that on many occasions Far Eastern managers (unlike American managers) lack full authority to make a deal, and because their cultural values are in favor of avoiding conflict and embarrassment caused by the failure of negotiation (Cassee 1980; Tung 1984).

On the other hand, Latin American managers show a reasonable degree of assertiveness and often "fight for the floor" during the conversation. They also appear to use the tactic of "making a calculated delay" as a way of putting pressure on the other party. Such behaviors may result from the traditional Latin American views of negotiation, in which "being tricky" is not considered to be a serious transgression of negotiation ethics (Graham and Herberger 1983).

Finally, managers from Arab countries seem to combine assertiveness and a "wait-and-watch" attitude. Like the Latin American managers during this stage of the negotiation process, they also resort to "fighting for the floor," and like American managers, they also tend to use threat and warning to end the negotiation. In general, their approach at this stage of the negotiation process is to secure the most favorable outcome by being assertive but slow and unhurried.

Differences at the Concession and Outcome Stage

In general, the negotiating behaviors of the managers was not significantly different at the concession and agreement stage of the negotiation process. However, there were some major differences in terms of a few negotiating behaviors. American managers, for example, use the strategy of "taking an extreme position" least often. They tend to start bargaining from a position that is very close to what they want and expect to achieve. As a result, they do not leave room for subsequent concessions—a fact that has been noted as one of the major shortcomings of American negotiators (Adler and Graham 1989; Barnum and Wolniasky 1989).

Latin American managers, on the other hand, start from a somewhat extreme position and leave themselves room to maneuver. Similarly, Arab managers also expect to make a series of concessions and often use the tactic of "creating/seeking favors" to secure concessions. Managers from Far Eastern countries rely more on the tactic of "normative appeal" to make the other party offer concessions.

CONCLUSIONS

This study investigated how managers from different cultures differ in terms of the negotiating behaviors displayed by them during different stages of the business negotiation process. The study also examined the effect of these differences on the negotiation process. Consistent with Graham and Herberger's (1983) comments, results of this study clearly show that what is considered to be "the heart of the matter in a business negotiation" varies across cultures.

From the point of view of the American managers, "the heart of the matter" is the third stage—pursuading. American negotiators show only "business-like" interest in the people they are negotiating with and are interested in quick trading of task-related information. Therefore, they go through the first two stages quickly and spend considerable time at the third and fourth stages.

For Latin American managers "the heart of the matter" in a business negotiation is to get to know the people involved, and to develop a strong relationship based on personal understanding and rapport. As such, they spend significant time at the first stage of negotiation—relationship building. The importance of building personal relationships also spills over into the information exchange stage (the second stage), where considerable time is spent discussing nontask related issues.

The Far Eastern managers view negotiation as "a coooperative effort." This is in sharp contrast to the "competitive," "adversarial" view of negotiation adopted by American managers (Barnum and Wolniasky 1989). The negotiating behaviors of managers from these countries is marked by persistent efforts, at all stages, to arrive at solutions which will further the interests of both parties. Therefore, instead of treating negotiation in stages, they take an "holistic approach" that is marked by intense effort to develop and reach understanding (Graham and Herberger 1983). Finally, Arab managers view negotiation as a means of establishing long-term relationships, with a strong emphasis on developing trust. They prefer a cautious and slow approach to negotiation and are willing to spend considerable time bargaining and making concessions.

These findings could serve, in several ways, as the basis for some useful guidelines. Such guidelines could assist practitioners to be better prepared for international business negotiations and, consequently, enhance their chances of success. First, the findings may be helpful in creating greater cultural self-awareness among managers of specific cultures. By allowing managers to reflect on their own negotiating behaviors, they might recognize their own shortcomings. Second, by identifying the differences in the emphasis placed by managers of different cultures at different stages of negotiation, the study could assist practitioners in understanding both the negotiation strategies and styles of managers from other cultures.

REFERENCES

Adler, N.J. 1991. *International Dimensions of Organizational Behavior.* Boston, MA:PWS-Kent.
Adler, N., and J.L. Graham. 1989. "Business Negotiations: Canadians Are Not Just Like Americans." *Canadian Journal of Administrative Sciences* 4(3):211-238.

Barnum, C., and N. Wolniasky. 1989. "Why Americans Fail at Overseas Negotiations." *Management Review* 78(October):55-57.

Beliaev, E., T. Mullen, and B.J. Punnett. 1983. "Understanding the Cultural Environment: U.S.A.-USSR Trade Negotiations." *California Management Review* 27(2):100-112.

Cassee, P. 1980. *Training for Cross-Cultural Mind.* Washington, DC: SIETAR.

Dupont, C. 1982. "La Negociation: Conduite, Theorie, Application." Paris: Dalloz. [Quoted in N. Adler's "Cross-Cultural Interaction: The International Comparison Fallacy." *Journal of International Business Studies* (Fall):515-537.]

Fisher, G. 1980. *International Negotiation.* Yarmouth, ME: Intercultural Press.

Fisher, R.. and W. Ury. 1981. *Getting to Yes.* Boston: Houghton Mifflin.

Fouraker, L.E., and S. Siegel. 1963. *Bargaining Behavior.* New York: McGraw-Hill.

Glenn, E.S., D. Witmeyer, and K.A. Stevenson. 1977. "Cultural Styles of Persuasion." *International Journal of Intercultural Relations* 1(3):52-66.

Glover, K. 1990. "Do's and Taboos: Cultural Aspects of International Business." *Business America* 111(August):2-6.

Graham, J.L. 1989. "An Exploratory Study of the Process of Marketing Negotiations Using a Cross-Cultural Perspective." In *Developing Communicative Competence in a Second Language,* edited by R. Scarcella and E. Anderson. Rowley, MA: Newbury House.

———. 1985. "The Influence of Culture on the Process of Business Negotiations: An Exploratory Study." *Journal of International Business Studies* 16(Spring):81-96.

———. 1983. "Brazilian, Japanese, and American Business Negotiations." *Journal of International Business Studies* XIV(1):47-61.

Graham, J.K., and R.A. Herberger. 1983. "Negotiators Abroad: Don't Shoot From Hips." *Harvard Business Review* 61(July-August):160-168.

Graham, J.L., D.K. Kim, C.Y. Lin, and M. Robinson. 1988. "Buyer-Seller Negotiations Around the Pacific Rim: Differences in Fundamental Exchange Process." *Journal of Consumer Research* 15:48-54.

Graham, J.L., and Y. Sano. 1984. *Smart Bargaining: Doing Business with the Japanese.* Cambridge, MA: Ballinger.

Harnett, O.L. 1980. *Bargaining Behavior: An International Study.* Houston, TX: Dane Publications.

Hawrysh, B., and J. Zaichkowsky. 1990. "Cultural Approaches to Negotiations: Understanding the Japanese." *International Marketing Review* 7(10):28-42.

Insley, R., K. Kumar, and S. Nonis. 1990. "International Negotiation: Differences in Verbal and Non-Verbal Persuasion Tactics." Paper presented at the 55th annual conference of the *Association of Business Communication,* San Antonio, TX.

Perlmutter, H. 1983. Quoted in N. Adler's "Cross-cultural Interaction: The International Comparison Fallacy." *Journal of International Business Studies* 20(Fall):515-537.

Rackham, N. 1976. *The Behavior of Successful Negotiator.* Reston: VA: Huthwaite Research Group.

Raider, E. 1982. *International Negotiations: Training Programs for Corporate Executives and Diplomats.* Brooklyn, NY: Ellen Raider International.

Ronen, S., and O. Shenkar. 1985. "Clustering Countries on Attitudinal Dimensions: A Review and Synthesis." *Academy of Management Review* 10(July):444-453.

Sawyer, J., and H. Guetzkow. 1965. *Bargaining and Negotiation in International Relations.* In *International Behavior: A Social Psychological Analysis,* edited by H.C. Kelman. New York: Rinehart and Winston.

Stewart, S., and C. Kewon. 1989. "Talking with Dragon: Negotiating in People's Republic of China." *Columbia Journal of World Business* 24(3):68-72.

Tung, R.L. 1984. "How to Negotiate with Japanese." *California Management Review* 26(4):62-77.

Van Zandt, H.F. 1977. "How to Negotiate in Japan." *Harvard Business Review* 55:72-80.
Wright, P. 1981. "Doing Business in Islamic Markets." *Harvard Business Review* 59(1):31-34.
Wolniansky, N. 1989. "We Do (Do Not) Accept Your Offer." *Management Review* 78(12):54-55.

A DISCRIMINANT ANALYSIS OF CROSS-CULTURAL DIFFERENCES IN MANAGEMENT STYLES FOR FIVE ASIAN COUNTRIES

David M. Boje, Charles M. Vance, and Dan Stage

INTRODUCTION

Are there fine-grain differences among managerial styles between Asian countries? Much of the international management style research has compared the United States with so-called Asian styles of management (Evans and Sculli 1981; Evans, Hau, and Sculli 1989; Evans, Sculli, and Hau 1987; Doktor 1990; Weihrich 1990), as if the management styles manifest within different Asian countries were similar enough to suggest a singular Asian management style. These studies may contribute to the assumption that there are no significant differences in style across Asian countries.

Our position is that the intertwining of cultural and industrial factors affects the styles of management that predominate in a particular country. Table 1 summarizes some of the major industrial and cultural differences in five Asian

International Research in the Business Disciplines, Volume 1, pages 91-106.
ISBN: 1-55938-538-3

Table 1.   Summary Comparison of Industrialization and Culture Factors

Culture Factors

Hong Kong   No predominant religion
                 Most top level managers receive a Western-style education
                 Firms often run on "family lines"
                 Population density among highest in the world
                 Chinese (mostly Cantonese) are 97% of population
                 Mostly urban.

Malaysia   Major religions: Islam, Buddhism, Taoism, Hinduism, Christianity
                 Government constitutional monarchy legislature: Parliament
                 Family is a pivotal institution
                 Literacy (1988): 76% of adult population
                 Population is 17.4 million, 35% urban, 65% rural.
                 Language: Bahasa

Indonesia   Major religions: Islam, Christianity, Hinduism
                 Government: republic-legislature: People's Consultative Assembly
                 Family viewed as central to daily life and provides job opportunities
                 Literacy (1988): 74% of adult population
                 Population: 184.6 million, 26% urban, 74% rural.
                 Language: Bahasa

Philippines   Major religions: Roman Catholicism, Protestantism, Islam
                 Government republic-legislature: National Assembly
                 Family is a prime unit in order to establish economic stability
                 Literacy (1988): 88% of adult population
                 Population (1989): 64.9 million: 39% rural, 61% urban.

Thailand   Major religions: Buddhism, Islam
                 Government constitutional monarchy-73 provinces, legislature: National
                     Assembly
                 Family involvement in business decreasing
                 Literacy (1985): 91% of adult population
                 Population 55.6 million: 17% urban, 83% rural.

Industrial Factors

Hong Kong   Economic growth 13.6%
                 Exports: manufactured textiles and clothing, electronic equipment, metal
                     goods, and plastic products imports: food, machinery, steel, iron, and raw
                     materials

Malaysia   Economic growth 4.7%
                 Exports: petroleum, timber and equipment (electronic components)
                 Imports: intermediate materials and components, and capital goods and
                     equipment
                 GNP (1987 est.): $28.4 billion
                 Per capita: $1,721
                 Foreign trade(1987 est): imports $16.6 billion; exports $20.8 billion
                 Principle trade partners: United States, Japan, Singapore

(continued)

Table 1   (Continued)

Indonesia	Economic growth 3.5%
	Exports: oil and liquefied natural gas, rubber, and coffee
	Imports: capital goods and raw materials
	GNP (1987 est.): $59 billion
	Per capita: $330
	Foreign trade (1987 est): imports $12.3 billion; exports $17.2 billion
	Principle trade partners: Japan, United States, Singapore
Philippines	Economic growth 5.05%
	Exports: semiconductors and other electronic equipment
	Imports: petroleum and other mineral fuels, intermediate goods and raw materials
	GNP (1987 est.): $33.94 billion
	Per capita: $460
	Foreign trade (1988 est): imports $7.68 billion; exports $6.59 billion
	Principle trade partners: United States, Japan, Hong Kong, West Germany, Taiwan
Thailand	Economic growth 6.6%
	Exports: tin and clothing
	Imports: raw materials and petroleum products
	GNP (1987 est.); $48.2 billion
	Per capita: $881
	Foreign trade (1987): imports $12.8 billion; exports $11.5 billion
	Principle trade partners: Japan, United States, Singapore, West Germany, Netherlands, Malaysia

settings: Hong Kong, the Philippines, Malaysia, Indonesia, and Thailand. If we accept convergence theory, as industrialization progresses, a pattern of technical and market constraints emerge that make the management style becomes highly similar to that of Western Countries (Shenkar and Ronen 1987).

This has also been referred to as strategic predisposition. Industrialization, for example, makes people less dependent upon the family. But, as people become more independent of the traditional family and seek alternative values in the work place, they are still rooted in deep religious values and beliefs. This observation supports a second theory: divergence. In divergence, the culture of a society deeply affects management style even as industrialization progresses (Hofstede 1980, 1987; Ratiu 1987; Evans, Hau, and Sculli 1989). In divergence theory, the host country's culture is assumed to dominate managerial style, such that there may even be poly-styles (i.e., poly-centric) that are more situationally effective within subcultures.

We would like to propose a way to combine aspects of convergence and divergence theories by investigating which one explains unique variations in managerial style across our sample of Asian countries. We will do this by

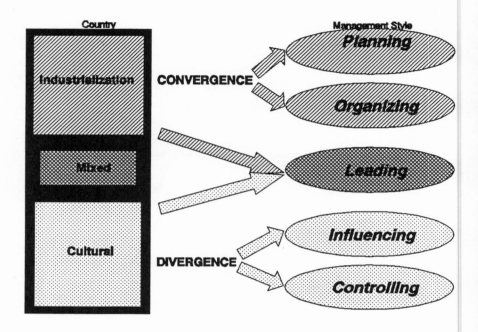

Figure 1.   Proposed Integration of Convergence and Divergence Theories

explaining statistically significant empirical comparisons of managerial styles across these Asian countries using qualitative indicators convergence and divergence for each country. Our assemblage of qualitative factors comes from a review of the international literature. Our general theory of relationships between facets of managerial style and a country's pattern of convergence and divergence arising from inherent levels of industrial development and cultural milieu has been summarized in Figure 1.

Our managerial style facets are the widely accepted classical functions of Henri Fayol (1949, pp. 43-110): planning, organizing, influence, command (leadership), and control. Consistent with convergence theory, our review of the Asian management literature suggests that patterns of industrialization are typically talked about with reference to planning and organizing styles. Authors describing less industrialized societies often suggest that managers operate with significantly longer planning cycles and within more family-based organizations. Divergence theory, however, suggests that style must still be responsive to a country's cultural milieu. For example, religious values dictate one style of influence and control over another. Finally, authors who write about the leadership function suggest aspects of both industrialization and cultural milieu are correlates.

METHODS

Respondents and Procedures

This study is based on data from 736 English-speaking nationals from five Asian countries. 81.7 percent of the sample are male managers. 92.6 percent of the sample lived over twenty years in their country. 72.1 percent had never worked outside their own country. This is a pivotal statistic, since we are assuming that most of these managers do not work for multinational firms which frequently reassign managers. Of these managers, there were 79 from Hong Kong, 185 from Indonesia, 192 from Malaysia, 96 from the Philippines, and 184 from Thailand. Participants were given a 28-item questionnaire measuring participant perceptions of their country's predominant behavioral management style on seven-point bipolar scales. For purposes of this study, we have selected only those questions dealing directly with the five classical management principles.

Three concerns must be raised. First, the group of participants cannot be considered representative of all managers in each country. Second, there are definite variations in economic and social conditions within each country that have not been measured. Third, by picking respondents who are English-speaking, we have not shown that our sample response would not vary from non-English-speaking managers.

Data Analysis

We performed *F*-tests on the nineteen management-style items. As all *F*-tests but one were significant to the .001 level (the other was significant at the .01 level), we proceeded to use *t*-tests to compare differences between countries. These univariate measures are presented one principle at a time to allow us to make qualitative statements concerning industrial development and cultural patterns (see Table 1). We will also discuss a question we included concerning religion. These univariate results are explained within the context of qualitative observations of the relationship of industrialization and culture on particular facets of managerial style. Finally, we discuss a multiple discriminant analysis where we look at interrelationships among the variables.

RESULTS AND DISCUSSION

Since Henri Fayol, many management scholars have accepted the observation that managers perform basic functions of planning, organizing, influencing, commanding (leading), and controlling.

Planning

Planning "is the managerial function of establishing the basic directions and organizational objectives, and laying out a design for reaching them" (Gray and Smeltzer 1989, p. 16).

Tables 2 and 3, question 1, illustrate the differences in long-term and short-term planning. The mean score for Hong Kong falls on the "short-term planning" side of the scale, whereas the mean for Indonesia is significant and reflects a preference for long-term planning. Table 1 indicators of industrialization suggest Hong Kong to be a more Westernized society and more advanced industrially than our comparison countries.

Table 2, questions 4 and 20, summarize the country's method of initiating plans and risk involvement. Thailand initiates plans quickly and easily while frequently taking more risks than the other countries. Malaysia tends to be more conservative and allows more time for the development of plans. The differences in the economic growth percentages (Table 1) could possibly reflect the extent to which these countries take risks as well as affecting their planning horizons.

Organizing

Organizing "involves determining the several activities necessary to accomplish plans, grouping them, assigning them to specific positions and individuals, and delegating the requisite authority" (Gray and Smeltzer 1989, p. 16).

Tables 2 and 3, questions 2, 3, and 5 compare organizational techniques of management within the five Asian countries. Hong Kong tends to establish precise measurable, time-dated objectives, while the score for Malaysia shows that its objectives are not specific and are frequently modified. Because Hong Kong is more Westernized, we assume that this Western influence has affected its style of organizing. Hong Kong is far more industrialized and westernized than any other of the five Asian countries included in this study.

In questions 3 and 5, Malaysia appears to have a more individualistic approach to organization within management, and favors a more structured organization. Thailand prefers to develop objectives by group action and is less demanding as far as giving orders, and their organization tends to be more flexible. These mean scores do not accurately represent the current situation in Thailand. The country is currently undergoing a major reform in their conversion of family-style management to professional management following the western model.

Table 2. Management Style Questions

Function	Question		Scale	
Planning	Q1	Long term	1 2 3 4 5	Short term
	Q4	Initiates plans quickly and easily	1 2 3 4 5	Takes extensive time to develop plans
	Q20	Frequently takes risks	1 2 3 4 5	Conservative seldom takes risks
Organizing	Q2	Objectives are not specific and are frequently modified	1 2 3 4 5	Establishes precise measurable time dated objectives
	Q3	Set objectives for organization and gives orders	1 2 3 4 5	Develops objectives by group action
	Q5	Prefers to initiate rigid, highly structured organizations	1 2 3 4 5	Prefers to initiate flexible and adaptive organizations
Controlling	Q10	Emphasizes control by group norms and individual values	1 2 3 4 5	Emphasizes control by measurable company standards
	Q11	Focuses control on group and company performance	1 2 3 4 5	Focuses control on individual performance
	Q14	Believes that employees must be watched and controlled	1 2 3 4 5	Believes that employees can be trusted to do the job with minimal supervision
Influencing	Q6	Use human relation skills to influence others	1 2 3 4 5	Relies on positional authority to influence others
	Q7	Enjoys internal competition within the organization	1 2 3 4 5	Enjoys internal harmony and a friendly organization environment
Leading	Q12	Gives very infrequent performance evaluations	1 2 3 4 5	Frequently gives performance evaluations
	Q24	Motivates predominately by use of rewards and punishment	1 2 3 4 5	Motivates using recognition and praise
	Q19	Seldom involves subordinates in decisions related to their work	1 2 3 4 5	Fully involves subordinates in all decisions related to their work
	Q21	Emphasizes task- oriented supervision	1 2 3 4 5	Seldom emphasizes task-oriented supervision
	Q22	Seldom emphasizes relationship-oriented supervision such as recognition, morale, etc.	1 2 3 4 5	Emphasizes relationship-oriented supervision, using recognition and relationship-oriented techniques
	Q23	Maintains aloof distance from employees	1 2 3 4 5	Develops close personal relationships with employees
	Q26	Emphasizes formal written communication	1 2 3 4 5	Emphasizes informal face-to-face communication

Table 3. Means and F-tests for Management Style Questions

Function	Question	Indonesia	Thailand	Philippines	Malaysia	Hong Kong	F-Value
Planning	Q1	3.19	3.93bc	4.21ac	4.24ab	4.57a	11.35
	Q4	3.36ab	2.84c	2.98ac	4.32	2.98ac	19.00
	Q20	3.80b	3.61b	4.45a	4.89a	4.71a	16.00
Organizing	Q2	4.23abcd	4.49ad	4.30acd	3.90bc	4.59a	3.34
	Q3	3.60abc	4.40d	3.91cd	3.58abc	3.84ac	5.20
	Q5	5.22a	5.25a	5.25ab	3.82	4.77b	22.00
Controlling	Q10	4.03a	5.10	4.53b	4.21ab	3.27	17.30
	Q11	3.38ab	4.61	3.70ab	3.72a	3.65a	10.30
	Q14	3.84a	3.28	3.99a	4.05a	2.71	10.80
Influencing	Q6	3.12b	2.40a	3.35b	4.41	2.44a	35.40
	Q7	4.65a	4.30ab	4.94a	4.08b	5.90	16.90
	Q12	3.99ab	5.51	4.38cd	4.20ac	3.81a	20.70
	Q24	4.87ab	4.91ac	4.48bc	3.98	5.23a	11.40
Leading	Q19	4.28b	4.86	4.37b	3.87a	3.56a	10.80
	Q21	2.61a	3.05b	2.69ab	3.44	4.08	19.40
	Q22	4.65a	5.18	4.73a	3.97	4.38a	16.70
	Q23	4.97b	5.17b	5.09b	4.06a	4.39a	12.60
	Q26	4.81b	3.39c	4.68b	3.92a	3.61ac	20.00

Note: Means sharing subscripts are not significantly different at .05 level. All F-values are significant.

Influencing

Influencing "is principally the managerial function of supervising and guiding subordinates toward the accomplishment of organizational objectives. It also involves interacting with people, both inside and outside the organization, over whom the manager has no authority" (Gray and Smeltzer 1989, p. 16).

In Tables 2 and 3, question 6, the human relations skills are compared among the five countries. Thailand and Malaysia show significant differences in their mean values. Previously Thailand has been reported to place much more emphasis on family involvement in business practices (Rainat 1989). Thailand is also about two years into a ten-year cycle of real GNP growth that will exceed 7 percent a year (Rainat 1989). While their low mean value on question 6 supports this statement, recent data shows that the rapid economic development in the country has altered this concept of the use of family in business. The more advanced stage of industrialization in Hong Kong may well explain an increase in the competitive level within the organization. The use of the family in business has declined but has not been completely ruled out. In Figure 1, therefore, we have suggested that the cultural role of the family is a more salient influence than the industrial factors.

The results from question 7 indicate that Malaysia has more internal competition within the organization, while Hong Kong favors internal harmony and a pleasant organization environment. Even though there is a need for harmony within the organization, we also believe that Hong Kong is in fact competitive. The preference for harmony stems from the cultural fabric of the country.

Leading

Fayol's term "Command," or the more popular term, "Leading," is the directing and coordinating of task-relevant activities (Fiedler 1967).

In Tables 2 and 3, the leadership within these countries and the extent of the manager-staff relationship is examined. Hong Kong and Malaysia report a more formal style of relationship. The country most opposite this style is Thailand, which can be seen in their overall response to question 23. However, Thailand does tend to have a more formal written communication system with their employees. This is represented in Tables 2 and 3 (question 26). In Table 3 the statistics for question 19 show that Thailand directly involves subordinates in work-related decisions. Hong Kong, however, rarely takes into consideration subordinates in making decisions related to their work.

The culturally prescribed role of women in each country has a direct affect on the job-related decision making. Traditionally, Asian women have been viewed as decision makers within the family, but have not been recognized as leaders in the work force. Sex-role segregation starts early in the educational process. This segregation formulates an image that women are nonachievers (Wong and Cheung 1987). Thus, in spite of the rising level of education, women still occupy only a small percentage of the higher paid professional, administrative, executive, and managerial jobs. Equally significant is the observation that often those countries that are not as advanced industrially tend to have few highly educated women. Thus, industrialization and cultural standards both have an influence on the leadership role of women in business (see Figure 1).

Controlling

Controlling "is the managerial function of measuring and correcting the activities of subordinates to assure that events conform to plans" (Gray and Smeltzer 1989, p. 16).

Tables 3 and 4 address the managerial principle of control in these Asian countries. Question 10 deals with how control should be emphasized with respect to business decisions. Hong Kong emphasizes control by group norms and individual values, while the mean value for Thailand indicates a preference to measure control by company standards. Hong Kong runs its firms mainly on "family lines" and includes cultural factors in the use of control. This is an interesting result, since Hong Kong is considered advanced industrially.

Question 11 of Table 2 deals with the focus of control within the company. In Thailand there tends to be more attention given to the individual performance, whereas in Indonesia the focus is mainly on the performance of the company. In Thailand the recent adaptation of Western influences supports their decision to focus on the performance of the individual rather than the company.

In Table 2, question 14 discusses the level of trust within each of these countries. Hong Kong is the country which places the least amount of trust in their employees. Managers from Hong Kong indicated by their mean score that they prefer a high degree of close supervision. This could be because of the changing cultural values within this country.

Our findings on control are consistent with the Evans, Hau, and Sculli (1989) review of the literature, where they conclude: "management style is a function of the level of industrialization, but is tempered by cultural characteristics" (p. 12). Our results, however, suggest that planning and organizing are more a function of industrialization, while influencing and controlling are tempered more by the cultural milieu. The fifth function, leadership, appears to reflect both the convergence of industrialization and the divergence of culture.

Table 4. Intercorrelations

Function	Question	Q1	Q4	Q2	Q3	Q5	Q6	Q7	Q12	Q24	Q19	Q21	Q22	Q23	Q26	Q10	Q11	Q13	Q14
Planning	Q1	-06																	
	Q4	-09	23																
Organizing	Q2	-38	-06	-03															
	Q3	-03	-11	-08	16														
	Q5	05	-34	-19	05	23													
Influencing	Q6	11	-06	16	-15	-31	-40												
	Q7	01	-09	-01	17	07	20	-20											
	Q12	-12	-14	01	13	12	17	-24	-02										
	Q24	-11	-23	-08	16	20	22	-37	15	24									
Leading	Q19	-10	-17	-06	17	28	31	-30	06	26	28								
	Q21	17	09	04	-11	10	-13	12	02	-09	-07	-12							
	Q22	-16	-17	-06	22	16	14	-28	16	19	19	27	-22						
	Q23	-12	-22	-04	14	12	28	-33	16	32	40	33	-13	31					
	Q26	17	-08	-10	-13	-06	28	-02	08	-01	08	04	-11	02	20				
Control	Q10	-01	-08	-06	16	14	06	-11	-02	19	-02	10	-13	18	05	-15			
	Q11	23	-07	-09	-15	-06	14	-06	-11	16	04	02	06	-02	06	04	04		
	Q13	07	-17	-13	-08	06	12	-02	-13	11	15	05	01	01	02	-02	21	20	
	Q14	-06	08	-05	09	08	02	-05	03	15	13	13	-02	17	17	09	03	-13	-09
		Q1	Q4	Q2	Q3	Q5	Q6	Q7	Q12	Q24	Q19	Q21	Q22	Q23	Q26	Q10	Q11	Q13	Q14

Note: * All correlations above 0.05 are significant at $p < .05$; all correlations above 0.08 are significant at $p < .01$; $n = 736$. Decimals omitted.

Table 5.   Breakdown of Religion of Manager by Country

Religion	Hong Kong	Indonesia	Malaysia	Phillippines	Thailand	%
Buddhism	1	8	9	0	102	19.8
Christianity	6	40	17	3	40	17.5
Confucianism	0	1	0	1	7	1.5
Hindu	0	1	8	0	1	1.7
Sikh	0	0	1	0	0	.2
Islam/Muslim	0	37	55	0	7	16.9
Protestant	1	9	0	2	0	2.0
Catholic	2	72	2	67	17	26.4
Shinto	0	0	0	0	2	.3
No Religion	69	0	14	1	2	14.2
Col %:	13.1	27.8	17.5	12.2	29.4	(605)

Note: 605 cases responded out of 736.

Religion

To give more insight into the cultural differences among managers we have included the responses to a question on religion in Table 5. Participants were asked an optional "Religious" affiliation question. Despite the optional nature of the question, 82 percent of the participants gave a response. Most Philippine managers were Catholic. Most Thailand managers were Buddhist. Indonesia is split between Catholics, Christians, and Islam/Muslims. Hong Kong expressed "no religion" as their write-in choice. In this case, since Confucianism is not considered by many Chinese to be a so-called "religion," the no religion response is interesting and informative. We make no claims that our distribution of religious percentages reflects the demographics of each country. We do, however, suggest that there are significant and impactful differences in religion that must be accounted for in cultural divergence. For example, in Hong Kong, modern skyscrapers are still located with the aid of a geomacer to ensure their locations does not disturb any spirits living on the site.

Multivariate Results

Given our list of style questions, we wanted to examine their combined ability to distinguish between managers from different Asian countries. The mathematical objective of the procedure is to weight the style variables such that the country patterns are forced to be as statistically distinct as possible. Results of the Discriminant Analysis are displayed in Table 6.

The eigenvalues and associated canonical correlations suggest that three functions adequately discriminate among managers by country. Higher eigenvalues mean a function is statistically more relevant than those with weaker eigenvalues.

Table 6.   Results of Discriminant Analysis Between Countries

Function	Eigenvalue	Percent of Variance	Canonical Correlation	Degrees Freedom	Level Significance
0				76	*
1	.53	38.1	.59	54	*
2	.49	35.8	.58	34	*
3	.30	21.9	.48	16	*

Note: $* p < .001$.

Table 7.   Pooled Within-Groups Correlations
between Discriminant Variables

Variable	Function 1	Function 2	Function 3
Q13	.51		
Q12	.44		
Q10	.38		
Q22	.35		
Q20	−.33		
Q19	.32		
Q11			
Q3			
Q6		.44	
Q7		−.34	
Q1		.33	
Q4		.30	
Q2			
Q5			−.48
Q26			−.44
Q21			.41
Q1			.36
Q23			−.30
Q24			

Note: Variables ordered by size of correlation within function. Only
correlations $< .295$ are shown.

In Table 7, the pooled within-groups correlations between discriminant
variables and each function are displayed. In Function One, the variables seem
to stress measurable controls, performance controls, recognition, conservat-
ivism in risks, as well as involving subordinates in all decisions related to their
work. We could therefore interpret Function One as related to tight control
and feedback on work. Function Two combines questions that deal with
position authority, promoting internal competition, giving minimal

supervision, and spending extensive time on planning. We interpret this group of questions to reflect a more detached style, where the pattern of organization and plans affecting worker behaviors. Finally, in Function Three, we find rigid and highly structured organizations, formal written communications, task-oriented supervision, short-term planning, and an aloof distance with employees. We interpret this to be more of a Theory X style with the stress on structure, short-term focus, and interpersonal distance.

The group centriods (country scores on a given function of weighted variables) reveal the statistical ordering of the countries on a given function. For example, in Function One, which we are labeling "Feedback and Control" the ordering is as follows:

Feedback and Control (Function One)

Hong Kong	−.89
Malaysia	−.49
Philippines	−.25
Indonesia	−.17
Thailand	1.19

In Function Two: Detached and Planners, Hong Kong is at one end of this dimension and Malaysia is at the other.

Detached and Planners (Function Two)

Hong Kong	−1.80
Thailand	−.26
Philippines	.23
Indonesia	.34
Malaysia	.56

In Function Three, Theory X and Structure, Indonesia is at one end of this dimension and Malaysia is at the other.

Theory X and Structure (Function Three)

Indonesia	−.82
Philippines	−.22
Hong Kong	.07
Thailand	.17
Malaysia	.68

In short, the analysis seems to suggest that the five principles of classical management are arrayed in three underlying dimensions to differentiate the countries under study. In some Asian countries giving workers more feedback and exercising more control over them is apparently a more acceptable practice. On a separate dimension being more detached and planning out the work for the workers is more or less an acceptable style, depending upon the Asian

Table 8.   Discriminant Analysis Classification Results

Actual Country	Number of Cases	Hong Kong	Indonesia	Malaysia	Philippines	Thailand	Percent Correct
			Predicted Country Memberships				
Hong Kong	79	59	3	15	0	2	74.7
Indonesia	185	5	123	31	0	26	66.5
Malaysia	192	4	33	136	0	19	70.8
Philippines	96	4	44	32	0	16	0.0
Thailand	184	7	24	26	0	127	69.0

Percentage of grouped cases correctly classified: 60.46

country we are looking at. Finally, being more aloof, more Theory X and exercising definite structure is more or less the approach across these countries. The point, therefore, that we are concluding is that there are real differences in Asian management styles.

In Table 8, 60.46 percent of the managers were correctly classified from looking at the pattern of scores on their management style. 74.7 percent of Hong Kong managers were correctly classified as compared to none of the Philippine managers. This result can occur when the discriminant technique can not locate questions that differentiate a group uniquely. Rather, the other countries overshadow the pattern for the Philippines. We see that the discriminant functions split them between Indonesia, Malaysia, and Thailand. Despite this shortcoming, overall the discriminant functions do classify significantly more managers than would have occurred by chance. The finding is therefore consistent with the purpose of our study in four of the five countries.

CONCLUSIONS

We conclude that in the case of planning and organizing the rate of industrialization provides a useful rationale for differences in Asian managerial styles. In the case of influencing and controlling, the results suggest that the pace of industrialization is tempered by a diversity of culturally preferred styles. The most pronounced instance is Hong Kong, where we find that, despite advanced industrialization, there is a fairly controlling style of influence and control. Finally, in the instance of leadership, both culture and industrialization are equal contributors.

Overall, our study contributes to international management theory by showing conclusively that there are stylistic differences among Asian countries. We believe that it is inappropriate to say that Asians have this style or that. Rather, it is more appropriate to say that there are strong cross-country variations reflecting culture and industrialization. In future studies, we think there is a need to look at differential acceptance of female leadership across Asian countries. In addition, regional style variations within a given Asian country are certainly worth looking at in future research.

REFERENCES

Doktor, R. 1990. "Asian and American CEOs: A Comparative Study." *Organizational Dynamics* 18(3):46-56.

Evans, W.A., H.C. Hau, and D. Sculli. 1989. "A Cross-Cultural Comparison of Managerial Styles." *Journal of Management Development* 8(3):5-13.

Evans, W.A., and D. Sculli. 1981. "A Comparison of Managerial Traits in Hong Kong and the U.S.A." *Journal of Occupational Psychology* 54:83-186.

Evans, W.A., D. Sculli, and W.S.L. Yau. 1987. "Cross-Cultural Factors in the Identification of Managerial Potential." *Journal of General Management* 13(1):52-59.

Fayol, H. 1949. *General and Industrial Management.* London: Sir Isaac Pitman and Sons.

Fiedler, F.E. 1967. *A Theory of Leadership Effectiveness.* New York: McGraw-Hill.

Gray, E.R., and L.R. Smeltzer. 1989. *Management: The Competitive Edge.* New York: Macmillan.

Hau, K.C. 1989. " A Cross-Cultural Comparison of Managerial Styles." *Journal of Management Development (U.K.)* 8(3).

Hofstede, G. 1980. "Motivation, Leadership and Organization: Do American Theories Apply Abroad?" *Organizational Dynamics* (Summer).

————. 1987. "The Applicability of McGregor's Theories in South East Asia." *Journal of Management Development* 6(3):9-18.

Rainat, J. 1989. "New Fields Await Foreign Investors: SET Aspires to Be a Super-Star." *Asian Finance* 15(10).

Ratiu, I. 1987. "Introduction." Special Issue on Management Development and Culture, *Journal of Management Development* 6(3).

Sculli, D. 1987. "Cross-Cultural Factors in the Identification of Managerial Potential." *Journal of General Management* (UK) 13(1):52-59.

Shenkar, O., and S. Ronen. 1987. "Structure and Importance of Work Goals Among Managers in the People's Republic of China." *Academy of Management Journal* 30(3):564-576.

Weihrich, H. 1990. "Management Practices in the United States, Japan, and the People's Republic of China." *Industrial Management* 32(2):3-7.

Wong, A. 1987. "Changing Role and Status of Woman." *The ASEAN Success Story: Social, Economic, and Political Dimensions,* pp. 28-34.

AUTONOMY AND LOCALIZATION OF AMERICAN, EUROPEAN, AND JAPANESE MNC SUBSIDIARIES IN SINGAPORE

Joseph Putti, Kulwant Singh, and William A. Stoever

INTRODUCTION

This paper hypothesizes that a multinational corporation's (MNC's) home country—its headquarters nationality—is an important determinant of both the degree of autonomy and the degree of localization found in its overseas subsidiaries. It examines the degree of autonomy and of localization of American, European, and Japanese subsidiaries in one newly industrializing country, Singapore.

Although some authors treat autonomy and localization as similar, conceptually they are quite different. Autonomy refers to the extent to which overseas subsidiary managers are allowed to make decisions on important strategic and operational matters without having to obtain specific authorization from their corporate headquarters. Localization refers to the

International Research in the Business Disciplines, Volume 1, pages 107-123.

extent to which the subsidiaries place host-country citizens in high executive positions, adopt local management practices, and otherwise shape their practices and procedures to the local environment. A foreign subsidiary could be allowed a great deal of latitude in decision making but maintain management practices and/or personnel very similar to the parent's: autonomy without localization. Conversely, its personnel could be entirely local and most of its practices and procedures follow local norms, but the content or outcome of its decisions could be quite closely controlled by the parent: localization without autonomy. The authors postulate that the characteristic relationship between autonomy and localization in the MNCs of one nationality may be significantly different from the characteristic relationship between them in MNCs of another nationality.

BACKGROUND

Singapore

Singapore is an appropriate place for the study because it has a significant number of MNC subsidiaries from each of these three countries/groups. Many of the subsidiaries are engaged in the same general type of operation, namely, using parent-company technology and know-how to manufacture products primarily for export but also for sale in the local market. Hence, the problem of variation among the types of industries owned by different foreign MNCs is minimized. The country allows essentially unrestricted entry to most imports and most multinational investments. It imposes very few restrictions on MNC operations and is quite liberal in granting work permits to foreign executives. Hence, MNCs are free to decide how much autonomy to grant their Singaporean operations, how many foreign versus local executives to employ, and the extent to which they wish to localize their management practices. At the same time, Singapore is not yet fully modernized or industrialized, and there are significant differences between local and most foreign management practices. Consequently, localization of an American, European, or Japanese company's management practices would involve substantial changes from headquarters practices that could be meaningfully assessed.

Although the empirical data was gathered in Singapore, we believe that the findings on differing characteristics of American, European, and Japanese MNCs should be applicable in many other less-developed host countries, and quite possibly in industrialized host countries as well.

Previous Studies

A substantial body of research focusing on structural relationships between MNCs and their foreign subsidiaries has emerged in recent years. It has examined such topics as the locus of decision making in MNCs (Goehle 1978; Larsson 1985); centralization and autonomy (Brooke 1984; Hedlund 1981; Garnier 1982; Yunker 1983), and control and influence (Hulbert and Brandt 1980; Leksell 1981; Doz and Prahalad 1981).

The degree of autonomy allowed to overseas subsidiaries has been found to vary by the extent of internationalization of the MNC (Stopford and Wells 1972; Aharoni 1966); by the ethnocentrism of MNCs' management; across functions (Alpander 1978; Hedlund 1981; Garnier 1982); by the strategic impact of decisions (Alpander 1978; Berenbeim 1983; Hedlund 1981; Yunker 1983); with subsidiary characteristics such as its capital intensity and geographic or product line structure (Berenbeim 1983), size (Berenbeim 1983; Daniels 1986; Hulbert and Brant 1980), and age (Youssef 1973); and by the nationality of the MNC (Hedlund 1981; Hedlund and Aman 1984; Hulbert and Brandt 1980; Negandhi and Baliga 1979; Negandhi et al. 1987).

Some studies specifically compared autonomy among U.S., Japanese, and European MNCs. Negandhi and Baliga (1979, 1981) found that managers in Japanese subsidiaries enjoyed greater autonomy than their American and West German counterparts. Negandhi and Welge (1984) also found Japanese subsidiaries to be the most autonomous, but they found similar patterns of autonomy across fifteen different types of decisions for American, German, and Japanese subsidiaries. Hedlund (1981), employing part of the Neghandi and Baliga (1981) data set, found that Swedish subsidiaries enjoyed significantly greater autonomy than American subsidiaries and slightly more than Japanese subsidiaries. In contrast, Negandhi et al. (1987) reported that Japanese subsidiaries operating in three Southeast Asian counties were closely controlled by their corporate headquarters.

Hulbert and Brandt (1980) identified the long European experience in managing international operations as the primary reason for the relatively high decentralization of power in European MNCs. These authors attributed the relative lack of autonomy in U.S. subsidiaries to the American desire for formalization in management practices. They also found that Japanese subsidiaries have less autonomy than European but more than American. Interestingly, the authors characterize the Japanese MNCs as being uncertain in their management of subsidiaries, as a result of their relative inexperience in international business.

Gates and Egelhoff (1986) found greater centralization in U.S. MNCs than in British or European. However, they found that centralization varied by function, with British MNCs being the most decentralized in marketing and manufacturing, but the most centralized in finance. This finding supports the view that the nature of the decision is an important determinant of the degree of autonomy allowed to subsidiaries.

Negandhi and Baliga (1979) and Negandhi et al. (1987) report that Japanese headquarters achieved high levels of control over their subsidiaries by many means, including the appointment of Japanese managers to almost all the senior management positions, visits by headquarters staff, regular reports to and from headquarters, and frequent communications. Appointing home-country nationals and establishing good communications channels were control devices employed by many of the 56 European subsidiaries in the United States studied by Pichard (1980), and by American and European MNCs studied by Berenbeim (1983). Generally, American and European subsidiaries have been found to employ local or third-country nationals more readily than Japanese subsidiaries (Lee 1985; Kobrin 1988).

Edstrom and Galbraith (1977) identified transfers of top managers from the parent to subsidiaries as an important means of exercising control. However, this measure has potentially serious implications for the utilization of corporate manpower resources, information management, host country relations, and the profitability of operations (Edstrom and Galbraith 1977; Kobrin 1988). The employment of foreign nationals has also been a source of conflict between MNCs and host governments and has been perceived as an indication of failure to localize (Berenbeim 1983). Brooke (1984), however, points out that the expatriate manager often brings with him (or her) greater autonomy for the subsidiary.

The extensive use of Japanese managers in foreign subsidiaries has been attributed to differences in the Japanese mode of operations (Negandhi and Baliga 1981) and to fundamental differences in Japanese management (Ouchi and Jaeger 1978). The latter authors contrasted the Japanese "Type J" organization (with its reliance on implicit, informal, and cultural control) to the American "Type A" (explicit formal and behavioral control). They then postulated that different national approaches to organization and management influence not only the degree of control exercised over subsidiaries, but also the type of measures employed to exercise it. Jaeger (1982) found that "Type A" organizations tended to rely more on formal and impersonal reports, directives, and telex messages, while "Type Z" organizations (defined as an emerging Western form similar to the "Type J") relied more on personal communications such as visits and telephone calls. Hedlund and Aman (1984) noted a similar preference among Swedish MNCs for extended personal networks among top management of MNCs and subsidiaries and for control through information sharing and informal personal contacts, rather than through hierarchical systems.

Some researchers foresee that differences in control relationships among MNCs from different countries will gradually diminish and eventually disappear (Hulbert and Brandt 1980). Negandhi (1983) argues that technological and environmental factors are becoming the dominant influences on organizations, ahead of sociocultural factors; this will eventually lead to greater similarity in organizational practices. Negandhi's position is consistent with the convergence hypothesis (Webber 1969), which holds that technology, education, and pragmatic philosophy will produce greater commonality in business and management practices across cultures. Bartlett and Ghoshal (1988) similarly see a trend towards globalization as a result of strong convergent forces. However, Vozikis and Mescon (1981) and Meleka (1985) foresee the erosion of these convergent forces and the rise of divergent forces.

A surprising omission in the literature is research on the consequences and outcomes of various levels of autonomy allowed to subsidiaries. Few studies have examined how the subsidiary's autonomy affects its strategy, structure, or operations. A number of studies have also dealt (explicitly or implicitly) with localization. Hrebiniak and Joyce (1985) defined localization as the process of adaption to the host country's environment, so as to align organizational capabilities with environmental contingencies.

Putti and Chong (1985), in their examination of managerial practices of U.S. and Japanese subsidiaries, found that U.S. firms transferred their home practices to Singapore to a large extent, while the Japanese did not. For example, Japanese did not extend the much-discussed "ringi-sho" system of collective decision- making beyond the closed group of Japanese top managers. Putti and Chong (1985) attributed their findings to the much greater American influence on the workforce, language differences for Japanese staff, and, interestingly, to Singapore's similarities to the United States in being a "unified yet heterogeneous nation" with a tradition of individualistic competition. This is consistent with Lee's (1985) findings that American subsidiaries in Singapore employed locals in managerial positions more often than European and Japanese subsidiaries. Low (1984) found significant differences in the philosophy, practices, and effectiveness of managements of U.S. subsidiaries and Singaporean companies. The local firms in this study were found to have more autocratic management styles, despite having similar structures.

Negandhi et al. (1987) also reported that there was little in common between the management styles adopted by subsidiaries in Singapore (or those in Malaysia and Thailand) and their parents in Japan. The subsidiaries' use of a different approach emphasizing high levels of control was attributed to both environmental and organizational factors.

On the other hand, Chong and Jain (1987) reported a convergence in human resource management practices between Japanese and local firms and a divergence in practices between subsidiaries and their parent corporations in Japan. They attributed these findings to the introduction of Japanese management practices into local companies and to the Westernization of Japanese subsidiaries' management. The authors concluded that Japanese subsidiaries do modify their practices to suit the local environment.

Chong (1984), in his comparative study of twelve U.S. and Japanese subsidiaries in Singapore, found similarly that U.S. subsidiaries generally followed home practices, while Japanese subsidiaries modified theirs. He attributed these differences to reasons similar to those identified by Chong and

Jain (1987), namely, the strong American influence in Singapore and the Japanese corporations' belief that modification was required because of language and educational differences.

In contrast, in his study of 49 French subsidiaries, Lasserre (1985) found that Singapore generally lived up to its reputation as a highly attractive site that catered well to the needs of foreign businesses. Nevertheless, these subsidiaries faced problems in implementing their operations, arising largely out of differences between Singapore and France in the availability of skilled workers, consumer characteristics, and the government's intervention in the economy.

Lee (1985) found that six Japanese subsidiaries in Singapore were closely controlled by their parent corporations; they essentially transplanted their entire set-up and environment including supervisors and suppliers from the home to the host country. She also detected a preference for Japanese managers and a tendency to concentrate power in the foreign staff. The present study seeks to examine the effects of nationality of MNCs on subsidiary autonomy and localization. This study is part of a larger exploratory project conducted in 1989 on the levels of and relationship between autonomy and localization among subsidiaries in Singapore.

METHODOLOGY

Questionnaires were distributed to executives of 78 corporations operating in Singapore, of which 34 were subsidiaries of American MNCs, 28 of European, and 16 of Japanese.[1] The sample was selected to obtain a broad range of business types and product lines. Respondents were asked to complete a twelve-page questionnaire designed to collect data on company background as well as to measure autonomy and localization. Semi-structured follow-up interviews were conducted with 11 subsidiaries; these ranged from 40 to 70 minutes each. Table 1 provides a profile of the sample.

Respondents estimated the relative degree of local autonomy versus headquarters influence over 26 different types of decisions affecting their subsidiaries[2] (see Table 2).[3] They rated each item on a five-point scale ranging from 1 (decisions influenced totally by headquarters) to 5 (influenced totally by subsidiary). Thus, a higher score (closer to 5) indicates a higher perceived degree of autonomy. The average over all 26 types of decisions provides a general measure of autonomy. This approach also allowed us to measure autonomy in various functions: six items were characterized as strategic or planning, seven items as finance, three as marketing, seven as personnel-related, four as production or operations, and seventeen as operations (see Table 3).

Table 1. Sample Profile

Characteristic	American	European	Japanese
Number of Subsidiaries	24.8	37.0	19.0
MNC Sales (S$ '000 million)	4956	13620	18610
Subsidiary Age	14.0	15.6	11.5
% of Respondents Fully owned by MNC	88.2	78.6	81.3
Type of Industry (%)	61.8	63.0	75.0
Manufacturing type			
Service Type	38.2	37.0	25.0
% of Output Sold Locally	47.0	46.3	36.5

Table 2. Subsidiaries' Autonomy by Decision Type

	American			European			Japanese		
Decision Type	Rank	Mean	SD	Rank	Mean	SD	Rank	Mean	SD
Workers' participation	1	4.61	.67	1	4.67	1.07	2	4.63	.62
Union relations	2	4.60	.75	1	4.52	1.08	5	4.54	.52
Short-term plans	3	4.38	.89	4	4.15	1.32	7	4.19	.75
Wage/salary increases	4	4.18	.83	8	3.92	1.13	4	4.56	.77
Employee benefits	5	4.00	1.02	11	3.82	1.30	1	4.81	.40
Personnel lay-off policies	6	3.91	1.33	6	3.96	1.25	6	4.50	.76
Appointment of key staff	7	3.85	1.20	12	3.81	1.27	22	3.34	1.54
Marketing programs	8	3.85	1.40	7	3.96	1.25	15	3.73	1.39
Advertising programs	9	3.84	1.53	9	3.89	1.24	10	4.00	1.60
Product/service quality	10	3.77	1.21	14	3.44	1.42	11	3.94	.85
Management style	11	3.71	1.27	3	4.37	1.21	14	3.88	1.26
Production/sales levels	12	3.66	1.29	5	4.11	1.22	12	3.94	1.00
Pricing of products/serv.	13	3.62	1.44	10	3.85	1.41	9	4.06	1.12
Annual budget	14	3.56	1.08	13	3.52	1.31	13	3.88	1.09
Product/service range	15	3.56	1.34	15	3.44	1.55	18	3.50	.97
Operating rules/regs.	16	3.35	1.50	16	3.19	1.44	8	4.19	.75
Profit targets	17	3.29	1.27	18	3.07	1.33	21	3.38	1.03
Strategic plans	18	3.12	1.12	21	2.70	1.33	24	3.07	.96
Type technology employed	19	2.91	1.45	20	2.96	1.60	20	3.40	1.21
Executive benefits	20	2.88	1.24	19	3.00	1.52	3	4.63	.62
Setting of transfer prices	21	2.86	1.46	23	2.64	1.43	19	3.50	1.00
Borrowing/use of funds	22	2.82	1.31	17	3.16	1.43	17	3.56	1.21
Reports to corporate HQ	23	2.82	1.55	25	2.37	1.46	23	3.33	1.29
Remittances to MNC	24	2.73	1.13	24	2.46	1.42	16	3.67	1.18
Significant capital exp.	25	2.59	.99	26	2.12	1.14	25	3.06	1.00
Conduct of R&D	26	2.04	1.13	22	2.68	1.67	26	2.15	.89
Average		3.60	.70		3.57	.74		3.98	

Table 3.   Localization by Functions and Strategic Levels

Function	American		European		Japanese		
	Mean	SD	Mean	SD	Mean	SD	Prob.
Personnel	3.65	.94	3.56	.63	3.84	.60	.516
Marketing	3.20	1.09	3.18	.67	3.27	1.12.	831
Production/							
Operations	2.70	.89	2.73	1.04	3.29	1.01	.109
Finance	2.49	1.10	2.77	.83	3.22	.95	.052
Operational							
Decisions	3.39	.76	3.34	.60	3.64	.63	.352
Strategic							
Decisions	2.49	.98	2.69	.74	2.78	1.03	.501

Note: Probability represents the level of significance of differences across nationality groups.

Table 4.   Localization of Subsidiary Operations by Decision Type

Area of Operations	American			European			Japanese		
	Rank	Mean	SD	Rank	Mean	SD	Rank	Mean	SD
Union relations	1	4.44	.98	1	4.30	.93	1	4.46	.52
Relationships with public	2	4.09	1.10	3	3.89	.86	7	3.89	1.28
Employee welfare schemes	3	3.97	1.29	2	4.07	.83	4	4.11	.88
Lay-off policies	4	3.97	1.38	7	3.63	1.17	13	3.44	1.32
Employee benefits	5	3.94	1.23	5	3.85	.99	2	4.32	.58
Productivity programs	6	3.84	1.14	15	3.27	.96	8	3.71	.92
Staff innovation	7	3.79	1.30	11	3.37	1.01	5	3.94	.90
Communications openness	8	3.49	1.33	13	3.35	1.06	9	3.71	1.11
Staff reporting relationship	9	3.47	1.31	6	3.78	1.16	12	3.53	1.02
Marketing programs	10	3.44	1.32	12	3.36	.91	15	3.29	1.26
Advertising programs	11	3.42	1.41	10	3.48	.92	10	3.71	1.44
Management style	12	3.35	1.20	14	3.33	1.11	17	2.79	1.08
Personnel performance									
evaluation criteria	13	3.27	1.48	16	3.22	1.09	11	3.47	1.07
Executive benefits	14	3.27	1.36	8	3.52	.98	6	3.90	.81
Operating rules/regulations	15	3.18	1.26	9	3.49	1.12	3	4.05	1.03
Corporate culture	16	2.85	1.35	17	3.00	.96	18	2.78	1.17
Planning procedures	17	2.82	1.49	4	3.89	1.22	20	2.68	1.00
Sourcing/uses of funds	18	2.63	1.24	18	2.96	1.10	14	3.44	1.10
Product/service quality	19	2.48	1.24	20	2.59	1.08	24	2.53	1.23
Budget practices	20	2.38	1.35	21	2.59	1.15	16	3.00	1.16
Product/service quality	21	2.37	1.00	19	2.93	1.17	19	2.77	1.15
Type of technology employed	22	2.26	1.24	23	2.44	1.00	21	2.65	1.17
Conduct of R&D	23	2.22	1.31	22	2.52	1.03	22	1.77	.83
Subsidiary performance									
evaluation criteria	24	2.09	1.08	24	2.37	.93	23	2.58	1.12
Average		3.20	.74		3.20	.55		3.45	.62

Respondents also estimated the relative degree of localization in 24 different operating areas (see Table 4)—that is, the extent to which they believed that the subsidiary's operations had been modified from the parent's practices and had been made more similar to what they (the respondents) perceived as local practices. Again, each item was rated on a five-point scale ranging from 1 ("Identical to MNC") to 5 ("Totally Local"). In one subcategorization, we considered five matters to be strategic and nineteen operational. Separately, we categorized eighteen of the items by function: personnel (10 items), production (3 items), marketing (3 items), and finance (2 items) functions.

RESULTS

Autonomy versus Localization

Subsidiaries of all three nationalities/groups saw themselves as having a higher degree of autonomy than of localization; Americans, Europeans, and Japanese rated themselves at 3.60, 3.57, and 3.98 respectively on autonomy (Table 2) but only at 3.20, 3.20 and 3.45 on localization (Table 4). These differences may be large enough to suggest the possibility of a negative relationship between autonomy and localization. At the very least, they suggest that allowing greater autonomy to a subsidiary does not necessarily mean that its personnel and management practices will be more localized. Furthermore, it is possible that some parent companies are willing to allow more autonomy to their subsidiaries precisely because the subsidiaries have a number of home-country nationals in top management positions and their management practices remain comfortably familiar to the parent—that is, the subsidiaries are less localized. Our interview evidence, while not extensive on this point, tended to confirm this analysis for some subsidiaries (particularly Japanese).[4] Differences between autonomy and localization in strategic versus operational decisions are discussed in the following section.

Differences among American, European, and Japanese MNCs

Managers of Japanese subsidiaries ranked themselves as having a higher degree of both autonomy and localization than managers in American and European subsidiaries. The overall average score for autonomy among Japanese managers was 3.98, significantly higher than the autonomy ratings of American and European managers (which were essentially similar at 3.60 and 3.57 respectively—Table 2). Similarly, the Japanese rated themselves at an overall average of 3.45 on the localization scale, significantly higher than the Americans and Europeans (both 3.20 on Table 4). Furthermore, the Japanese subsidiaries exhibited a somewhat greater desire than the Americans or Europeans to localize their operations still further. In response to one question on how they would modify their operations if given the authority to do so ("Localize Much Less" to "Localize Much More"), the average Japanese score was 3.69, whereas the Americans and Europeans each scored 3.57. However, our interviews revealed that the actual degree of both autonomy and localization (at least as most non-Japanese would understand the terms) was considerably less in the Japanese subsidiaries than in either the American or European subsidiaries. Thus, the first point at which our findings were unexpected was in the differences between the reported (statistical) degrees of autonomy and localization among the Japanese subsidiaries and the actual degrees as revealed in interviews of Japanese managers. The implications of these findings are discussed below.

Table 5 compares autonomy across strategic levels and across functions. Not surprisingly, it indicates that Singaporean subsidiaries of all three nationalities/ groups of MNCs believe that they have significantly more autonomy on operational matters than on strategic. Also not surprising, in light of the above findings, is that Japanese managers rated themselves as having more autonomy on both strategic and operational matters (scores of 3.15 and 4.08 respectively) than did American and European managers (whose scores were essentially identical at 3.01/3.00 for strategic decisions and 3.57/3.58 in operational decisions).

More remarkable is the finding that the gap between strategic and operational autonomy was substantially larger for Japanese subsidiaries than for American or European. To the extent that it is true, this finding would imply that Japanese MNCs are more likely than American or European to follow the management philosophy of having the corporation's top management set the corporation's overall objectives or strategy and then

Table 5.   Subsidiary Autonomy by Function and Strategic Level

	American		European		Japanese		
Function	*Mean*	*SD*	*Mean*	*SD*	*Mean*	*SD*	*Prob.*
Personnel	3.85	.80	3.89	.78	4.32	.53	.096
Marketing	3.57	1.34	3.74	1.06	3.72	1.55	.872
Production/							
Operations	3.41	.84	3.46	1.09	3.89	.65	.208
Finance	3.06	.76	2.99	.83	3.60	.47	.026
Operational							
Decisions	3.57	.65	3.58	.68	4.08	.82	.019
Strategic	3.01	.85	3.00	.93	3.15	.51	.831
Decisions							

Note: Probability represents the level of significance of differences in means across nationality groups.

leaving lower-level managers free to make the operational decisions on how to achieve the objectives. This implication is doubtful, however, in view of the discussion below on how Japanese subsidiaries' actual autonomy and localization is less than the statistical findings appear to indicate.

Table 3 compares localization across functions and strategic levels. All three nationalities/groups believed themselves to be more localized on operational decisions than on strategic.

Once again, the Japanese saw themselves as having localized both their strategic and operating practices more than the Americans or Europeans.[5] However, the differences among the nationalities are not as striking as in the case of autonomy, which could suggest that the degree of localization depends more on characteristics of the host-country environment, while the granting of autonomy depends more on characteristics of the MNC's home nationality.

Actual versus Perceived Autonomy and Localization

A further examination of the data reveals that the degree of autonomy and localization enjoyed by Japanese subsidiaries is less than the statistical findings would appear to indicate. This is because of the predominance of Japanese nationals in top management positions in most Japanese subsidiaries in Singapore and of these managers' close ties to and frequent interactions with their headquarters. Table 6 presents the frequency of home national CEOs and management staff for the three groups of MNCs. The much higher percentages of Japanese CEOs and managers in their subsidiaries is consistent with other studies that found that Japanese MNCs employ home-nationality managers in order to retain control over their subsidiaries. The high proportion of Japanese managers contradicts their self-reported high degree of localization.

Similarly, Japanese subsidiaries reported submitting reports to and receiving visits from corporate headquarters very frequently (Table 7). Despite the high proportion of Japanese nationals managing subsidiaries in Singapore, these subsidiaries submitted reports almost as frequently as the American subsidiaries, whose greater reliance on formalized control measures has been well documented (Jaeger 1982; Ouchi and Jaeger 1976). The Japanese

Table 6. Nationality of Management Staff

Variable	American	European	Japanese	Prob.
% of home national CEOs	26.5	50.0	93.8	.000
% expatriate managers	13.0 (.16)	28.3 (.30)	49.0 (.26)	.000

Note: Figures in parentheses are standard deviations.

Table 7.   Frequency of Reports and Visits by MNCs' Nationality

	American		European		Japanese		
Frequency	*Mean %*	*SD*	*Mean %*	*SD*	*Mean %*	*SD*	*Prob.*
Reports to HQ	3.64	.81	3.13	.96	3.53	.688	.061
Visits from HQ	3.27	1.11	3.44	1.25	3.80	1.01	3.26

Note: Frequencies of reports and visits were rated as follows:

  6 = Weekly (or more often)   5 = Monthly
  4 = Quarterly   3 = Semi-annually
  2 = Annually   1 = Less often than annually

subsidiaries also received visits more frequently than the other subsidiaries. This may reflect a Japanese preference for face-to-face dealings and behavioral control, compared to the American preference for more formal controls (Hayashi 1978; Ouchi and Jaeger 1978; Yoshino 1976), or more mundanely, it could simply reflect the greater ease of travel between Japan and Singapore. Nonetheless, these findings certainly tend to gainsay the Japanese subsidiaries' reported high degrees of autonomy and of localization.[7]

Interviews with executives also indicated that Japanese subsidiaries did not have as much autonomy and did not localize as much as superficially indicated by the survey. For example, a Japanese executive admitted that he found it difficult to understand the question of subsidiary autonomy—"Why should the subsidiary not follow the headquarters?"—but stated that it was his corporation's firm policy to localize, and that it would localize its management when it could find Singaporeans who speak Japanese well and who understand his corporate headquarter's complex operating systems. However, he could not see this happening soon. Another Japanese executive pointed out that the rules, culture, and systems in his corporation were largely undocumented and were learned through many years of service. This factor, and the unwillingness of most non-Japanese to commit themselves to a single employer for their entire career, made it most unlikely that the subsidiary would reduce the proportion of Japanese managers. He readily agreed that the same factors provided his corporate headquarters with almost total control over the subsidiary.

One Singaporean executive graphically illustrated the close relationship between Japanese managers in the subsidiary and their headquarters by pointing to the round face of his watch and saying that if his CEO's boss in Tokyo were to say that the watch was square, all the Japanese managers in Singapore would agree with him. Even though he was the only Singaporean manager in the subsidiary, he said he was almost always left out of the decision-making process because of his unwillingness "to see square watch faces." He felt he was tolerated only because of his ability to deal with Singaporean workers, whom the Japanese often found difficult to handle.

Yet another example: A local executive told of a Japanese engineer from the Japanese subsidiary of an American MNC who refused to release technical details to fellow engineers from other subsidiaries of the same company, apparently because they were not Japanese. While this may be an isolated incident and may reflect a whole host of factors, it does indicate that the desire of Japanese executives to interact with and adapt to foreign practices may be less than they themselves perceive.

DISCUSSION

This study should be very helpful in clearing up the confusion between (a) those earlier studies that reported that Japanese subsidiaries enjoy greater autonomy and/or are more localized than American and European subsidiaries, and (b) those that found that Japanese subsidiaries are in fact closely controlled by the parent headquarters, possess little autonomy, and have not localized their practices or personnel very much.

In the first place, many studies in this stream of research appear to have relied excessively on quantifiable data. Their results have tended to be similar to our statistical findings, as indicated in the notes accompanying our tables above. However, other authors have recognized that this approach fails to account for many important but non-quantifiable factors. For example, several authors have emphasized the use of non-quantifiable factors when examining power relationships: Brooke (1984) and Goehle (1978) assert that power relationships are inherently non-quantifiable and are dependent on a multitude of intangible interpersonal processes. Ballon (1983) argues that the "objectivist/ functionalist paradigm" with its "inherent(ly) Western concepts of management and organization" is an inappropriate vehicle for analyzing Japanese corporations. Western authors have commented on the enigmatic nature of the Japanese concept and application of power, the Japanese employee's loyalty to his employer above almost all else (Ballon 1983), and the impact that the acculturation and socialization processes have on employees in Japanese organizations. Yet these factors have not received adequate attention in MNC-subsidiary management studies.

Second, our observations and interviews confirmed earlier findings on an essential difference in the mindset of Western versus Japanese multinationals (see, e.g., Edstrom and Galbraith 1977; Kobrin 1988; Negandhi et al. 1987). In Western MNCs, a subsidiary is viewed as a distinct legal and organizational unit with a separate management, over which the MNC has to make conscious efforts to exert control. Such Western MNCs frequently have host-country citizens in almost all managerial posts except possibly a few critical positions such as the local CEO, the chief financial officer, and some highly technical assignments. Home-country nationals usually make up a very small portion of the subsidiary's management. In contrast, many Japanese subsidiaries (especially in LDCs) are more accurately viewed as extensions of the MNC itself (even though they may technically be separately incorporated, self-standing legal entities). Most such subsidiaries' top management consists almost entirely of Japanese nationals who have undergone extensive service and socialization in their parent companies and who will in all probability return to serve with the MNCs for the rest of their careers. They are therefore not so much the subsidiaries' managers as the MNCs' representatives. Thus, they can be allowed considerable "autonomy," with the knowledge that such discretion will be utilized in accordance with the parents' wishes. In one sense, therefore, the "subsidiary" as such can be viewed as commencing at the level below the core of Japanese managers. This sub-subsidiary is likely to be closely controlled and monitored, with little if any autonomy.

Studies in Singapore have found that almost all the CEOs and almost half of all managers in the local subsidiaries of Japanese companies are home-country nationals. Some researchers attributed the extensive use of Japanese managers to language and educational differences between the two countries (Chong 1984; Chong and Jain 1984) or more generally to environmental differences (Negandhi et al. 1987). We believe that the reasons may go beyond these differences; the use of Japanese managers appears to reflect a strong emphasis in Japanese MNCs on control over all aspects of their operations. A Japanese MNC in effect transplants part of its hierarchy or structure to the subsidiary, so that while appearing to grant considerable autonomy, it is in fact merging the subsidiary's management with the parent's. Control of these subsidiaries is therefore largely a matter of communications and information management, rather than one of behavior and power.

Finally, it should be noted that our questionnaires, and even the interviews, did not attempt to assess the actual amount of subsidiary autonomy or of adjustment to local practices; rather, they assessed the respondents' *perceptions* of autonomy and of localization of management. It could be argued that the Japanese managers perceived their autonomy to be much greater than Western managers would have felt in similar conditions. It is also possible that the Japanese were highly ethnocentric in their management practices, while the Americans and Europeans were more willing to accommodate to other countries' ways of doing things. Thus, the Japanese might have viewed even slight deviations from home-company practices as major adjustments to local practices, while the other nationalities could have made greater absolute changes but assessed them as less significant.[8] Assessment of the actual amount of subsidiary autonomy and the actual degree of managerial localization would require more careful definition and a more exact measuring instrument than our questionnaires and interviews. We must, regretfully, leave these tasks for another study.

NOTES

1. It was believed appropriate to lump together MNCs from different European countries for several reasons: the sample size of any European group (except possibly British MNCs) would have been too small (British MNCs make up about half the sample of "European" companies); several Singaporean subsidiaries were joint ventures with participation by MNCs from more than one European country ("mixed nationality"); the similarities among Singaporean subsidiaries of different European countries tended to be more noticeable than the differences among them; and other authors have lumped together subsidiaries of different European MNCs without any substantial loss of validity.

2. Brooke (1984) identifies two approaches for measuring autonomy. The "locus of decision making approach" essentially aims to identify the specific position within the MNC hierarchy where a decision is made. The "influence approach" attempts to measure the relative degrees of influence that the subsidiary and the corporate headquarters have over the outcome of major decisions. Our study was closer to the latter.

3. The authors are preparing a separate write-up analyzing the significance of the different nationalities' different rank orderings of autonomy in the various types of decisions and areas of operations and of localization in the various subcategories (strategic/operational and by function).

4. Brooke (1984) found that subsidiaries with expatriate managers—that is, less localized— were likely to have greater autonomy.

5. This finding is consistent with the results obtained by Chong (1984), who found that American MNCs tended to adopt home practices, while Japanese corporations modified theirs to Singapore.

6. Other studies have also the importance that Japanese MNCs place on control of subsidiaries through home nationals (Edstrom and Galbraith 1977; Kobrin 1988; Negandhi et al. 1987), and on the American MNCs' more frequent employment of Singaporeans to head their operations (Lee 1985).

7. European subsidiaries submitted formal reports much less frequently than either the Americans or Japanese, approximately semiannually.

8. We are not asserting that the Japanese did in fact perceive their autonomy to be greater than Americans or Europeans would have perceived in the same situations, nor that the Japanese are in fact more ethnocentric than the other nationalities. We have no basis for judgment one way or another on these points; we are merely noting the possibilities.

REFERENCES

Aharoni, Y. 1966. *The Foreign Investment Decision Process*. Division of Research, Harvard Business School.

Alpander, G.G. 1978. "Multinational Corporations. Homebase Affiliate Relations." *California Management Review* 20(3):47-56.

Bartlett, C.A., and S. Ghoshal. 1988. "Organizing for Worldwide Effectiveness: The Transnational Solution." *California Management Review* 30(Fall):54-74.

Berenbeim, R.E. 1983. *Operating Foreign Subsidiaries*. Conference Board Report 836, New York: The Conference Board.

Ballon, R.J. 1983. "Non-Western Work Organization." *Asia Pacific Journal of Management* 1(1):1-14.

Brooke, M.Z. 1984. *Centralization and Autonomy. A Study in Organization Behavior*. New York: Praeger.

Chong, T., and F. Hong. 1984. "A Comparative Study of American and Japanese Management Practices in Singapore." Unpublished project report, National University of Singapore.

Chong, L.C., and H.C. Jain. 1987. "Japanese Management in Singapore: Convergence of Human Resource Management Practices." *Asia Pacific Journal of Management* 4(2):73-89.

Daniels, J.D. 1986. "Approaches to European Regional Management by Large U.S. Multinational Firms." *Management International Review* 26(2):27-42.

Doz, Y., and C.K. Prahald. 1981. "Headquarters Influence and Strategic Control In MNCs." *Sloan Management Review* 23(1):15-29.

Edstrom, A., and J. Galbraith. 1977. "Transfer of Managers as a Coordination and Control Strategy in Multinational Corporations." *Administrative Science Quarterly* 22:248-263.

Garnier, G. 1982. "Context and Decision-Making Autonomy in the Foreign Affiliates of United States Multinational Corporations." *Academy of Management Journal* 25(2):893-908.

Gates, S.R., and W. Egelhoff. 1986. "Centralization in Headquarter-Subsidiary Relationships." *Journal of International Business Studies* 17(2):71-92.

Ghertman, M. 1984. "Decision Making in Multinational Enterprises: Concepts and Research Approaches." Working Paper No. 31, ILO, Geneva.

Goehle, D.G. 1978. *Decision Making in Multinational Corporations.* Ann Arbor, MI: University Microfilms.

Hayashi, K. 1978. "Corporate Planning Practices in Japanese Multinationals." *Academy of Management Journal* 21(2):211-226.

Hedlund, G. 1981. "Autonomy of Subsidiaries and Formalization of Headquarters-Subsidiary Relationships in Swedish MNCs." Pp. 25-78 in *The Management of Headquarters-Subsidiary Relationships in Multinational Corporations,* edited by L. Otterbeck. Stockholm: Gower.

Hedlund, G., and P. Aman. 1984. *Managing Relationships with Foreign Subsidiaries.* Vastervik: Sveriges Mekanforbund.

Hrebiniak, L.G., and W.F. Joyce. 1985. "Organizational Adaptation: Strategic Choice and Environmental Determinism." *Administrative Science Quarterly* 30:336-349.

Hulbert, J.M., and W.K. Brandt. 1980) *Managing the Multinational Subsidiary.* New York: Holt, Reinhart and Winston.

Jaeger, A.M. 1982. "Contrasting Control Modes in the Multinational Corporation: Theory, Practice, and Implications." *International Studies of Management and Organization* 12(1):59-82.

Kobrin, S.J. 1988. "Expatriate Reduction and Strategic Control in American Multinational Corporations." *Human Resource Management* 27(1):63-75.

Lasserre, P. 1985. "Singapore as a Regional Centre: The Experience of French Enterprises." *Euro-Asia Business Review* (May):26-31.

Larsson, A. 1985. *Structure and Change: Power in the Transnational Enterprise.* Stockholm: Uppsala.

Lee, J.G.C. 1985. "The Process of Technology Transfer by the Multinationals in the Electronic Industry in Singapore." Unpublished project report, National University of Singapore.

Leksell, L. 1981. *Headquarter-Subsidiary Relationships in Multinational Corporations.* Stockholm: Stockholm School of Economics.

Low, P.S. 1984. "Singapore-Based Subsidiaries of U.S. Multinationals and Singaporean Firms: A Comparative Management Study." *Asia Pacific Journal of Management* 2(1):29-39.

Meleka, A.H. 1985. "The Changing Role of Multinational Corporations." *Management International Review* 25(4):36-45.

Negandhi, A.R. 1983. "Management in the Third World." *Asia Pacific Journal of Management* 1(1):15-25.

Negandhi, A.R., and R. Baliga. 1979. *Quest for Survival and Growth.* New York: Praeger.

_____. 1981. *Tables are Turning: German and Japanese Multinational Companies in the United States*. Cambridge, MA: Oelgeschlager, Gunn and Hain.

Negandhi, A.R., and M. Welge. 1984. *Beyond Theory Z: Global Rationalization Strategies of American, German and Japanese Multinational Companies*. Greenwich, CT: JAI Press.

Negandhi, A.R., E.C. Yuen, and G. Eshghi. 1987. "Localization of Japanese Subsidiaries in Southeast Asia." *Asia Pacific Journal of Management* 5(1):67-79.

Ouchi, W.G. 1981. *Theory Z: How American Business Can Meet The Japanese Challenge*. Reading, MA: Addison-Wesley.

Ouchi, W.G., and A.M. Jaeger. 1978. "Type Z. Organization: Stability in the Midst of Mobility." *Academy of Management Review* 3(2):305-314.

Pichard, J. 1980. "Organizational Structures and Integrative Devices in European Multinational Corporations." *Columbia Journal of World Business* 15(1):30-35.

Stopford, J.N., and L.T. Wells. 1972. *Managing the Multinational Enterprise: Organization of the Firm and Ownership of the Subsidiary*. New York: Basic Books.

Vozikis, G.S., and T.S. Mescon. 1981. "Convergence or Divergence? A Vital Quest Revisited." *Columbia Journal of World Business* 15(2):79-87.

Webber, R. 1969. "Convergence or Divergence." *Columbia Journal of World Business* 3(2):75-83.

Welge, M.K. 1981. "The Effective Design of Headquarter-Subsidiary Relationships in German MNCs." Pp. 79-106 in *The Management of Headquarters-Subsidiary Relationships in Multinational Corporations*, edited by L. Otterback. Stockholm: Gower.

Yoshino, M. 1976. *Japan's Multinational Enterprises*. Cambridge, MA: Harvard University Press.

Youssef, S.M. 1973. "Contextual Factors Influencing Control Strategy of Multinational Corporations." *Academy of Management Journal* 18(1):136-143.

Yunker, P.J. 1983. "A Survey Study of Subsidiary Autonomy, Performance Evaluation and Transfer Pricing in Multinational Corporations." *Columbia Journal of World Business* 17(3):51-64.

SURVEY RESEARCH TECHNIQUES:
APPLICATION IN DATA COLLECTION FROM
DEVELOPING COUNTRIES (DCs)

Esmail Salehi-Sangari and Bob Lemar

INTRODUCTION

The importance of collecting data in marketing has been emphasized time and again in Industrialized Countries (ICs), since it is regarded as a major mode of providing information which will assist managers in decision making. As international business gains momentum, the acquisition of market research information from other countries is growing more and more important; it is also increasing rapidly as business boundaries lose their significance. In addition, because of differences (culture, language, familiarity with concept of research, etc.) within DCs, the applicability of one data collection technique in one environment (country) might not necessarily be justified in another. In view of the above factors, and owing to the fact that DCs are gaining leverage in international business activities, this paper sets out to assess the use of different methods of survey research techniques initiated in ICs in marketing research practices in DCs.

International Research in the Business Disciplines, Volume 1, pages 125-133.
Copyright © 1993 by JAI Press Inc.
ISBN: 1-55938-538-3

STATUS OF MARKETING RESEARCH IN DCs

According to some scholars (Goodyear 1982; Kaynak 1987; Saleki-Sangari 1991; Stanton 1967) who have dealt with the problems associated with conducting marketing research in DCs, obstacles exist in the application of different methods of data collection in DCs. Kaynak (1987) stresses the fact that businesses and governments in DCs are nervous about the data gathered by marketing research. This is because these data might reveal the inefficiency of the government and business community. Other problems which cause difficulties in the employment of different techniques of data collection are, according to Kaynak:

- restrictions on sample selection and data collection;
- bureaucratic attitudes existing within the economic and social environments of DCs;
- existence of a high degree of illiteracy; and,
- lack of sufficient means of communication (i.e., telephone and mail service).

In a comparison between the application of qualitative versus qualitative research methods in marketing in DCs, Goodyear (1982) concluded that;

- qualitative research is often needed, due to the absence of data banks in DCs, and that
- since qualitative research is more easily monitored, it will result in faster and cheaper results.

Evaluation of the views provided by the others (see Salehi-Sangari 1991; Stanton 1967) shows that the employment of a qualitative approach using survey techniques of data collection is strongly suggested.

TECHNIQUES IN DATA COLLECTION

Communication with respondents, in order to obtain information, can be achieved by the application of different techniques. Evaluation of the literature, however, shows that there is general agreement among scholars regarding the types of communication techniques available, with minor variations of course. For this reason the literature covered in this paper has been restricted, but in order to provide a comprehensive picture of proposed ideas in this field, views have been selected from three different decades: from the 1960s—Mattson, Buzzell, Levitt and Frank (1969), Green and Tull (1966), and Stanton (1967); from the 1090s—Wentz (1972), Boyd and Massy (1972), Erdos (1974), Kaynak

(1987); from the 1980s—Tull and Hawkins (1984), Abeysekera (1985), and Aaker and Day (1986).

However, generally speaking, the combined views of the above-mentioned authors indicate that the sources of data can be divided into survey research, secondary data, and experimentation— of which the last two are beyond the scope of this paper and thus will not be discussed. Survey research has been categorized by the literature as personal interview, telephone interview, and mail interview (questionnaire). Tables 1, 2, and 3 provide a summary of the views of the authors cited in this paper, concerning survey research techniques.

Table 1. Personal Interview

Advantages	Disadvantages
Obtains a better sample	Most expensive technique
Most flexible	Requires more technical skills
Ability to accommodate unstructured questions	Slow if large area is covered
Obtains more information	

Table 2. Telephone Interview

Advantages	Disadvantages
Faster method	Questions must be relatively short
Low cost per completed interview	Format is less flexible
Can reach greater number of respondents	Quantity of data is limited
Can cover larger geographical area	Limited to telephone subscribers

Table 3. Mail Questionnaire

Advantages	Disadvantages
Easy to conduct	Slow replies
Low cost	Low response rate
Eliminates bias created by interviews	Usually difficult to compile a good list of accurate addresses
Centralized control	
Respondents anaonymity	
Wider distribution	
More considered replies	

The extracted data from literature, which are in part presented in Tables 1, 2, and 3, were the basis for the designed questionnaire which was given to the participants in this study.

METHODOLOGY

To obtain the necessary data for this study, three different cases of actual marketing research conducted in DCs, employing different techniques of survey research were selected. The principal researcher in each case has been contacted first by a designed mail questionnaire. To verify the gathered data, the researchers, at a second stage, were contacted by telephone. In each case, different types of language (vernacular, international, etc.) have been used. Table 4 presents the characteristics, approach, and languages employed in each case.

Table 4.   Characteristics of Cases Evaluated in This Study

Research Field	Countries Where Research Is Conducted	Countries Vernacular Language	Type(s) of Language(s) Employed in Questionnaires	Researcher's Native Language	Total Rate of Return
Case 1					
Industrial Marketing	Saudi Arabia	Arabic	Translation of Arabic	Farsi	60%[1]
	Syria	Arabic	Translation of Arabic		
	United Arab Emirates	Arabic	Translation of Arabic		
	Kuwait	Arabic	Translation of Arabic		
	Iran	Farsi	Farsi		
Case 2					
Industrial Marketing	Saudi Arabia	Arabic	English	Farsi	41%
	Kuwait	Arabic	English		
	United Arab Emirates	Arabic	English		
	Qatar	Arabic	English		
	Indonesia	Malayai	English		
	Thailand	Thai	English		
	Singapore	Malayai Chaines, English			
Case 3					
Marketing	Sri Lanka	Sinhales	English	Sinhales	51%[2]

Notes: [1]Personal distribution was employed

[2]Cash remuneration was given

Total number of questionnaires mailed in cases 1, 2, and 3 was 500, 600, and 700, respectively. Total number of conducted interviews in cases 1, 2, and 3 was 50, 23, and 10, respectively.

RESULTS AND DISCUSSION

Evaluation of the replies from the cases shows that the use of telephone interview in DCs should be ruled out, owing to the high costs involved and the existence of time-consuming problems in DCs' communication systems. According to the reviewed literature, mail questionnaire and personal interview have different degrees of reliability in terms of handling complex questions, accuracy on sensitive questions, time required, and soon. The results gathered in these connections are summarized in Table 5.

Concerning the rate of return of mail questionnaires from DCs, which is usually low compared to that of Industrialized Countries, different approaches can be seen when the gathered data are analyzed (see Table 6).

A comparison between the findings provided by the respondents, with regard to personal interview and mail questionnaire, reveals that:

- Personal interview will provide better results in terms of ability to handle complex questions, ability to collect large amount of data, accuracy on sensitive questions, and so forth, and that
- When cost is a consideration the mail questionnaire is to be preferred.

When the gathered information, with regard to the mail questionnaire, was tested against the views provided by the literature, contradictions were found. These are summarized in Table 7.

To summarize, using the replies of open-ended questions from questionnaire, it might be concluded that the views suggested by literature with regard to the advantages of personal interviews are confirmed by all three cases. The advantages of telephone interviews suggested by literature are supported to some extent. Differing views can be identified in connection with time-saving, and with questionnaires' ability to provide opportunity for respondents to give more attention to the questionnaire. To increase the motivation of the respondents in DCs, different suggestions have emerged from each case:

- assure the respondents that the information provided will not be used against them;
- overcome the suspicions of the respondents regarding industrialized countries; and,
- create a feeling that the end results of the research are useful for the respondents too.

Regarding the use of different languages in questionnaires and personal interviews, the use of native languages has been reported to produce the best results in terms of rate return, understanding of the questions, and quality of responses. If the highest quality is desired by the researchers in collection of

Table 5. Adequacy of Personal Interview and Mail Questionnaire When They are Employed in DCs

	Mail Questionnaire				Personal Interviews			
	Poor	Fair	Good	Excellent	Poor	Fair	Good	Excellent
1. Ability to handle complex questionnaire		1	2, 3				1, 3	2
2. Ability to collect large amounts of data	1	3	2			1	3	2
3. Accuracy on sensitive questions	1,	2	3			3	1	2
4. Control of interviewer effects		1	2, 3			1	2, 3	
5. Degree of sample control		1, 2, 3				1	2, 3	
6. Time required		2			1		2	
7. Probable response rate	1	2					2, 3	
8. Cost		1		2	2, 3			

Note: Numbers 1, 2 and 3 represent responses from different cases.

130

Table 6. Suggestions for Increasing the Rate of Return
of the Questionnaire When it is Employed in DCs

Case 1	Personal distribution, indication of advantages of results for the respondents
Case 2	Gift, follow up letters, precontacts, indication of advantages of results for the respondents
Case 3	Cash rewards, follow up letters, indication of advantages of results for the respondents

Table 7. Cross Checks between the Findings of this Study and Suggested
Views by Literature, Concerning Mail Questionnaires used in DCs.

Extracted Suggestions from the Literature	*Extracted Results from the Cases*
Centralized Control	Agree
Time saving	Disagree
Respondents anonymity	Agree
Low cost per completed questionnaire	Agree
No interview bias	Agree
Opportunity for respondents to give more attention to questions	Disagree
Wider distribution	Agree
Less distribution bias	Agree

data, the best approach for achieving this is the translation of the questions into the respondent's native language. Concerning the quality of information obtained, evaluation of the replies shows that the best results, in terms of quality, can be achieved by the use of personal interview in DCs, when marketing research is concerned. It can also be concluded that the size of the companies (number of employees) has a direct impact on the rate of return of the questionnaire. In other words, the bigger the company, the greater is the possibility of response to the mail questionnaire. This might be due to the fact that the larger companies have achieved a higher degree of research culture, or it might be related to the fact that the larger companies are trying to create a better image in terms of public relations. Thus, one possible strategy could be collaboration with the outside environment by providing responses to the research requests. It also emerged from the results that secondary data provided by DCs are limited and lacking in importance. This type of data base is not easily available, nor reliable, nor sufficient.

CONCLUSIONS

Assuming that the research is conducted in Developing Countries and the researcher is located in Industrialized Countries, use of mail questionnaires and/or personal interviews is highly recommended. Regarding the use of telephone interviews, this technique has not been found useful, owing to the existence of technical problems within DCs' communication systems, language, and the high associated cost. To increase the low rate of return of mail questionnaires from DCs, it is suggested that such approaches as personal distribution, follow-up letters, cash remuneration; and gifts be used. The appropriate size of questionnaires, which has direct impact on the rate of return and the quality of response, is identified within a six-page limit.

If the approval of the top management of an organization in DCs can be obtained for the research activities, the lower-level management will cooperate fully, which will result in:

- higher rate of return for questionnaire;
- increase in quality of response; and,
- possibility of availability of document, if needed for research.

It should be noted that only in very rare cases will companies in DCs grant permission to an outsider to examine their files. In other words, it is almost impossible to have access to the DCs' companies' files, when document analysis as a tool of investigation in marketing research is concerned. Even if the obstacle mentioned, access to the files, could be overcome, the unfamiliarity of an outside researcher with the vernacular language of the DCs is still a problem. As mentioned, the use of secondary data compiled by DCs is not recommended owing to the existence of a high degree of unreliability.

REFERENCES

Aaker, D.A., and G.S. Day. 1986. *Marketing Research.* New York: Wiley.

Abeysekera, J.D., and H. Shahnavaz. 1985. " A Brief Guide to Questionnaire Design." University document, Lulea University.

Boyd, J., W. Happer, and F.M. William. 1972. *Marketing Management.* New York: Harcourt Brace Jovanovich.

Erdos, L.P. 1974. "Mail Surveys." *Handbook of Marketing Research.* New York: McGraw-Hill.

Goodyear, M. 1982. "Qualitative Research in Developing Countries." *Journal of Marketing Research Society* (UK) 24(2):86-96.

Green, E.P., and S.D. Tull. 1966. *Research for Marketing Decisions.* Englewood Cliffs, NJ: Prentice-Hall.

Kaynak, E. 1987. "Difficulties of Undertaking Marketing Research in the Developing Countries." *European Research* (UK) 6(6):251-259.

Matthews, J., J.B. Buzzell, D. Robert, T. Levitt, and R.E. Frank. 1964. *Marketing: An Introductory Analysis.* New York: McGraw-Hill.

Salehi-Sangari, E. 1991. "Industrial Buying Behavior of Developing Countries: A Study of Malaysia and Thailand." Sweden: Lulea University.

Stanton, W.J. 1967. *Fundamentals of Marketing.* New York: McGraw-Hill.

Tull, D.S., and D.I. Hawkins. 1984. *Measurement and Methods* New York: Macmillan.

Wents, W.B. 1972. *Marketing Research: Management and Methods.* New York: Harper & Row.

PART IV

GLOBAL FOCUS STUDIES

INTRODUCTION TO PART IV

The fourth and final section of this volume is directed at questions and issues which are truly global in scope. The articles address a variety of substantive topics which, by and large, focus on very broad questions. Consequently, the observations of the authors may provide a better starting point for future research than the previous sections of this book. In many respects these articles are thought pieces; intended to provoke interest, to initiate discourse, and to foster future inquiry. If they fulfill even part of these functions the editors will be satisfied.

When is a firm truly global? In an effort to answer this question and provide academic researchers with a more useful statistical tool to determine the nature and extent of globalization, Drs. Quinton and Neves propose a new model to test whether a firm's activities are more or less globalized. This model explores the relationship between two areas of global strategic consideration: (1) the firm's degree of international involvement (Internationalization Process), and (2) the amount of the firm's dispersion of activities (Global Market Diversification).

In proposing a new Global Diversification Measurement (GMD), the authors incorporate a variety of financial performance indicators, internationalization factors, and market diversification variables to provide a more sensitive measure of the differences between national and regional markets. The preliminary results of the pilot study of 45 firms suggests the

International Research in the Business Disciplines, Volume 1, pages 137-139.
Copyright © 1993 by JAI Press Inc.
All rights of reproduction in any form reserved.
ISBN: 1-55938-538-3

possibility that more globally diverse firms may grow at a slower pace than less globally diversified firms. If so, then firms that seek to be truly global may be compelled to strategically operate with a longer time frame. Firms that are primarily interested in an immediate profit return had better have some second thoughts about going global.

The author of the second study in this section observes that the decades of the 1960s and 1970s was one of confrontation between investors and nations in the area of foreign direct investment (FDI) as host nations restricted FDI. In the post-1980 period, the attitude of host countries has become more pragmatic and they are now encouraging foreign investment. Dr. Movassaghi finds that this "reversal" resulting from the liberalization of FDI policies is "virtually across the board" in the 52 nations that are the primary recipients of FDI by U.S. firms—23 industrialized nations and 29 developing nations. Tax incentives are identified as the principal tool used to attract FDI. The author predicts that the race to attract foreign capital has just begun and that new competitors are entering the race for foreign investors—the Eastern European economies. In his opinion, the future "challenge" for the world's financial markets will be to satisfy this growing and insatiable demand for capital.

The third study in Part IV focuses on a popular subject: Self-Managed Work Teams (SMWTs). The four authors, Drs. Metheny, Bentson, Beyerlein, and Frey identify and analyze some of the challenges confronting corporate human resources departments when the firm decides to establish and operate SMWTs. This study differs from all of the other studies in this volume because it does not discuss SMWTs in the context of any specific nation or region or compare successes or failures due to cultural differences. Instead, the authors discuss some of the pitfalls that can confront any firm in any country that is interested in the idea of employing SMWTs. In this regard, the authors approach their subject as though there were a universal management denominator in human resource management. For the practitioner interested in becoming more competitive in the global arena and making better use of his/her organization's human resources, this study will provide a much-needed examination of SMWT basics.

The fourth study continues the section's change of pace by providing a conceptual overview designed to explain the internationalization process of a firm. Dr. Farhang identifies three different approaches that might be employed to construct a recognizable framework for analysis: the behavioral/incremental model, the economic model, and the strategic model. The advantages and disadvantages of each model are discussed. The author concludes that all three models are being used by enterprises when appropriate, since each model is distinct and mutually exclusive. What is needed but is not proposed by the author is a "new" model that either subsumes the previous three models or is a single-model substitute for the previous approaches.

The fifth paper in this section provides a specific example of a nation experiencing the impact of global change, India. Dr. Siddiqi presents the factors which he believes have moved India away from an introspective view of their economic situation to all but embracing a global perspective. Given the potential which nations with developing economies represent, his portrayal of India's changing view of globalization provides a benchmark from which to gauge future activity.

The last paper in Part IV, and in this first volume, is by one of the editors of the series. It is best described as "way out"—literally way out in space. Dr. Ryan contends that our current definition of global is obsolete and that "technological developments have placed an entirely new territory within the grasp of private enterprise": outer space. The author deplores the current business gap between U.S. interest in commercial space activities and that of Japan, France, the Soviet Union, and China. To generate interest in doing "cutting edge" research the author proposes a wide variety of research areas such as organizational behavior, finance, risk management, and so forth, that have space potential. For the practitioner, Dr. Ryan provides one of the clearest and most concise overviews of the opportunities and challenges open to business firms interested in opening the newest global market.

TOWARD THE MEASUREMENT OF
GLOBAL MARKET DIVERSIFICATION

Alfred P. Quinton and Joao S. Neves

SUMMARY

Although the globalization of a firm's business should be given serious consideration within the firm's strategic planning process, the measurement of the globalization phenomenon and its relationship to a firm's financial growth performance has received limited attention in both the professional management and academic literature. The term global has been used incorrectly to enhance the title of many business writings, when the subject or concept is not even close to being worldwide in scope. This paper recommends and applies a new measurement of global market diversification which tests whether a firm's activities are more or less globalized.

In this measurement, geographic, cultural, and economic distances are combined with two commercialized country potential evaluation methods, to provide a more sensitive measure of the differences between national and regional markets. Although these differences between home and host country have been recognized as critical factors in developing international market entry strategies, they have not been applied previously to globalization. In this

International Research in the Business Disciplines, Volume 1, pages 141-151.

expanded application, the differences between the various host countries is considered in addition to the differences between home and host countries. The difficulties which firms have in reaching out to more distant operating environments has been recognized by Omhae (1985) and Geringer, Beamish, and daCosta (1989). In these works, the concept of a business distance hurdle has been noted. Corporate financial growth performance can be affected when a business distance peak is reached.

The model developed in this study considers the differences between various national operating environments as well as the influence of these differences on management effectiveness. Preliminary results of a pilot study support the possible existence of a threshold at which point corporate growth performance is diminished. This possibility is based on findings indicating that firms with above average global diversification had significantly lower five-year sales growth ratios. If sales for more globally diversified firms are growing at a slower pace than less globally diversified firms, this implication supports the negative impact of increased geographic, cultural, and economic distances.

INTRODUCTION

The globalization of markets and the trend towards an increasingly integrated worldwide economy have compounded the effects of a more intense competitive environment. This trend will continue into the twenty-first century (Naisbitt and Aburdene 1990). Recent political and economic upheavals in Eastern Europe and the U.S.S.R., may on the other hand, strengthen arguments for regionalism and the "global impasse" expressed by Ohmae (1985). Can U.S. multinational enterprises (MNEs) that reach out into numerous unfamiliar host countries expect to perform at the same levels as they have while operating in more familiar environments? This argument is supported by the findings of Geringer, Beamish, and daCosta (1989), whose results indicate that: " . . . as the degree of internationalization of multinationals reached higher values, performance also exhibited increased values but then peaked and exhibited diminished levels of performance" (p. 117).

The value of global strategies appears to have been widely supported by academics and professionals alike (Grant 1987) without a clear definition or understanding of the extent to which they can be and are applied. Worldwide standardization of products and brands (Levitt 1983a, 1983b) has been critically viewed by many who favor a more adaptive localization strategy (Fisher 1984; Kotler 1985). However controversial this topic may be, it represents only a small part of the tremendous trend in business to attempt to apply the global concept to even the broadest aspects of corporate strategy not only for large MNEs but for firms of all sizes. The application of broad-based global expansion strategies to almost every business segment and industry must be continually examined (Caldwell 1986), and their effectiveness must be supported by empirical studies.

DEFINING GLOBAL MARKET DIVERSIFICATION

Terms such as "global" and "globalization" have been applied to numerous aspects of international business without a clear explanation of their exact meaning and usage. Most agree that these terms connote a worldwide perspective, yet we do not find any measurement of globalness (i.e., the amount of diversity in location of the firm's worldwide activities) applied to definitions of global industries, global corporations, or global strategies. These terms are frequently applied to "worlds" that are usually much smaller than any of the Earth's seven continents. In many cases, these "worlds" are defined in terms of a few target markets, the host countries receiving direct foreign investment, or regions of natural resource abundance.

Current researchers are investigating the globalization framework in an attempt to link the concept of industry and technology globalization with the application or usefulness of global strategies (Yip 1990; Light 1989; Henderson 1989; Muroyama and Stever 1988; Grunwald and Flamm 1985; Davidson 1982). These studies present varied approaches and useful insights, however they do so without a clear and precise measure of globalness. Geringer, Beamish, and daCosta (1989) have dealt with various individual aspects of the strategic diversification options available to MNE managers such as the diversification of product offerings (related versus unrelated lines), or diversification of international operations (exporting, licensing, management contracts, and all the forms of foreign direct investment), while Kim, Hwang, and Burgers (1989) have integrated these concepts into the framework of global strategies.

Globalness has been measured by country counting (Cohen 1972), and the percent of foreign sales to total sales (Rugman 1979) or domestic sales (Wolf 1975, 1977) has also been used as a proxy for international diversification. Miller and Pras (1980) used the entropy measure combining these factors which added a perspective of the size of foreign operations. They stated: "A more precise measure of multinational diversification would be based on corporate diversification of assets, rather than the number of subsidiaries." The established viewpoints of international diversification can be classified as: (a) the internal environment (i.e., organizational or developmental as measured by the orientation stages of the internationalization process and corporate development) (Keegan 1989); (b) the industry or product market environment as measured by the number and diversity of the industries in which the firm operates (Rumelt 1974); and, (c) the geographic or locational market environments in which the firm researches, develops, produces, sells, and/or distributes its offerings (Wolf 1975).

Kim (1989) and Kim, Hwang, and Burgers (1989) proposed an entropy measure which combined industry diversification with geographic market diversification. However, it has been illustrated (Neves and Quinton 1990) that their results can be distorted by changing the sequence in which these two factors are ordered when calculating a global diversification measure. Differences in geographic distance, cultural distance, or economic distance between the home country and the host countries in which foreign operations exist or between the various foreign host countries have not been explicitly addressed in terms of global market diversification.

One can reason that the difference in business distance (physical, cultural, and economic) (Luostarinen 1980) between home and/or host markets should take precedence over diversification of industry-based factors. After all, the transfer of product-based core knowledge into foreign markets has been recognized as the special ability that makes the MNE unique.

JUSTIFICATION FOR A NEW METHOD

Researchers at the University of Uppsala in Sweden have focused on business distance differences in their studies of the internationalization process (Johanson and Wiedersheim-Paul 1975; Johanson and Vahlne 1977), export activity, increased uncertainty in international business (Wiedersheim-Paul 1972) and foreign buyer-seller interaction (Hallen and Wiedersheim-Paul 1984). An expanded measurement of global market diversification should employ this concept in order to account for these differences between national, regional, and continental markets.

The differences between national markets has also been part of the global market segmentation process (Day, Fox, and Huszagh 1988). In trying to determine the extent to which global marketers can pursue the same strategy across national borders, Day, Fox, and Huszagh sought to segment global markets by grouping countries according to the degree of economic development differences. The level of economic development has been used as an indicator of market potential (Haner 1980; Cundiff and Hilger 1984) and several classification schemes have been developed by Rostow (1960), Sethi (1971), Terpstra (1983), and Cateora (1983).

The need to incorporate external data to measure the geographic, cultural, and economic differences between home/host countries or host/host countries is evident if any analysis of global market diversification is truly going to assess the effects on operating conditions. This is consistent whether the countries are target markets for export sales, locations for foreign production and consumption, foreign production for export to regional markets or foreign export back to the home market. The selection of external variables does however bring into play some subjectivity but this seems inevitable for this type of analysis.

While exploring the internationalization process in Swedish firms, Johanson and Wiedersheim-Paul (1975) proposed the use of the psychic distance concept (Beckerman 1956; Linnemann 1966; Wiedersheim-Paul 1972) when considering the extension of the firm's activities into new international markets. This concept, defined as "the factors preventing or disturbing the flows of information between the firm and each foreign market" includes differences in language, culture, political systems, education levels, and levels of industrial development and is correlated with geographic distance (Johanson and Wiedersheim-Paul 1975). The application of this concept was furthered by Luostarinen (1980) through the construct of lateral rigidity that is defined as a behavioral characteristic of the firm which causes inelasticity in the firm's strategic decision-making behavior.

In Luostarinen's (1980) business distance framework, the concept of distance is three dimensional, that is, (1) physical (geographic distance), (2) economic (industrial development), and (3) psychic (Beckerman 1956), cultural, or institutional (Luostarinen 1980). The third grouping may be labeled "cultivated distance" for the sake of simplicity. Luostarinen (1980) has operationalized these terms under the heading of business distance and has empirically tested several hypotheses regarding target market determination.

The country potential model developed by Haner (1980) as a market entry forecasting system also encompasses human variables (e.g., temperament, economic activity, social structure, and political framework) and physical variables (e.g., natural resources, climate, geography, and infrastructure development). The advantage in using Haner's system is that these variables have already been rated for 60 countries and then the countries are ranked and grouped into five regions, namely, Europe, Far East, Latin America, Middle East, and North America by a team of twelve experts (Haner 1980).

Haner (1980) also measured and adjusted these country potential ratings against a commercial environmental risk assessment service (BERI, Washington, DC). An adjusted rating score was then used to classify countries into three categories, that is, achievers, underachievers, and those achieving potential. A final analysis developed profit opportunity recommendations (PORs) for the 60 countries in the study. PORs based on each country's performance and potential ratings were classified into four broad categories: (1) POR1 Capital Investment Recommended, (2) POR2 Non-dividend cash flow investments recommended, (3) POR3 Export trade only, and (4) POR4 No business relations are recommended.

The introduction of external variables similar to Luostarinen's business distance concept provides the missing framework needed to expand from an internal factors method (number of countries and foreign activity ratios) of market diversification measurement to a broader, more encompassing measure of global market diversification.

RECOMMENDATIONS FOR A NEW METHOD

A new model is recommended that will explore the relationship between two areas of global strategic consideration, that is, (1) the firm's stage of development within the Internationalization Process, which measures the degree of international involvement, and (2) the firm's level of global market diversification, which measures the dispersion of activities. The proposed global market diversification measurement (GMD) incorporates a combination of both internal variables such as the ratios of foreign sales, profits, and assets to total sales, profits, and assets as well as external variables, that is, business distance, which combines geographic, cultural, and economic factors (Luostarinen 1980), country potential ratings (Haner 1980), and profit opportunity recommendations (Haner 1980). Specifically:

$$GMD = BDD1 + BDD2 + CPRD1 + CPRD2 + PORD1 + PORD2$$

BDD1 is the difference in the business distance variable between the home country and host countries. BDD2 is the difference in the business distance variable between the host countries. CPRD1 is the difference in the country

Table 1. Description of Variables

Corporate Financial Performance Variables

CSALES: five-year compounded growth rate of sales.
    CNI five-year compounded growth rate of net income.
    CEP five-year compounded growth rate of earnings per share.

  CFPR = CSALES + CNI + CEPS

Internationalization Variables

    EXPSR: total exports to total sales.
    EXTSR: total exports to total foreign subsidiary sales.
    FORSR: total foreign subsidiary sales to total sales.
  FORINCR: total foreign income to total income.
  FORINVR: total foreign investments to total investments.

      IPS = EXPSR + EXTSR + FORSR + FORINCR + FORINVR

Market Diversification Variables

    BDD1: business distance (geographic, cultural, economic factors) between home country and each country with reported foreign operation.
    BDD2: business distance between the countries with foreign operations.
  CPRD1: differences between country potential rating for home country and each country with foreign operations.
  CPRD2: differences between country potential rating for the countries with foreign operations.
  PORD1: differences between profit opportunity recommendations for home country and each country with reported foreign operations.
  PORD2: differences between profit opportunity recommendations for the countries with foreign operations

potential ratings between the home country and host countries. CPRD2 is the difference in the country potential ratings between the host countries. PORD1 is the difference in the profit opportunity recommendations between the home country and the host countries. PORD2 is the difference in the profit opportunity recommendations between the host countries (Table 1).

OBTAINING GEOGRAPHICALLY SEGMENTED DATA

The difficulty of obtaining firm-level data by geographic or national segments has been noted by several researchers including Miller and Pras (1980), Horst (1973), Dunning (1973), Cohen (1972). The fact that firms operating in the United States must report under the Financial Accounting Standards Board Statement #14, 1983, all foreign revenues or assets equal to 10 percent or more of the firm's consolidated total revenues or assets by significant geographic regions has been recognized and utilized by other researchers (Collins 1990). There are limitations to the degree of segmentation of the data that is available. The data used in this pilot study has been collected from *Compustat PC Plus* (Standard & Poors) and refers to the FY 1987/88. The geographically segmented portion of this data include net sales, operating profits, and overseas investments that are reported according to five continents (e.g., Africa), two regions (e.g., Middle East), and eleven major countries (e.g., France). This system of categorization certainly has limitations when measuring global diversification.

METHODOLOGY

The data for this study consists of three dependent variables—compounded corporate performance measures over a five-year period and eleven independent variables—five measuring internationalization, and six measuring global market diversification. (See Table 1 for a detailed description.)

The data measuring the independent variables was combined into two primary measurements, that is, Internationalization Process Stage (IPS) and Global Market Diversification (GMD). Both IPS and GMD were then divided into high and low groupings based on their means. A two-sample *t*-test was performed on each independent variable against the corporate performance measures. In addition, simple regression was used to examine the relationship between financial growth performance and the two components of globalization.

RESULTS AND DISCUSSION

The statistical results outlined in Table 2 indicate that our pilot sample contained 45 firms, of which 18 were above average in global market

Table 2.   Sample Profile (*n* = 45)

Economic Activity Reported for FY 1987/88 (MM$):

	Sales	Net Income	Assets
Average	4440.2	289.2	4637.2
Maximum	32917.0	2337.0	36960.0
Minimum	8.6	.7	7.3

	Sales, Export	Sales, Domestic	Sales, Foreign
Average	372.3	3207.5	1567.1
Maximum	4196.0	20866.0	12896.0
Minimum	4.4	4.9	3.6

	Average	Std. Dev.	Max.	Min.
Performance Indicators (5 Year Growth Rates)				
Sales	.1295	.1546	.7390	−.058
Net Income	.2004	.2513	.9840	−.10
Earnings/share	.1962	.2249	.97	−.136
Combined	.5261	.54912	.293	−.183
Internalizationation Indicators				
Exports to Total Sales	0.09	0.08	0.52	0.01
Exports to Foreign Sales	0.37	0.37	1.59	0.03
Foreign Sales/Total Sales	0.36	0.42	2.97	0.07
Foreign Profit/Net Income	0.75	0.58	2.58	0.11
Foreign Invest./Tot. Assets	0.26	0.10	0.55	0.07
Foreign Profit/Dom. Profit	0.61	0.98	3.73	2.79
Foreign Invest./Dom. Invest.	0.42	0.23	1.20	0.08
Internationalization Stage	1.83	0.84	5.02	0.95
Global Market Diversification Indicators				
Business Distance Home/Host	0.46	0.19	0.92	0.15
Business Distance Host/Host	0.30	0.20	0.67	0.00
Country Potential Home/Host	0.39	0.21	0.89	0.02
Country Potential Host/Host	0.23	0.21	0.80	0.00
Profit Opportunity Home/Host	0.35	0.15	0.65	0.12
Profit Opportunity Host/Host	0.17	0.16	0.67	0.00
Global Market Diversification	1.90	1.00	3.80	0.41

diversification and 27 were below average, while 17 were above average in internationalization and 28 were below average.

The average five-year sales growth percentage for the above-average globally diversified firms was .07 compared to .17 for the below-average firms. The two-sample *t*-test indicated a significant difference in sales growth: firms with high

Table 3.   Statistical Results: Impact on Sales Growth

	Global Market Diversification	
	Above Average (*GMD* < *1.90*)	*Below Average* (*GMD* < *1.90*)
Sample Size	18	27
Average	7.01	16.90
Std.Dev	7.19	18.41
T-Value	2.517	(0.0166)

	Level of Internationalization	
	Above Average (*IPS* < *1.825*)	*Below Average* (*IPS* < *1.825*)
Sample Size	17	28
Average	17.27	10.32
Std.Dev.	17.58	14.01
T-Value	1.384	(.1892)

levels of global market diversification exhibited lower financial growth performance. In the case of internationalization, the differences were not significant. Firms with a high level of internationalization had an average five-year sales growth percentage of .17, whereas firms with low levels of internationalization had .10, but the two-sample *t*-test result was not significant.

In regard to sales growth (Table 3), the GMD measure provides preliminary support for the global impasse theory (Ohmae 1985) and the internationalization threshold concept (Geringer, Beamish, and daCosta 1989). The same significance was not found however in the other performance factors, particularly net income.

If sales for more globally diversified firm's are growing at a slower pace than less globally diversified firms, this may confirm the negative impact of increased business distance and support Haner's potential and opportunity ratings. Since the net income variable was not significant in these preliminary results, we cannot state that this study confirms or conflicts with the Kim, Huang, and Burgers 1989. Their results indicated no difference in profit growth for firms with high global diversity in related product markets, but a higher profit growth for firms in unrelated product markets. The primary purpose of this paper was to argue in favor of a more detailed measure of global market diversification. The model we have proposed does support the need for a more complex measure to assist global analysts in understanding this multi-faceted phenomenon.

REFERENCES

Beckerman, W. 1956. "Distance and the Pattern of Intra-European Trade." *Review of Economics and Statistics* 28.

Caldwell, P.K. 1986. "U.S. Firms Can Add to Their Profits By Developing Global Marketing Plans." *Business America* (November 24), pp. 7-11.

Carlson, S. 1975. "How Foreign is Foreign Trade? A Problem in International Business Research." *Acta Universitatis Upsaliensis Studia Oeconomiae Negotiorum 11,* Uppsala, Sweden.

Cateora, P.R. 1983. *International Marketing,* 5th ed. Homewood, IL: Irwin.

Cohen, B.I. 1972. "Foreign Investment by U.S. Corporations as a Way of Reducing Risk." Mimeo, Yale University, Economics Growth Center, Discussion Paper No. 51, September.

Collins, J.M. 1990. "A Market Performance Comparison of U.S. Firms Active in Domestic, Developed and Developing Countries." *Journal of International Business Studies* 21(2):271-287.

Cundiff, E.W., and M.T. Hilger. 1984. *Marketing in the International Environment.* Englewood Cliffs, NJ: Prentice-Hall.

Davidson, W.H. 1982. *Global Strategic Management.* New York: Wiley.

Day, E., R.J. Fox, and S.M. Huszagh. 1988. "Segmenting the Global Market for Industrial Goods: Issues and Implications." *International Marketing Review* 5(3):14-27.

Dunning, J.H. 1973. "The Determinants of International Production." *Oxford Economic Papers* 25(November):289-336.

Fisher, A.B. 1984. "The Ad Biz Gloms Onto Capital." *Fortune* (November 12).

Geringer, J.M., P.W. Beamish, and R.C. daCosta. 1989. "Diversification Strategy and Internationalization: Implications for MNE Performance." *Strategic Management Journal* 10:109-119.

Grant, R.M. 1987. "Multinationality and Performance Among British Manufacturing Companies." *Journal of International Business Studies* 18(3):79-89.

Grunwald, J., and K. Flamm. 1985. *The Global Factory: Foreign Assembly in International Trade.* Washington, DC: The Brookings Institution.

Hallen, L., and F. Wiedersheim-Paul. 1984. "The Evolution of Psychic Distance in International Business Relationships." Pp. 15-27 in *Between Market and Hierarchy,* edited by I. Hagg and F. Wiedershain-Paul. Uppsala, Sweden: University of Uppsala.

Haner, F.T. 1980. *Global Business Strategy for the 1980s.* New York: Praeger Publishing.

Henderson, J. 1989. *The Globalization of High Technology Production: Society, Space, and Semiconductors in the Restructuring of the Modern World.* New York: Routledge, Chapman & Hall.

Horst, T.O. 1973. "Firm and Industry Determinants of the Decision to Invest Abroad: An Empirical Study." *Review of Economics and Statistics* 54(August):258-266.

Johanson, J., and F. Wiedersheim-Paul. 1975. "The Internationalization Process of the Firm—Four Swedish Cases." *Journal of Management Studies* 12(3):305-322.

Johanson, J., and J.-E. Vahlne. 1977. "The Internationalization Process of the Firm—A Model of Knowledge Development and Increasing Foreign Market Commitment." *Journal of International Business Studies.*

Keegan, W. 1989. *Global Marketing Management,* 4th ed. Englewood Cliffs, NJ: Prentice-Hall.

Kim, W.C. 1989. "Developing a Global Diversification Measure." *Management Science* 35(3):376-383.

Kim, P.W., P. Hwang, and W.P. Burgers. 1989. "Global Diversification Strategy and Corporate Profit Performance." *Strategic Management Journal* 10:45-57.

Kotler, P. 1985. "Global Standardization—Courting Danger." Panel discussion 23, American Marketing Association Conference, Washington, D.C.

Levitt, T. 1983a. "The Globalization of Markets." *Harvard Business Review* (May-June):92-102.

_____. 1983b. *The Marketing Imagination*. New York: The Free Press.

Light, C.D. 1989. "The Globalization of the Automobile Industry: A Look at the Effects on Product Strategy." *Proceedings of the 1989 Conference of the Association for Global Business*, New Orleans, November 9-11.

Linnemann, H. 1966. *An Econometric Study of International Trade Flows*. Amsterdam: North-Holland.

Luostarinen, R. 1980. *Internationalization of the Firm*. Helsinki: Finland: Helsinki School of Economics.

Miller, J.C., and B. Pras. 1980. "The Effects of Multinational and Export Diversification on the Profit Stability of U.S. Corporations." *Southern Economic Journal* 46:792-805.

Muroyama, J.H., and H.G. Stever, eds. 1988. *Globalization of Technology: International Perspectives*. Washington, DC: National Academy Press. ·

Naisbitt, J., and P. Aburdene. 1990. *Megatrends 2000*. New York: William Morrow and Co.

Neves, J.S., and A.P. Quinton. 1990. "Measuring Global Market Diversification." Unpublished paper, submitted to the Academy of Marketing Science, International Marketing Track, 1991 Conference, Miami, FL.

Ohmae, K. 1985. *Triad Power, The Coming Shape of Global Competition*. New York: The Free Press.

Rostow, W.W. 1960. *The Stages of Economic Growth*. New York: Cambridge University Press.

Rugman, A.M. 1979. *International Diversification and the Multinational Enterprise*. Lexington, MA: Heath.

Rumelt, R.P. 1974. *Strategy, Structure, and Economic Performance*. Boston, MA: Division of Research, Harvard Business School.

Sethi, S.P. 1971. "Comparative Cluster Analysis for World Markets." *Journal of Marketing Research* 8(3):348-354.

Terpstra, V. 1983. *International Marketing*, 3rd ed. New York: Dryden Press.

Wiedersheim-Paul, F. 1972. *Uncertainties and Economic Distance–Studies in International Business*. Uppsala, Sweden: Almqvist & Wiksell.

Wolf, B.M. 1975. "Size and Profitability Among U.S. Manufacturing Firms: Multinational Versus Primarily Domestic Firms." *Journal of Economics and Business* 28(1):15-22.

_____. 1977. "Industrial Diversification and Internationalization: Some Empirical Evidence." *The Journal of Industrial Economics* 26:177-191.

Yip, G.S. 1990. "An Exploratory Test of a Globalization Framework." Working paper #90-01, George Washington University, School of Business. Presented at the American Marketing Association Summer Educator's Conference, Washington, D.C., August.

CHANGING CLIMATE IN REGULATION AND PROMOTION OF FOREIGN DIRECT INVESTMENT:
A GLOBAL SURVEY

Hormoz Movassaghi

INTRODUCTION

Foreign investment legislation and programs designed to regulate and attract foreign direct investment (FDI) emerged for the first time in a number of less developed countries (LDCs) between the late 1950s and 1960s (National Industrial Conference Board 1969; Salehizadeh 1983). The principal objectives of such programs were to attract and screen inflows and shape the activities of foreign firms. This was done in order to bring them into closer harmony with the national economic goals and objective of the host countries. By the late 1970s nearly all nations, major developed countries (DCs) included, had instituted promotional schemes of different scopes (OECD 1983). Some were also actively engaged in competition to attract FDI by offering lucrative investment incentives like tax holidays and subsidies and minimizing

International Research in the Business Disciplines, Volume 1, pages 153-166.

imposition of requirements such as foreign equity limitations and local content (Guisinger 1985). The 1980s has been an era of noticeable liberalization in the FDI promotional polices of many countries irrespective of their position across the ideological and economic development spectrums ("India Opens Up" 1982; "How Columbia Aims" 1984; Demirsar 1988; Wain 1989).

The main objective of this study is to review the major elements in the FDI promotional programs of various countries that comprise the bulk of the U.S. FDI and identify recent patterns in their incentive and requirement schemes as reflected in the "Benchmark Surveys" of the U.S. Department of Commerce. Data from these surveys is presented which indicate rather consistent changes in the host governments' policies both in granting incentives of various types and the imposition of different requirements. The principal proposition advanced here is that the 1980s can be termed as a decade of liberalization in the attitudes of host governments toward foreign investors. The notable aspect of this policy "reversal" is the virtual, across-the-board nature of this phenomenon as manifested in approximately 50 nations that comprise the bulk of U.S. FDI. These trends are discussed relative to the available empirical evidence on the effectiveness of such promotional programs in various countries.

FOREIGN DIRECT INVESTMENT PROGRAMS IN LDCs AND DCs

Foreign direct investment incentive programs refer to any host government that is designed to raise the rate of return on FDI over and above what it would be in the absence of such intervention. These incentives are often used to attract foreign investment into a country, a particular industry or geographic location, or to induce firms to comply with specific performance requirements.

Investment Incentives

The most common investment incentives are:

1. *Tax and Tax-related Concessions.* These include outright reduction in or exemption from corporate income taxes, accelerated depreciation allowance and investment credits among others.
2. *Import Concessions.* These refer to rebates on customs duties associated with the importation of raw materials and capital equipment, "drawbacks," and protective tariffs or quotas on competing imports for the firms' final output(s).
3. *Subsidies.* These consist of investment grants, cash support for R & D and training of local labor, low-interest loans, provision for infrastructure and administrative assistance.

Performance Requirements

Performance requirements, on the other hand, refer to any measure imposed on a foreign firm in order to regulate certain aspects of the firm's operations. The most common performance requirements are:

1. *Minimum Local Content.* This refers to a predetermined percentage of the firm's total production expressed in monetary, physical, or value-added terms which must be procured from local suppliers or produced locally in the host country by the foreign firm.
2. *Minimum Export Level.* This refers to an obligation to export a certain level of the firm's total production stated in value or quantitative terms.
3. *Local-Equity Participation.* This consists of the minimum level of equity specified in terms of the percent ownership that should be held by the host country nations or state-owned enterprises.
4. *Employment, Size, Location, and Financing Restrictions.* These include use of local labor in manual or managerial positions, minimum or maximum size, location in economically depressed regions, and limits on access to local financing.

Several surveys provide descriptions of the different incentives/requirements offered by the developed countries (DCs) and the LDCs as promulgated in the various laws, regulations and decrees governing FDI into those countries (Price-Waterhouse 1976; LICIT 1981). Much less information, however, is available on the *actual incidence* of FDI incentives, and so forth, in various countries or industries. One major source of data on programs affecting the subsidiaries of U.S. companies is the *Benchmark Survey of U.S. Direct Investment Abroad.* To date, two surveys of U.S. firms having direct investment abroad have been conducted, the first in 1977, the other in 1982. In both surveys, non-bank affiliates of non-bank U.S. parent companies were asked about the type(s) of investment incentives that they received and/or any kind of performance requirements that they were subject to. The 1977 survey indicated that 27 percent of the affiliates in LDCs and 25 percent of those located in DCs received at least one type of incentive (U.S. Department of Commerce 1981). Tax concessions have been the most common form of investment incentive among all countries. Tariff incentives are most often used in LDCs while subsidies are more frequently offered in DCs. This pattern was exhibited both in 1977 and again in 1982 as shown in Table 1.

Furthermore, there are inter-industry differences in terms of the incidence of these incentives and restrictions. In 1977, for example, 41 percent of the U.S. manufacturing affiliates received some type of incentive as compared to 29 percent in mining and 21 percent of petroleum affiliates. Within the manufacturing sector, electrical machinery, food processing, and transportation

Table 1.   Incidence of Investment Incentives
By Type and Country in 1977 & 1982

Incentives	Tax Concessions		Tariff Concessions		Subsidies		Other Concessions	
	1977	1982	1977	1982	1977	1982	1977	1982
All Countries	20.5	24.8	8.4	9.8	9.0	14.2	5.2	7.4
Developed Countries	19.7	24.5	5.6	6.7	11.2	17.5	5.3	6.8
Less Developed Countries	22.6	26.3	14.8	16.4	4.9	8.7	5.2	8.8

Table 2.   Incidence of Investment Incentives by Type and Industry in 1982

Industry	Tax Concessions	Tariff Concessions	Subsidies	Other Incentives
Petroleum	18.8	5.2	8.0	6.0
Manufacturing	38.2	17.3	26.4	12.7
Food	43.9	18.0	25.5	11.2
Chemicals	42.0	21.0	26.1	15.2
Primary and Fabricated Materials	31.9	12.5	26.8	8.7
Non-electrical Machinery	36.5	8.2	27.2	15.1
Electrical Machinery	44.6	22.7	26.5	14.1
Transportation Equipment	38.8	22.0	35.6	15.0
Mining	27.4	11.2	10.1	8.0

equipment received more incentives than others. In comparison, the same survey found that performance requirements were applied much more in the LDCs than DCs, 29 percent vs. 6 percent respectively.

As Table 2 indicates, the most frequently used performance requirements were minimum export restrictions and local content requirements.

Analysis of the performance requirements by industry revealed that firms in the mining industry were more often subject to such requirements (27%) followed by manufacturing (19%) and petroleum industries (16%). With the manufacturing industry, U.S. affiliates in transportation equipment (27%), electrical machinery (21%), and food processing (21%) were most often subject to such requirements compared to others (U.S. Department of Commerce 1981).

METHODOLOGY

This study examines changes in FDI positions of U.S. firms from a sample of countries. (Refer to Tables 3 and 4 for countries used in the study.) These 52 countries, 23 industrialized and 29 developing, contain the bulk of direct investment by the non-bank affiliates of non-bank U.S. parent companies. The *only* source of information on the *actual* frequency of investment incentives and performance requirements experienced by U.S. firms in various countries is the *Benchmark Survey of U.S. Investment Abroad.* The Benchmark Surveys are the most comprehensive information on the universe of U.S. FDI abroad. In the two previous surveys U.S. companies were asked if they had received any incentives or were subject to one or more performance requirements.

RESULTS

Tables 3 and 4 show the percent of the "non-bank affiliates of non-bank U.S. parents" that indicated receipt of one or more of the major types of investment incentives from their host countries in 1972 and 1982.

Table 3. Percent of U.S. Companies Receiving Different Types of Incentives from the Most Developed Countries in 1972 and 1982

	Tax Concessions		Tariff Concessions		Subsidies	
	1977	*1982*	*1977*	*1982*	*1977*	*1982*
All Countries	21	25	8	10	9	14
Developed Countries	20	25	6	7	11	18
Canada	14	17	5	7	6	10
Europe	3	26	5	5	14	21
European Communities	21	25	4	4	16	22
Belgium	15	29	4	5	18	29
Denmark	19	19	6	1	14	15
France	12	22	3	4	10	15
Germany	11	16	3	3	15	20
Ireland	67	68	*	8	*	49
Italy	23	23	4	6	20	25
Luxembourg	35	29	*	0	*	16
Netherlands	25	30	4	3	8	31
United Kingdom	26	24	4	4	18	19
Other Europe	20	27	6	9	8	15
Austria	*	34	*	10	*	22
Finland	*	27	*	7	*	13
Norway	8	9	2	3	6	6
Spain	35	45	13	21	13	29
Sweden	26	30	2	3	15	24
Switzerland	11	14	2	1	2	1
Japan	8	12	3	5	1	5
Australia	35	35	13	15	11	18
New Zealand	37	50	18	23	5	8
South Africa	33	42	14	20	10	15

Notes: * Missing information or data suppressed to avoid disclosure of companies involved.
Source: Calculated by the author from U.S. Department of Commerce (1981, 1985).

Table 4.   Percent of U.S. Companies Receiving Different Ttypes of
Incentives from the Host Developing Countries in 1977 and 1982

	Tax Concessions		*Tariff Concessions*		*Subsidies*	
	1977	*1982*	*1977*	*1982*	*1977*	*1982*
Developing Countries	23	26	15	16	5	9
Europe						
Greece	*	44	*	25	*	30
Portugal	*	39	*	21	*	25
Turkey	*	36	*	32	0	13
Latin America	24	28	16	17	4	11
Argentina	30	41	12	16	11	19
Brazil	38	44	20	23	13	25
Chile	*	16	*	11	*	12
Columbia	16	23	16	18	10	16
Ecuador	*	25	22	33	*	12
Peru	28	34	26	19	3	7
Venezuela	23	23	24	26	2	6
Mexico	23	28	13	14	7	15
Panama	19	21	13	13	1	4
Bahamas	*	8	3	10	0	0
Bermuda	19	23	*	1	*	0
Jamaica	*	11	*	17	*	1
Trinidad-Tobago	*	14	*	17	*	6
Africa	*	17	*	17	*	2
Egypt	*	23	*	25	0	0
Libya	*	10	*	0	0	0
Liberia	20	11	10	7	0	0
Nigeria	14	10	16	15	*	3
Middle East	20	24	12	10	7	7
Israel	*	29	17	14	30	25
Saudi Arabia	*	38	*	9	*	6
United Arab Emirates	*	10	*	12	*	0
Other Asia and Pacific	*	29	*	17	*	6
Hong Kong	4	6	*	1	0	1
India	32	44	11	20	10	23
Indonesia	*	16	*	26	4	2
Malaysia	27	41	28	34	3	7
Philippines	13	18	14	21	1	6
Singapore	22	37	7	7	6	10
South Korea	52	53	27	23	*	3
Taiwan	40	51	24	37	*	9
Thailand	14	21	7	21	4	12

Note: * Missing information or data suppressed to avoid disclosure of companies involved.
Source: Calculated by the author from U.S. Department of Commerce (1981, 1985).

Across all countries and for all subsidiaries combined, there was a general increase in the proportion of the subsidiaries of U.S. companies receiving tax and tariff incentives and subsidies. In 1982, 25 percent of those firms received tax incentives while 10 percent enjoyed tariff concessions and 14 percent obtained subsidies. The percentage growth in the number of firms receiving subsidies (55.6%) exceeded the combined increases of those receiving tariff concessions (25.0%) and tax incentives (19.1%). This was true in DCs as well as in LDCs. Tax and tariff incentives were more popular among the LDCs. In contrast, more U.S. subsidiaries in DCs receive subsidies than other forms of incentives. This pattern was found in 1972 and again in 1982.

Investment Incentives

Tax Incentives

Tax incentives have, by far, been the most pervasive type of policy tool utilized by governments of both DCs and LDCs to attract FDI. This can be seen by comparing the percentage of U.S. firms that received these types of incentives as compared to other incentives in the various host countries as reported in 1972 and 1982. Among the DCs, the proportion of U.S. firms that received various forms of tax incentives ranged from a low of 9 percent in Norway to 16 percent in Germany, 35 percent in Australia, 50 percent in New Zealand and 68 percent in Ireland in 1982. Corresponding numbers for the LDCs ranged from a low of 6 percent in Hong Kong to 16 percent in Chile, 37 percent in Singapore, 44 percent in Brazil and 53 percent in South Korea. Nearly the same pattern was observed in host countries' reliance on tax incentives for DCs and LDCs in 1977.

Tariff Incentives

Tariff incentives are also widely used, more so by LDCs than by DCs. 1982, the percent of U.S. firms in DCs receiving various types of customs concessions ranged from none in Luxembourg to 20 percent in South Africa. The corresponding data across LDCs ranged from none in Libya to 15 percent in Nigeria, 26 percent in Indonesia and 37 percent in Taiwan. Relative to other areas, Southeast Asian, Pacific, and South American nations preferred these types of incentives. The regional pattern of competing nations is particularly noteworthy.

Subsidies

Subsidies have also been increasingly utilized by governments of both DCs and LDCs in order to attract inflows of foreign capital. As noted before, these types of incentives are understandably more common among DCs than LDCs. This is in spite of the increased rate in the percentage of U.S. firms receiving subsidies in DCs rather than LDCs. There remains extensive variation across both groups of countries in the use of subsidies as a policy tool.

Performance Requirements

Tables 5 and 6 show the percent of non-bank affiliates of non-bank U.S. parent companies that indicated that they were subject to one or more major types of performance requirements in 1977 and 1982. Table 5 displays the percentage of U.S. firms in DCs subject to various performance requirements. Table 6 summarizes comparable information for affiliates operating in LDCs.

In general, the number of firms subject to these requirements is low in both DCs and LDCs. This is particularly true in DCs. Parent equity limitations and local labor requirements are the most pervasive form of performance requirements for countries within the sample. Subsidiaries of American companies in LDCs had a relatively higher incidence of local content and minimum export requirements. There is a noticeable decline in the percentage of firms subject to various performance requirements across all countries between 1977 and 1982. This was particularly evident across LDCs with respect to parent company equity limitations and local labor requirements.

Minimum Export Requirements

Across all countries, only 2 percent of U.S. firms were subject to minimum export requirements. This was the same for 1977 and 1982. Moreover, there were no notable differences between the host DCs and LDCs. In this regard, only 1 percent and 3 percent in those countries respectively were required to export a given level of their production in 1982. Some DCs, such as Denmark and Italy, do not even have such restrictions. At the other extreme, 20 percent of American firms operating in Portugal were expected to fulfill a given export quota. Among LDCs, and contrary to conventional wisdom, over time many countries have dropped such requirements. By 1982, the percentage of American firms subject to this type of requirement ranged from none in countries such as Chile, Nigeria and Hong Kong to only 9 percent in Brazil and 12 percent in the Philippines.

Maximum Import Requirements

Similar to the minimum export requirement, the incidence of American firms subject to import limitations was low across all countries. In 1982, between 3 percent to 5 percent of American companies were subject to this type of requirement in LDCs and DCs respectively. Among the latter, this ranged from

Table 5. Percent of U.S. Companies Receiving Different Types of Requirements from the Host Developed Countries in 1972 and 1982

	Min. Exp. Rqmt.		Max. Imp. Rqmt.		Loc. Con. Rqmt.		Loc. Lbr. Rqmt.		For. Eqty. Rqmt.	
	1977	1982	1977	1982	1977	1982	1972	1982	1972	1982
All Countries	2	2	3	2	3	1	8	8	5	5
Developed Countries	9	1	1	5	1	.5	3	4	2	1
Canada	.3	.2	1	.6	1	.9	2	3	2	1
Europe	1	1	.8	.3	.9	.4	4	5	2	1
European Communities	.8	.7	.3	.1	.6	.3	3	4	.8	.7
Belgium	0	.4	*	.2	.4	.2	6	9	.8	.7
Denmark	0	0	0	0	0	0	*	.9	0	0
France	1	2	.6	.2	.4	.5	4	7	2	1
Germany	*	.2	*	.2	0	.4	11	2	.3	.6
Ireland	14	7	*	0	*	2	13	17	*	2
Italy	.6	0	.6	0	1	0	4	6	2	2
Luxembourg	0	0	0	0	0	0	*	9	0	2
Netherlands	*	.2	*	0	*	.2	2	2	*	.5
United Kingdom	.3	.1	.4	.1	.7	.1	2	2	.7	.1
Other Europe	.8	3	.7	.1	2	.8	7	5	5	3
Austria	0	.8	*	.8	*	0	*	6	0	0
Finland	*	0	*	0	*	0	*	2	*	2
Norway	0	0	0	0	*	0	3	3	3	.9
Spain	7	8	4	2	4	2	10	8	2	9
Sweden	0	.5	0	0	0	0	1	1	2	2
Switzerland	.4	0	.4	.6	.7	.5	6	5	1	.2
Japan	0	0	1	.5	1	1	2	1	8	3
Australia	.7	4	.7	.6	4	3	3	3	5	3
New Zealand	*	5	9	4	4	3	6	5	11	4
South Africa	*	1	8	3	3	2	2	5	1	1

Note: * Missing information or data suppressed to avoid disclosure of companies involved

Source: Calculated by the author from U.S. Department of Commerce (1981, 1985)

161

Table 6. Percent of U.S. Companies Receiving Different Types of Requirements from the Host Developing Countries in 1977 and 1982

	Min. Exp. Rqmt.		Max. Imp. Rqmt.		Loc. Con. Rqmt.		Loc. Lbr. Rqmt.		For. Eqty. Rqmt.	
	1977	1982	1977	1982	1977	1982	1972	1982	1972	1982
Developing Countries	3	3	*	3	*	2	19	15	13	10
Europe										
Greece	*	7	0	1	*	7	*	0	*	0
Portugal	*	9	*	0	*	12	*	10	*	6
Turkey	*	16	*	4	14	20	*	4	*	4
Latin America										
Argentina	3	3	6	5	7	3	15	18	13	10
Brazil	1	.6	5	1	5	2	5	5	4	.5
Chile	3	9	7	19	9	4	31	32	4	5
Columbia	0	0	6	1	*	0	*	12	*	1
Ecuador	4	6	*	0	4	.6	28	19	13	9
Peru	*	0	6	7	9	7	25	17	25	13
Venezuela	2	1	5	0	11	3	35	27	28	11
Mexico	1	.6	6	2	11	4	43	41	27	15
Panama	5	5	10	5	10	4	17	3	30	30
Bahamas	3	1	2	0	2	1	15	14	1	1
Bermuda	*	0	*	0	*	0	8	13	*	1
Jamaica	.9	0	0	0	*	2	2	6	*	.3
Trinidad and Tobago	*	4	*	0	*	2	*	4	0	0
	0	0	0	0	6	0	*	27	10	20

162

Africa	7	.4	7	2	4	1	19	19	12	10
Egypt	0	0	*	0	5	0	*	24	*	10
Libya	**	0	0	0	0	0	50	7	12	7
Liberia	*	0	7	0	4	0	22	7	8	3
Nigeria	*	0	3	3	3	4	36	22	34	45
Middle East	4	1	2	.8	3	.8	14	8	13	9
Israel	18	5	*	2	6	2	7	3	8	0
Saudi Arabia	*	0	*	.6	*	1	*	13	*	19
United Arab Emirates	*	1	*	0	*	0	*	3	*	4
Other Asia and Pacific	5	3	*	1	*	2	12	10	16	13
Hong Kong	*	0	0	0	0	0	*	0	*	8
India	20	7	37	8	22	5	26	17	60	54
Indonesia	2	2	7	2	8	3	20	19	22	19
Malaysia	9	6	*	1	7	4	22	33	19	18
Philippines	3	12	7	3	3	3	8	3	20	14
Singapore	4	1	0	0	3	0	8	2	*	.5
South Korea	15	9	11	1	11	7	9	7	32	31
Taiwan	11	10	3	0	5	2	5	15	5	8
Thailand	0	1	3	0	5	1	15	11	15	11

Note: * Missing information or data suppressed to avoid disclosure of companies involved.

Source: Calculated by the author from U.S. Department of Commerce (1981, 1985).

no restrictions in countries such as Denmark and Norway to 4 percent in New Zealand and 10 percent in Portugal. In LDCs, many countries had no restrictions, including Peru, Liberia, and Singapore. However, 5 percent of American firms in Mexico, 8 percent of firms in India and 19 percent in Brazil reported maximum import requirements. These types of restrictions were greatly reduced or eliminated by many nations, particularly LDCs, in the period between the two surveys.

Local Content Requirements

Local content requirements was one of the least pervasive restrictions across all countries regardless of LDC or DC status. Perhaps indicative of a changing regulatory focus fewer firms were subject to such restrictions in 1982 as compared to 1972. Among DCs, the range of firms affected was from 0 percent in countries such as Austria, Italy, and Sweden, to 6 percent in countries such as Portugal. LDCs reflected a similar distribution, with no firms affected in countries such as Chile and Singapore to 7 percent of U.S. firms affected in countries such as Ecuador and South Korea.

Local Labor Requirements

As previously stated, this requirement is one of the most common across all countries. While similar to previous requirements, the incidence of firms required to employ a minimum of local personnel has dropped over time in most countries. This is particularly true among LDCs. For all countries combined, there were no differences in the percentage of firms subject to this type of requirement between 1972 and 1982. Across all DCs, the percentage of American firms required to employ local personnel increased from 3 percent to 4 percent. Among LDCs, the percentage of affected firms decreased from 19 percent in 1977 to 15 percent in 1982. For DCs in 1982, the percentage of American firms subject to this type of requirement ranged from 1 percent in Sweden and Japan, 9 percent in Belgium, to 17 percent in Ireland. Within LDCs, the same number varied from 0 percent in Hong Kong, 19 percent in Indonesia, 33 percent in Malaysia to 41 percent in Venezuela. Host LDCs exhibited a much greater level of variation in their imposition of such requirements on foreign firms than did host DCs.

Parent Equity Limitations

By far, this is the most prevalent form of control exercised upon foreign firms, particularly in LDCs. As the data in Tables 5 and 6 illustrate, the incidence of firms subject to this form of requirement is higher in LDCs than DCs. In 1982, 1 percent of American firms in DCs were subject to this type of requirement as compared to 10 percent in LDCs. Within DCs, Portugal, Austria, and Denmark had no such restrictions. Alternatively, 4 percent of American firms operating in countries such as Turkey and New Zealand were subject to this requirement. Across LDCs, the percentage of affected firms ranged from 0 percent in Israel and Jamaica, 15 percent in Venezuela, 30 percent in Mexico, 45 percent in Nigeria to 54 percent in India. As noted before, there has been a remarkable decline in the overall number of American firms subject to this type of requirement. This decline is particularly evident in LDCs. Noteworthy in this regard are Ecuador, Peru, and Venezuela in South America; Liberia and Nigeria in Africa; and the Philippines and Thailand in Asia.

DISCUSSION

In the 1980s, it appears, the FDI policy position of the host countries has been noticeably relaxed. This is in sharp contrast to the maze of rules and restrictions that governed entry of foreign capital into various nations in the 1960s and 1970s. At that time, the principal concern shared by many governments was to limit the foreign exchange cost and foreign investor control over the host country's economy. A logical question, at this point, is whether these investment incentives and performance requirements have indeed achieved what their architects hoped they would accomplish. Several empirical studies designed to examine the effectiveness of such schemes have produced mixed results. Reuber et al. (1973), Agodo (1978), Lim (1983), and Robinson (1983) found little or no support for the contention that these programs had swayed the location decisions of foreign investors. The overriding conclusion was that each foreign investment project had to stand economically on its own. Incentives, although critical in some instances, were found to have marginal impact at best. On the other hand, Root and Ahmed (1978), Situmeang (1978), and Guisinger (1985) found evidence in support of one or more types of incentives. Generally, the "up-front" incentives, that is, cash incentives, loans at subsidized rates, duty-free import of raw materials and capital equipment, have been identified as important. other incentives whose effectiveness is contingent on future profitability of the firms' operations, such as tax incentives, have been discounted. While it is not the purpose of this paper to evaluate the above studies, it appears that certain incentives are more effective than others depending on the industry and the orientation of the investment projects involved.

The race to attract foreign capital has gathered momentum in the last decade. The global debt crisis continues unabated. Many banks no longer participate in any new lending and the shrinking resources of the World Bank and the IMF are not possibly enough to fill the void. With the recent opening of Eastern European economies to foreign investment and the prospect of post-1992

European economic unification, the worldwide demand for foreign capital is certain to increase for the foreseeable future. Consequently, many countries, particularly LDCs, will continue to make themselves more attractive host countries than ever before. Indeed, demand for capital may be the greatest "challenge" for the world's financial markets in the coming decade.

REFERENCES

Agodo, O. 1978. "The Determinants of U.S. Private Manufacturing Investment in Africa." *Journal of International Business Studies* (Winter):95-107.

Demirsar, M. 1988. "Foreign Investors Flooding Into Turkey." *Wall Street Journal* (December 20), p. A10.

Guisinger, S. 1985. *Investment Incentives and Performance Requirements-Patterns of International Trade, Production and Investment.* New York: Praeger.

"How Colombia Aims to Attract Foreign Investment." *Business Week* (August 24), pp. 48-51.

"India Opens Up." *Time* (August), p. 59.

Labor-Industry Coalition on International Trade (LICIT). 1981. *Performance Requirements.* Washington, DC: Author.

Lim, D. 1983. "Fiscal Incentives and Direct Foreign Investment in Less Developed Countries." *The Journal of Development Studies*: 207-212.

National Industrial Conference Board. 1969. *Obstacles and Incentives to Private Investment, 1967-1968,* Vols. I and II. Studies in Business Policy no. 130. New York: National Industrial Conference Board.

Organization for Economic Cooperation and Development (OECD). 1973. *Investment Incentives and Disincentives and the International Investment Process.* Paris: OECD.

Price-Waterhouse Inc. 1976. *U.S. Corporations Doing Business Abroad.* New York: Price-Waterhouse.

Reuber, G.L., H. Crook, M. Emerson, and G. Gallais-Pammona. 1973. *Private Foreign Investment in Development.* Oxford: Clarendon Press.

Robinson, R. 1983. *Performance Requirements for Foreign Business-U.S. Management Response.* New York.

Root and Ahmed. 1978. "The Influence of Policy Instruments on Manufacturing Direct Foreign Investment in Developing Countries." *Journal of International Business Studies* (Winter):81-94.

Salehizadeh, M. 1983. "Regulation of Foreign Direct Investment by Host Countries." South Carolina Essays in International Business No. 4, Center for International Business Studies, The University of South Carolina.

Situmeang, B. 1978. "The Environmental Correlates of Foreign Direct Investment with Reference to Southeast Asia." Unpublished Ph.D. dissertation, University of Oregon.

U.S. Department of Commerce. 1981. *The Use of Investment Incentives and Performance Requirements by Foreign Governments.* Washington, DC: U.S. Government Printing Office.

U.S. Department of Commerce. 1985. *U.S. Direct Investment Abroad: 1982 Benchmark Survey Data.* Washington, DC: United States Department of Commerce.

Wain, B. 1989. "Vietnam Luring Hardy Investors." *Wall Street Journal* (July 12), p. A14.

IMPLEMENTATION OF
SELF-MANAGED WORK TEAMS:
CHALLENGES FOR THE HUMAN
RESOURCES DEPARTMENT

William M. Metheny, Cynthia Bentson,

Michael Beyerlein, and Merle E. Frey

SELF-MANAGED WORK TEAMS

The concept of Self-Managed Work Teams (SMWT) dates back to the autonomous work groups introduced as part of Sociotechnical Systems interventions of the 1940s (Trist and Bamforth 1969). Since then, teams having similar characteristics have been called by a number of terms, including Autonomous Work Groups (Trist 1981), Semi-Autonomous Work Groups, Self-Regulating Work Teams, Self-Directed Work Teams (Orsburn et al. 1990), Cell Teams (Metheny 1990), and others. Often a particular term is chosen because of a preference for a key word or an objection to other terms. We will use Self-Managed Work Teams (Manz and Sims 1989) in this paper. A definition of the typed teams we discuss is presented below.

International Research in the Business Disciplines, Volume 1, pages 167-176.
Copyright © 1993 by JAI Press Inc.
All rights of reproduction in any form reserved.
ISBN: 1-55938-538-3

Widespread use of SMWT in both manufacturing and service companies is a relatively recent phenomenon (Harper and Harper 1989). There are two primary reasons why companies are starting to move to this unique organizational structure. First, Self-Managed Work Teams help companies to survive in an environment where competition is increasing at home and abroad (Reid 1990; Wellins et al. 1991). Second, companies are using the SMWT to allow them to make fuller use of the human resources in their organization. This helps them make maximum use of their intellectual capital (Stewart 1991). Participation of employees at work lies on a continuum with suggestion boxes at one end, quality circles near the middle, and SMWTs near the upper extreme. SMWTs are not all alike; some are truly cases of self-management, but others are less extreme levels of involvement and participation. A lot of the variation we see may be due to the type of product or service offered by the organization, the general history, culture, and personality of the organization, its place in the market, or simply the personal characteristics of the people responsible for the implementation. Regardless of these distinctive organizational characteristics and differences, self-managed work teams have several features in common:

- The teams are comparatively small (8-15 people) and have the authority and responsibility for producing a complete product or service;
- Team members rotate through all job tasks, and therefore compensation systems are usually connected to a pay-for-knowledge or pay-for-skill system;
- As the team matures, its autonomy in production or service delivery and in human resources issues usually becomes more complete (Wellins et al. 1991);
- The traditional roles of the supervisor are taken over by the team and the hierarchy of the organization becomes flattened and less bureaucratic in nature (Lee 1990);
- New leadership roles include acting as a resource person, as a listening post, as a group facilitator, and as a coach.

It should be quite obvious that SMWTs are a very distinctive job design. It should also be obvious that there will be a large impact on the role of the traditional human resources system. The next section takes a closer look at the characteristics of SMWTs, followed by a discussion of the various human resources issues impacted by the use of SMWTs.

SMWTs are somewhat analogous to the autonomous work groups of Europe, but raise participation to a higher level. Trist (1981) suggests that there is a relationship between forms of participation and national culture. Did the United States have trouble implementing quality circles as borrowed from the

Japanese because the cultural issues were too different? Will the Japanese have trouble implementing SMWTs for the same reason? Are SMWTS most appropriate for the United States because of the similarity of operating principles of the teams and the credo of the country? Will there be problems in the area of human resources management that eventually make it impossible to use them in this country? SMWTs seem to be flourishing in industry, but they are also spreading into the services and into public organizations; a few public schools are even trying to utilize the principles of SMWT (Slavin 1988). The specific structure of the work team may differ in each location, but most of them share several common characteristics. Each characteristic is discussed below.

Responsibility for a Complete Product

Teams generally assume responsibility for a complete product, whether they create a subassembly for a computer or provide Accounts Receivable services for customers. There is usually an identifiable beginning and an end to what they create, allowing them to view their work in its entirety. The product should be one which is well differentiated from other products created by the organization. Thus, the team will be uniquely qualified to handle its responsibilities with respect to the product. Such uniqueness enhances the team's autonomy. Responsibility for a product is part the team's responsibility on the technical side of the sociotechnical system.

Make Production Decisions

The members of a SMWT usually make most decisions about quality issues and how their product or service is created. Decisions may include layout of the production line in manufacturing, or searching for and solving problems in both service and industrial firms. The team will also schedule their work, order supplies, do the necessary troubleshooting, maintain their supplies and equipment, and modify their tasks, equipment, and work processes to ensure a high-quality product or service (Metheny 1990). This aspect of SMWT has been called "task control." It allows the group to have internal control over variances between standards and performance. Task control is another aspect of the team's responsibility for the technical side of the sociotechnical system.

Establishing Work Rules

Since the team performs the functions normally handled by management, members establish and police work rules regarding absenteeism, tardiness, breaks, use of the telephone, and so on. Thus, the group culture and norms may vary widely from team to team, according to group composition. What is acceptable in one group may be unacceptable in another. The participation of the entire group in establishing work rules increases worker commitment to abide by those rules. At one manufacturing site, one team established rules for use of the telephone during normal work hours. Since the group set the rules and all members clearly understood them, there has never been a violation of the rules. By setting such rules, the group is helping to establish the social context for its work.

Hiring Decisions

Since the teams are recognized as the experts in their jobs, they frequently play a major role in the selection of new members for the team. This can include the screening of applications, interviewing applicants, and providing recommendations to management on the hiring decision. As the teams mature, they completely take over these hiring activities and eventually become responsible for long-term staffing and planning decisions as well.

Performance Appraisals

SMWTs often take an active part in evaluating the performance of members. This activity can include establishing the criteria by which members are to be judged and the actual completion of evaluations. Cross-trained members are well qualified to pass judgment on how well other members are performing their many tasks. Also, only a team member can understand fully just how well another member works as part of the work team. Sometimes performance criteria are decided by a company-wide committee; on other occasions each team determines its own performance criteria (Orsburn et al. 1990).

Capable of Performing All Jobs

Normally, every member of a SMWT is capable of performing every function performed by the team. Often, members will rotate jobs to overcome boredom, to keep up their skill levels on other jobs, or to insure that no single person is solely responsible for the least attractive jobs. Since skills are redundant within the team, work may continue uninterrupted should a member be absent from work. Members are able to keep up their skills and morale through self-directed job enlargement. In the event that a bottleneck occurs at one position, team members can move quickly to help the team member who is overwhelmed.

JOB DESIGN

The Self-Managed Work Team is clearly a form of job design itself. The organization which chooses to use SMWT may have to redesign many long-standing Human Resources policies and practices to facilitate use of this organizational structure. For SMWT to work, there must be a clearly differentiated group task, a well-defined work area, and relevant measures of performance. The group task was discussed earlier. Providing a clearly differentiated work area helps the team gain a feeling of ownership for the area and, subsequently, what occurs in that particular work area. For performance measures to be relevant to the tasks assigned the team and appropriate for the needs of the company, the following two steps must be performed.

Job Analysis

Team members perform their individual jobs and the jobs of all other team members. Each of the individual jobs must be analyzed carefully to list the skills required of those performing them. However, this is not sufficient. Each team member must be at least partially capable of performing all jobs in the team. Thus a composite job of the team member must also be analyzed. This analysis must incorporate both the technical aspects of the job (e.g., soldering, assembly, etc.) and the process components (e.g., communication, cooperation, interaction, etc.).

Job Description

Once each job is analyzed, the organization must create complete job descriptions for the jobs. This will also guide the firm in its creation of the job description for a member of the SMWT. This composite job description must necessarily be quite different from the traditional job description which focuses on limited individual jobs. It must take into account the technical aspects of each of the team's jobs, and then include characteristics of the job such as interpersonal interaction that are more oriented to the process of work. Job descriptions will be important in selection, training, and appraisal of team members.

PERFORMANCE APPRAISAL

Appraisal by team members has both positive and negative aspects. Since each member of the SMWT is capable of performing the jobs of all other members, team members are uniquely qualified to assess the performance of other members from a technical viewpoint. Working closely with others in the team, members also are able to view behaviors that a traditional supervisor might never see. Thus appraisal within the SMWT could be an extremely thorough process.

However, there are potential problems associated with having team members evaluate each other. For instance, interaction with other team members might be a primary performance dimension in the team setting. It will be necessary to help team members learn to distinguish between aspects of interpersonal interaction which are appropriate to evaluate (e.g., cooperation, willingness to compromise) and those which are not (such as likability).

ASSESSMENT

There are significant assessment issues related to the use of SMWTs. Since team members must perform a wide variety of tasks, they must be capable of fulfilling the requirements of each job. As individuals who perform managerial functions, team members must be capable of arriving at good decisions. The administrative requirements of most tasks require competence at both reading and writing. Finally, the individual must be capable of working harmoniously in a group situation. The organization needs to be able to select individuals who are capable of functioning interdependently in a complex environment. And, as people are selected for the teams, their training needs must be assessed.

RECRUITING/SELECTION

Team members are often involved in helping to establish the job analysis and in helping to establish the job descriptions for team members. Because of their deep and personal involvement in the total product or service of the team, they are also very aware of what knowledge, skills, abilities, and personal characteristics are needed to help the team meet its goals. From their unique vantage point, they are an excellent resource to use in the selection process. Many teams interview prospective candidates, particularly with a view to how the candidate might work in a team situation. At one organization, team members serve as assessors in an assessment center designed for evaluating potential members.

This assistance in selection by team members places an additional burden on the company, however. The company must insure that team members are aware of the legal ramifications of the interview and selection process. Team members must be given the skills to pursue selection activities within those legal constraints. Of course, the human resources department is still responsible for other aspects of selection, such as receipt of applications, prescreening, and the administration of appropriate selection instruments.

TRAINING AND DEVELOPMENT

The greatly expanded roles of team members will often call for skills they do not initially possess. Most organizations implementing SMWT find that they must increase their levels of training expenditures to insure that their people are up to the task of self-management. One firm found that its spending on training had increased by 300 percent. The organization must begin with the job description and assess individuals to ascertain their current skill levels. This training needs analysis must then be compared to the team's training needs analysis, that is, what knowledge, skills, abilities, and personal characteristics are required by the team in order to produce its product or perform its service. After both of these needs analyses are completed, a training plan can then be formulated for the team members. Obviously, the training usually includes technical skills training such as soldering or writing purchase orders. Problem solving, team building, and improving quality are also common training topics for SMWTs (Wellins and George 1991).

Managerial personnel, too, will require some specialized training. It is difficult for most managers to relinquish a large degree of their decision-making authority to the workers. First-line supervisors, in particular, need to learn to be facilitators of the process rather than "the boss" in those companies which will retain them in those roles. Very different skills will be required of supervisors in a company with SMWTs (Smolek 1990). Firms which do away with the supervisor's position will need to prepare the supervisors for other jobs in the company.

Training can be a source of organizational flexibility. Employees who became team members with little skill and versatility have been developed into flexible members, which increases the redundancy of skills in the team and flexibility in the organization in responding to the demands for change from the external environment. For example, a defense plant facing a downturn in orders from the military may attempt to retool for the production of consumer goods. In this case, work teams who can perform a variety of overlapping tasks and are flexible enough to refocus their efforts and skills are vital to the organization's ability to remain competitive. Due to their special training and team flexibility, some SMWTs are capable of producing products tailored to specific customer requirements. This is often accomplished by making a team responsible for a flexible manufacturing station.

The potential disadvantage of giving workers extra skills is that the worker becomes more capable of obtaining employment elsewhere since he/she can bring along a valuable package of skills that exceeds those of the average production worker. Hence, turnover could possibly increase.

COMPENSATION

In order for compensation to be effective for the SMWT, it must be structured to reward team behavior as well as individual performance (Orsburn et al. 1990, p. 183). This compensation probably should include group incentive pay, as well as pay which rewards individuals for being able to perform multiple tasks. Firms also need to address how members may be rewarded for good service beyond pay raises. This need not be a costly proposition. One team generated a list of 200 non-pay rewards they felt were desirable. The most expensive item on the list cost $50.

When an organization moves to SMWTs, there are two critical compensation transitions to be made. The first is from the traditional pay-for-seniority and pay-for-job-title system to a pay-for-knowledge or gain-sharing system. A pay-for-knowledge system compensates individuals in relation to the job-related skills they possess. As team members learn to perform more of the team's tasks, they gain in their individual compensation. Gain-sharing systems reward teams or individuals in direct relation to increases in company value, such as earnings per share. There are a number of critical factors which would help a firm decide on whether to use gain-sharing. These are performance and financial measures, the size of the plant or facility, the type of production, the capacity of the firm to absorb the additional production, the potential impact of employee efforts, union-management relations, planned capital investments, the skills of local management, and continuity of top management.

After the difficult pay transition has been made, we find that as team members acquire all of the dozen or so skills for which they were to be compensated, they can reach a plateau or ceiling. As a result, a perception that rewards will no longer increase may lead to dissatisfaction and turnover. This is especially likely in a brownfield site with its years of traditional compensation plans. However, one organization has created a compensation system with so many performance-related steps that plateauing is unlikely.

It has been reported that when some supervisors have been asked to join the team, they have perceived it as a demotion (Street 1990) and left the organization. Therefore, the second critical compensation transition that must be made is to find other valuable and desirable rewards systems to supplement pay. Increased autonomy, increased opportunity to select next product or service lines, pride in a job well done, formal recognition in the organization (or the community or nation) may all be desirable reward systems that can augment pay and benefits. How the pay system is set up can have an immense impact on the long-term effectiveness of the SMWT.

LABOR UNIONS

The notions of workers assuming managerial duties and performing a multitude of tasks are anathema to most labor-management contracts. It takes careful explanation of the goals of the SMWT and cautious negotiating in order to convince labor unions that workers will gain rather than lose. Redesign of work within the unionized organization must include collaboration with the union from the beginning of the planning stage (Orsburn 1990, p. 195).

A major issue which often applies in union situations is handling those individuals who either refuse to function in the new structure ("dinosaurs" in some organizations, or "resisters," as employees at one plant call them), or are incapable of performing the additional duties. This could include supervisors who are unwilling to be brought into the team or managers who cannot handle the changes in leadership style. Does the company let them go? Does it find other places in the firm for these people? What are the EEO issues which may apply? In each case, the organization must find the unique and humane solution for this individual. In many companies, people could be transferred to other units which share the philosophy of the employee who does not fit the SMWT. Training and management development could either help people through the transition or prepare them for jobs in more traditional parts of the company. If employees must leave voluntarily or otherwise, because of SMWT implementation, the firm could offer outplacement services to help them find the appropriate next job. Whatever method is chosen to handle these people, it must be consistent with the enlightened philosophy that make SMWTs possible. A cursory firing would be a signal that the company does not practice the philosophy it is telling its employees to follow.

CONCLUSION

Implementation of SMWTs is difficult. It takes time. In a brownfield site, implementation requires major cultural changes, changes in work flow, training, selection, appraisal, compensation, job descriptions, and so on. Lawler (1986) seems to argue that quality circles, Quality of Work Life, and so on, are steps of increasing participation that build toward the SMWT. At the very least, SMWT is such a radical change for the brownfield, traditional organizations that it takes several years to make the transition, even for a small segment of the company. Greenfield sites have all of the problems of a start-up operation and then the problems of trying to implement (or even learn how to implement) SMWTs. Yet they are not fighting organizational traditions while having to deal with individual traditions.

Organizational change is always present and always difficult, but the implementation of SMWTs requires major cultural changes: changes in job analyses, job descriptions, recruitment and selection, training and development, assessment and appraisal, compensation, and reward systems. Indeed, the implementation of SMWTs requires us to rethink our ideas about work, organizations, and those people who make up the organization. But the benefits seem to be there: organizations are leaner and more efficient, there is less bureaucracy, there is increased communication within the organization, products and services are improved, turnover and absenteeism are reduced, and customer service is improved (Easton 1990).

The changes required of an organization which chooses to implement SMWTs seem daunting at first, but they are not insurmountable. Early evidence is mounting that the struggle is well worth it.

REFERENCES

Easton, S. 1990. "High Performance/High Commitment: Self-Managing Teams Respond to the Competitive Challenge!" Pp. 1-11 in *Proceedings of the 1990 International Conference on Self-Managed Work Teams,* edited by M. Beyerlein and C. Miller. Denton, TX: University of North Texas.

Harper, B., and A. Harper. 1989. *Succeeding as a Self-Directed Work Team.* Croton-on-Hudson, NY: MW Corporation.

Lawler, E.E. III. 1986. *High-Involvement Management: Participative Strategies for Improving Organizational Performance.* San Francisco, CA: Jossey-Bass.

Lee, C. 1990. "Beyond Teamwork." *Training* (June):25-32.

Manz, C.C., and H.P. Sims. 1989. *Superleadership: Leading Others to Lead Themselves.* New York: Prentice-Hall.

Metheny, W.M. 1990. "Implementation of Just-in-Time Manufacturing: Behavioral Changes Accompanying the Transformation." Unpublished Doctoral Dissertation, University of North Texas, Denton, TX.

Orsburn, J.D., L. Moran, E. Musselwhite, and J.H. Zenger. 1990. *Self-Directed Work Teams: The New American Challenge.* Homewood, IL: Irwin.

Reid, P.C. 1990. *Well Made in America: Lessons from Harley Davidson on Being the Best.* New York: McGraw-Hill.

Slavin, R.E. 1988. *Student Team Learning: An Overview and Practical Guide,* 2nd ed. Washington, DC: National Education Association.

Smolek, J. 1990. "Self-Directed Workforce Implementation: The Salaried Workforce." Pp. 77-82 in *Proceedings of the 1990 International Conference on Self-Managed Work Teams,* edited by M. Beyerlein and C. Miller. Denton, TX: University of North Texas.

Stewart, T.A. 1991. "Brainpower." *Fortune* (June 3), pp. 44-60.

Street, A. 1990. "Factors Related to Upper-Level Support for Organizational Redesign." Unpublished masters' thesis, University of North Texas, Denton, TX.

Trist, E.L. 1981. "The Evolution of Socio-Technical Systems: A Conceptual Framework and an Action Research Program." *Occasional Paper No. 2,* Ontario Ministry of Labour. Ontario: Quality of Work Life Centre.

Trist, E.L., and K.W. Bamforth. 1969. "Some Social and Psychological Consequences of the Longwall Method of Coal Getting." *Human Relations* 4:3-38.

Wellins, R.S., W.C. Byham, and J.M. Wilson. 1991. *Empowered Teams: Creating Self-Directed Work Groups that Improve Quality, Productivity, and Participation.* Pittsburgh, PA: Development Dimensions International.

Wellins, R., and J. George. 1991. "The Key to Self-Directed Teams." *Training and Development Journal* 45:26-31.

INTERNATIONALIZATION OF THE FIRM:
CONCEPTUAL OVERVIEW AND
EMPIRICAL EVIDENCE

Manucher Farhang

INTRODUCTION: INTERNATIONALIZATION
OF THE FIRM

The process by which companies internationalize their business has over the past decade been the subject of substantial research and theoretical development. Ever since researchers produced empirical evidence to suggest that firm's internationalization constitute a process of incremental and evolutionary build-up of foreign commitment over time (Johanson and Vahine 1977; Johanson and Wiedershaim-Paul 1975) there has been extensive research to support, and more recently to dispute, the proposed approaches to internationalization.

INTERNATIONALIZATION: THREE MODELS

Considering the wide range of research undertaken on the internationalization of the business firm it would be difficult to draw clearcut boundaries to identify

International Research in the Business Disciplines, Volume 1, pages 177-184.
Copyright © 1993 by JAI Press Inc.
All rights of reproduction in any form reserved.
ISBN: 1-55938-538-3

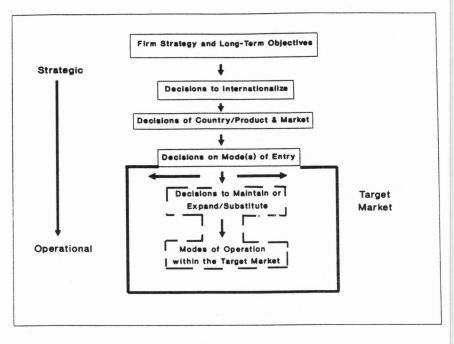

Figure 1.

the concept of internationalization. If we were to accept the definition most widely held, namely that internationalization involves the firm's entry and development in foreign markets, then all research that deals with the firm's decision to go abroad, its choice of country/product markets, selection of entry modes and finally substitution of methods of operation within the markets would be of relevance to the topic of internationalization (Figure 1).

Given the previous information, if we categorize the existing research on internationalization from a decision-making viewpoint, we can then identify three different approaches. In order to construct a recognizable framework for analysis, the main lines of current research will be discussed in terms of three models: the behavioral/incremental model, the economic model, and the strategic model.

The Behavioral/Incremental Model

This model, based on the behavioral theory of the firm (Aharoni 1966; Cyert and March 1963), was initially proposed by Swedish researchers (Johanson and Vahlne 1977; Johanson and Wiedersheim-Paul 1975) and later by others

(Bilkey and Tesar 1986; Cavusgil and Nevin 1981). According to this model, in a world characterized by uncertainty and imperfect information firms, when entering foreign markets, behave along a chain of development stages from export activity through agent and sales subsidiary to the formation of manufacturing subsidiary. In other words, internationalization is a passive, gradual, and evolutionary process with firms gradually developing a greater commitment to foreign markets over time with increasing international experience, foreign sales, and so on. Furthermore, factors preventing the free flow of information-the "psychic distance" (such factors as language, culture, political system, level of education, industrial development)—are crucial for the internationalization process.

The Economic Model

This model is based primarily on the choice of the most efficient mode, that is, it involves a comparison of costs and benefits of different entry and development modes in order to identify the market entry options that maximize long-run profits. Based on transaction cost analysis, Anderson and Gatignon (1986) have developed a model to aid management to choose the mode which maximizes long-run efficiency (risk-adjusted rate of return). Since control, according to these authors, is the most important determinant of both risk and return, market entry modes are differentiated accordingly by their level of control (example: export is a low-control mode; wholly owned subsidiary is a high-control mode). Jeannet and Hennessey (1988) have developed the economic model by devising a procedure to choose the entry mode through evaluating the expected sales, costs, and assets requirement over the planning horizon of the proposed venture.

According to the economic model, a firm's decision in a foreign market involves a rational trade-off, whereby the firm trades various levels of control for reductions in resource commitment, with the hope of increasing returns while reducing risks.

The Strategic Model

The strategic model is based on the assumption that when firms go international they pursue multiple objectives, and their choice of market entry and development is influenced by a set of internal and external factors (Dunning 1980; Reid and Rosson 1987; Root 1987). The most important internal factors constitute a company's products and its willingness to commit its management, capital, technology, production, and marketing resources to international business. The external factors include the target country's market, production, and environmental (economic, political, and socio-cultural) factors. Studies based on the strategic model deal either with identification of factors which explain choice of mode of entry (Goodnow and Hansz 1972; Green and Cunningham 1975); or stress the choice/trade-off between any two modes of entry: for example licensing versus FDI (Aliber 1970; Contractor 1984, 1985; Horst 1972; Hymer 1976; Mirus 1980). The strategic model allows managers to assess the relative attractiveness of different market entry methods and identify the appropriate market entry strategies.

INTERNATIONALIZATION: CONCEPTS BASED ON RATIONALITY, EFFICIENCY, AND FEASIBILITY

Each of the above models provides a different approach to how companies internationalize and establishes a different basis for managerial decision making. In other words, neither do the concepts address the same range of issues nor do empirical studies always present evidence sufficient to justify the level of generalizations that they claim. Furthermore, while many studies discuss, analyze and develop various approaches, there seems to be no empirical work which would explain why firms prefer to follow one pattern, as opposed to another, in their process of internationalization.

The models described do not seem to aim at answering the same questions. The behavioral model which addresses internationalization in broad terms attempts to answer which markets firms enter first (based on psychic distance) and how they organize at each stage of development within the new market. The economic model, on the other hand, addresses questions related to the more efficient between two alternative modes. Finally, the strategic model is based on what is most feasible, given the circumstances both at entry point and in expanding within the market. Whereas the behavioral model treats internationalization as a process, the economic model does not. The behavioral model implicitly assumes that all options are open to the firm to choose from in a foreign market, and does not account for factors such as competition, whereas the economic and strategic models do not make such implicit assumptions. With a view to the above, one could postulate that, whereas the behavioral model prescribes a rational choice, the economic model advocates an efficient (profitable) decision and the strategic model opts for a feasible alternative (Figure 2).

EMPIRICAL EVIDENCE

Increasing internationalization of firms and industries over the past decades has resulted in a growing amount of empirical research in this area. Whereas the behavioral/incremental model based originally on the experience of Swedish firms (Johanson and Vahlne 1977; Johanson and Wiedersheim-Paul 1975) and later supported by studies carried out on U.S., Japanese, Turkish,

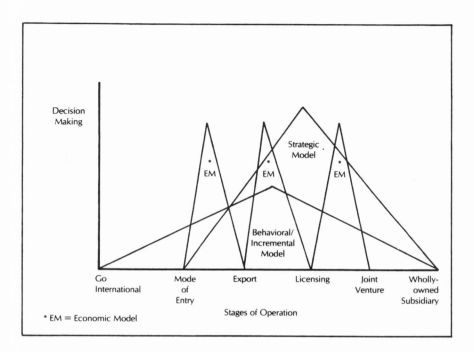

Figure 2.

and Australian Firms (Barrett 1986; Bilkey and Tesar 1986; Cavusgil 1980; Johanson and Nonaha 1983; Karfakioglu 1986) evidence from other empirical studies have disputed the pattern of foreign establishment espoused by this model. The latter studies indicate that: (a) market experience and psychic distance which play a crucial role in the behavioral/incremental model are no longer critical factors of internationalization for the fact that the world has become more homogeneous. Consequently, these studies conclude, lack of experience in a certain market is no longer a limiting factor (Hedlund and Kerneland 1985; Nordstrom 1991). (b) Most empirical studies that support the behavioral model come from the early stages of internationalization, and thus conclusions do not hold in higher stages of a firm's expansion in the market (Forsgren 1989).

In the empirical studies supporting the strategic model the emphasis has mostly been on determinants which influence choice of entry mode, rather than substituting one mode by another over time. Generally speaking, the two lines of empirical work which lend support to the strategic model are: (1) those that identify common factors which explain selection of entry mode (Goodnow and

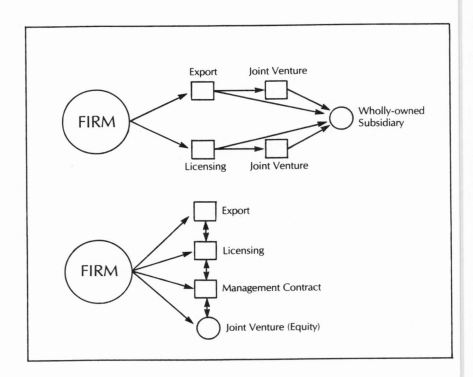

Source: Adapted from Farhang (1990, p. 12L).

Figure 3.

Hansz 1972; MaClayton et al. 1980); or (2) studies which stress the factors that lie behind the choice between two entry modes (Contractor 1984; Cunningham 1975; Horst 1972; Nigh 1985). With regard to the economic model, there are no independent empirical studies. Studies that reflect the strategic rather than the behavioral pattern of firm's internationalization however, usually incorporate an evaluation of sales, costs, and asset requirements to determine the most profitable entry mode for the firm in the target country.

CHOICE OF MODEL: CONCLUSIONS

From the previous discussion of conceptual and empirical evidence of a firm's internationalization, one may conclude that each model is distinct and mutually exclusive and that factors that encourage one pattern of internationalization would prohibit another pattern (Okorafo 1990). Recent empirical studies indicate, however, that: (a) whereas a firm may behave on an incremental basis, and thus rely on market experience (the behavioral/incremental model), this pattern may be replaced/superseded by a strategic pattern where the firm resorts to planning and systematic search thus leapfrogging in a non-incremental fashion (see Millington and Baylis 1990 on the experience of U.K. firms in the EC). (b) Experience of Swedish firms in the Middle East (Farhang 1990) also demonstrates that firms may move incrementally at first and non-incrementally later, depending on the nature of limitations placed on market entry by the host countries. Alternatively, firms may, right from the outset, adopt a strategy of mixed/multiple entry (i.e, exporting goods, selling technology and know-how, and hold equity share in the local joint venture) in order to compensate for psychic distance, hedge risk and maximize returns (Figure 3).

REFERENCES

Aharoni, Y. 1966. *The Foreign Investment Decision Process.* Boston, MA: Harvard University Press.

Aliber, R.Z. 1970. "A Theory of Direct Foreign Investment." In *The International Corporation,* edited by C. P. Kindelberger. Cambridge, MA: MIT Press.

Anderson, E., and H. Gatignon. 1986. "Modes of Foreign Entry: A Transaction Cost Analysis and Propositions." *Journal of International Business Studies* 17(3):1-26.

Barrett, N.J. 1986. "A Study of the Internationalization of Australian Firms." Unpublished dissertation, University of New South Wales.

Bilkey, W.J., and G. Tesar. 1986. "The Export Behavior of Smaller Sized Wisconsin Manufacturing Firms." *Journal of International Business Studies* (Spring):93-98.

Cavusgil, S.T. 1980. "On the Internationalization Process of Firm." *European Research* 8(6):273-281.

Cavusgil, S.T., and J.R. Nevin. 1981. "Internal Determinants of Export Marketing Behavior: An Empirical Investigation." *Journal of Marketing Research* 28(2):114-119.

Contractor, F.J. 1984. "Choosing Between Direct Investment and Licensing." *Journal of International Business Studies* 15(3).

Contractor, F.J. 1985. "A Generalized Theorem for Joint Venture and Licensing Negotiations." *Journal of International Business Studies* 16(2):23-50.

Cyert, R.M., and J.G. March. 1963. *A Behavioral Theory of the Firm.* New York: Prentice-Hall.

Dunning, J.H. 1980. "Towards an Eclectic Theory of International Production: Empirical Tests." *Journal of International Business Studies* 11(1):9-31.

Farhang, M. 1990. *Foreign Market Entry Strategy: Behaviour of Swedish Companies in the Middle East.* Lulea, Sweden: Lulea University of Technology.

Forsgren, M. 1989. *Managing the Internationalization Process.* London: Routledge.

Goodnow, J., and J. Hansz. 1972. "Environmental Determinants of Overseas Market Entry Strategies." *Journal of International Business Studies* (Spring):33-50.

Green, R.T., and W. Cunningham. 1975. "The Determinants of U.S. Foreign Investment: An Empirical Examination." *Management International Review* 15(2-3):113-120.

Hedlund, G., and A. Kverneland. 1985. "Are Strategies for Foreign Market Entry Changing? The Case of Swedish Investment in Japan." *International Studies of Management and Organization* 15:41-59.

Horst, T. 1972. "Firm and Industry Determinants of the Decision to Invest Abroad: An Empirical Study." *Review of Economics and Statistics* 54:258-266.

Horst, T. 1974. "American Exports and Foreign Direct Investment." Discussion paper no. 362, Harvard Institute of Economic Research.

Hymer, S.H. 1976. *The International Operations of National Firms: A Study of Direct Foreign Investment.* Cambridge, MA: MIT Press.

Jeannet, J.P., and H.D. Hennessey. 1988. *International Marketing Management: Strategies and Cases.* Boston: Houghton Mifflin.

Johanson, J., and J.E. Vahlne. 1977. "The Internationalization Process of the Firm: A Model of Knowledge Development and Increasing Foreign Market Commitments." *Journal of International Business Studies* 9(Spring):23-32.

Johanson, J., and Wiedersheim-Paul. 1975. "The Internationalization of the Firm: Four Swedish Case Studies." *Journal of Management Studies* (October):305-332.

Johanson, J., and J. Nonaka. 1983. "Japanese Export Marketing: Structures, Strategies, Counterstrategies." *International Marketing Review* 1:12-25.

Karafakioglu, M. 1986. "Export Activities of Turkish Manufacturers." *International Marketing Review* 3(4):34-43.

MaClayton, D., M. Smith and J. Hair. 1980. "Determinants of Foreign Market Entry: A Multivariate Analysis of Corporate Behavior." *Management International Review* 20(3):0-52.

Millington, A.I., and B. Baylis. 1990. "The Process of Internationalization: U.K. Companies in the E.C." *Management International Review* 30(2):151-161.

Mirus, R. 1980. "A Note on the Choice Between Licensing and Direct Foreign Investment." *Journal of International Business Studies* (Spring/Summer):86-91.

Nigh, D. 1985. "The Effects of Political Events on U.S. Direct Foreign Investment: A Pooled Time- Series Cross-Sectional Analysis." *Journal of International Business Studies* 16(1):1-17.

Nordstrom, K.A. 1991. *The Internationalization Process of the Firm: Searching for New Patterns and Explanations.* Stockholm: Stockholm School of Economics.

Okoroafo, S.C. 1990. "An Assessment of Critical Factors Affecting Modes of Entry Substitution Patterns in Foreign Product Markets." *Journal of Global Marketing* 3(3):87-103.

Reid, S., and P. Rosson, eds. 1987. "Managing Export Entry and Expansion: An Overview" In *Managing Export Entry and Expansion.* New York: Praeger.

Root, F. 1987. *Foreign Market Entry Strategies.* Lexington, MA: D.C. Heath.

INDIA'S LIBERALIZATION:
OPPORTUNITIES FOR MNCs

M.M. Shahid Siddiqi

INTRODUCTION

A series of cataclysmic socioeconomic and political events has occurred in the last decade changing a broad spectrum of business relationships. The long-term consequences, national, regional, and international, are difficult to gauge. The difficulties are due partly to the divergent and potentially conflicting elements involved in global activities and are partly a function of the level of activity, that is, macro versus micro issues. A general feeling now permeates management decisions that the world is getting smaller. Presumably this is a consequence of the rapid dissemination and use of communication technology. Even remote areas of the world are accessible and, hence, available to the demands of a developing global business economy. This perspective, coupled with the forces of change now in action, directly affects the internationalization of business.

Multinational corporations (MNCs), among the principal instigators of this process, are also influenced by it. Similarly, nation-states, which form the arena for MNC activity, also contribute in the creation and shaping of relevant

International Research in the Business Disciplines, Volume 1, pages 185-201.
Copyright © 1993 by JAI Press Inc.
All rights of reproduction in any form reserved.
ISBN: 1-55938-538-3

political and economic forces. This phenomenon is clearly visible in the case of India, the tenth largest industrial power. Its economic liberalization[1] is a direct result of the performance of its insulated economy being reevaluated in the context of a global perspective by its policymakers.

As world events coalesce into discernable patterns, the potential role of the MNC as a change agent becomes even more apparent. The effective transformation of developing and/or socially inclined economies into an efficient resource allocation system via the free market mechanism plays to the strengths of the MNC. The MNC possesses both the technical and managerial know-how needed for the conversion of real or potential national comparative advantage into its global counterpart. For individual MNCs the developing countries have offered tremendous opportunities. However, firms were frequently unable to exploit these opportunities because of the maze of rules, regulations, controls, and restraints operative in many countries. The problematics of dealing with inherently unstable business environments tended to destabilize the global objectives of MNCs. Gradual deregulation, the opening of previously restricted economies, and the increasing flexibility of many host countries is removing many obstacles in the design and management of workable worldwide business strategies.

However, these strategies cannot be formulated without concern for local strategic fit and an evaluation of evolving national comparative advantage. India presents a unique challenge for MNCs because of its size, location, economic stage, and the breadth of its industrial development. India seems to beckon to the MNC, yet frustrate its entry. Still, ample rewards await successful performance by an MNC. It is therefore a case worth examining. Prior to an examination of the growing prospects for the MNCs within the changing dimensions of India's economic structure and policy, it is important to review some of the salient forces at work. These forces, both international and domestic, have been critical to the reorientation of India's goal of self-reliance. Additionally, a brief look at the liberalization process itself will aid in understanding the scope of the questions investigated. Finally, an identification of various strategic approaches for exploiting emerging opportunities should provide a clearer perception of the factors needed for successful operations in India and elsewhere.

INDIA: TOWARDS AUTARKY

The world is a considerably changed place since India's independence in 1947. The United States was the dominant power after the Second World War, it remains so after the end of the Cold War. Yet, with the evolving complexity of industrial development, international trade and investment changes worldwide, the meaning of dominance has gradually acquired an economic connotation in contrast to its previous political basis. Having shrugged off the bondage of British colonial rule, Indian leaders reacted to the legacy of colonial dominance by focusing their attention inward (Chandra 1990).[2]

The goal of *self-reliance* was articulated as the moving spirit behind economic development. The previous orientation was seen as being impoverished and denuded by the passive dependency of the colonial relationship. Even if economic insulation (autarky refers to an insulated economy) was not the specific intent, the direct consequence of the goal of self-reliance was closure of the domestic economic system. However limiting, self-reliance was expected to yield bountiful results. India would be able to exploit its abundant natural and human resources in order to raise its economic standard. The hoped-for result would be attainment of parity with the developed countries. If the dependency equation vis-à-vis the global environment, was to be reversed and replaced with an equitable interdependency, central planning was believed to be imperative. The Russian command-oriented approach based on Five Year Plans was the model chosen to be emulated with due consideration given to India's own perspective of Fabian socialism.

In order to convert the abstract concept of self-reliance into concrete reality, an industrial policy was enunciated in 1948. It has gone through several revisions so as to keep abreast of environmental changes.[3] The last industrial policy statement was made in 1990. The purpose of the policy statements was that they serve as a normative plan. They defined the long-range industrial mission of the country. The policy is intended to form the foundation upon which national economic planning and control would ultimately be structured.

The general normative direction, as embodied in the industrial policy statement, was made specific and actionable through specific five-year strategic plans. Thus, the Five Year Plans, the first of which covered the years 1951-56, presented clear and quantifiable economic objectives. India is now supposed to be in the eighth plan (1991-96) (Chandra 1990). The plans encompassed a comprehensive system of resource allocation across a spectrum of agricultural and industrial objectives.

While the Russian approach to centralized planning had impact, India did not follow that model completely. It developed its own model, which can be best described as being a mix of controlled capitalism and a qualified command economy. India's quasi socialism (Scalapino 1989) envisioned both the pursuit of social goals and constrained market goals as well.

Predictably, small-scale industries formed an integral part of the economy. Of greater strategic importance was the role assigned to the public sector firms, that is, State-Owned Enterprises (SOEs). These enterprises were expected to control "the commanding heights" of the economy. However, private sector companies were still allowed a wide diversity of choices. There was even a common area where both the public and private sector could participate. Thus, India's policymakers responded on one hand to the objectives of social welfare which had been nurtured in the struggle for independence, and on the other, directed the expression of the culture's inherent spirit of entrepreneurship.

The resulting central planning system was believed to require significant types of regulation and control mechanisms if it was ever to reach its expected level of effectiveness. Therefore, an elaborate system of controls and incentives was developed so that the needs of a mixed economy could be finely balanced. *Industrial/capacity licensing* formed the cornerstone for the control of the private sector. Thus, a firm could not grow beyond its government-approved capacity. The expansion and diversification of the large firms were further constrained by the Monopolies and Restrictive Trade Practices Act (MRTP). A further limitation on corporate decision making was in price and distribution controls and labor relations (see, e.g., *India 1985* 1986; "Reforms Aim at Boosting Exports" 1990). Almost every dimension of economic development was regulated. Subject to particular scrutiny was the intensity of competition and the degree of interaction with the global environment.

The overwhelming restriction of the foreign sector created, in effect, an autarkic economy (an insulated economic system) having weak interaction with the global economic system. Included within the broad spectrum of international involvement, or lack of it, were issues of trade, investment, technology transfer, and foreign collaboration. Curtailment of imports was brought about through the establishment of an intricate regulatory system which included tariffs and nontariff barriers. Import licensing, phased manufacturing programs, and canalization were important elements of the system.[4] In short, the economy was designed to foster *import substitution industrialization* (ISI).

Apart from the restriction of imports, the insulation of the economy had two other critical dimensions. These were the issues of technology transfer and foreign collaboration on the one hand and foreign investment on the other. Given the confidence in its human capital and the commitment to endogenously created technology, as a general policy, foreign technology was discouraged. This was, in fact, a legacy of the swadeshi movement.[5] Consequently, foreign collaboration and technology transfer had meaning only when inventions could not be effectively reinvented locally. They were also permitted when the technology was of strategic importance.

Exports, imports, technology transfer, and foreign collaboration frequently form significant elements of an MNC's growth strategies. But one of their most distinguishing features remains their willingness and desire to undertake foreign direct investment (FDI) (Dunning 1988). Joint or full ownership of these income-producing assets are then organized so as to permit effective control. The latter is taken to be the sine qua non for the materialization of supranational strategies. India's policy toward FDI has evolved from being ambivalent and amorphous during the period 1948-1967 to becoming restrictive and definitive during the period 1968-1979. In the first two decades following independence foreign capital was required to fill the resource gap arising out of the economic consequence of independence. This phase witnessed the maturing of the centrally planned mixed economy approach to development. Considering the resource needs of the economy, local majority ownership was not insisted upon. At this time several hundred multinationals operated freely and profitably. The protected economy, even with scarcity, as a general rule had much to offer, given the predictability of the environment.

According to Kumar (1990), the restrictive period 1968-79 constituted the second of the three distinct phases in the evolution of India's policy on FDI. In fact, this second phase witnessed the severe delimiting of the role of the MNC in the Indian economy. In 1973 the insulation of the economy was completed with the establishment of a regulatory framework for FDI. A general ceiling of 40 percent foreign equity participation was instituted through the Foreign Exchange Regulation Act (FERA). Foreign companies with equity higher than 40 percent were required to conform to the ceiling. A case-by-case analysis yields a short list of about 150 companies out of a total of 881 which were permitted higher levels of foreign equity on special grounds, that is, technology renewal and improvement, contribution to the core sector, or export-based diversification. The rest either diluted their equity and were incorporated under the Indian Companies Act or departed from the Indian market. IBM and Coca Cola are well-publicized examples of those multinationals which left the market. These firms were control sensitive. To them effective control was necessary to the pursuit of their strategies and global objectives.

However, many multinationals remained behind to reap the benefits of the relatively closed and protected market. To these companies the joint venture was seen as an asset in a regulated foreign economy. These companies were also willing to Indianize themselves through a variety of means, including synchronization of domestic growth in priority areas suggested by national economic planning. For instance, Union Carbide was willing to venture into the manufacturing of jeans and ended up diversifying into the fishing business. The latter gave the firm an added synergy through the production of cellophane packages for its shrimp exports—a national priority area.[6] Unilever, Imperial Tobacco, and many others have found Indianization coupled with diversification to be an incredibly successful route to long-term growth and profitability in a market with little or no competition.

The third phase, the phase of liberalization, seems to have begun in the 1980s. An evolving set of factors at the global level and emerging pressures at the domestic level were instrumental in initiating and promoting the process of deregulation and deinsulation of the economy. This third phase heralds India's arrival as a player in the global economic system.

INFLUENCE OF SHIFTING GLOBAL FORCES

From the perspective of systems theory, the open system interacts with the environment, while the closed system does not. This is true for nations and companies alike. India's quest for self-reliance as a reactive response to British colonialism all but closed the economy. But in a world of interdependencies, no nation-state system is hermetically sealed. The global burst of technology, especially in communication, has had a profound effect in intermeshing nation-states. With the gradual diffusion of technology, India has been forced to reexamine and redefine its goal of self reliance. Along with this redefinition has crystallized a need for liberalization and deregulation. Involved within these processes are other concepts—delicensing, privatization, and decentralization—concepts alien to the spirit of the core denoted by self-reliance. Globalization, regionalization, the global retreat of socialism (or desocialization), the success of export-promotion (EP) industrialization along with the failure of IS industrialization, the changing perception of MNCs, and the worldwide movement toward privatization and liberalization (both processes being linked to desocialization) are some of the most critical factors to have had a resounding impact on India's reevaluation of its centralized approach to development.

Globalization

At the heart of this process of globalization is the multinational firm. Its prime concern with the acquisition of a global competitive edge has more often than not meant the utilization of international production as a strategic tool. When the location-specific advantage of a production base has matched national comparative advantage, it has helped the MNC in securing its global, regional, and local market share. At the same time, this process has produced at least two important consequences: global diffusion of production technology and worldwide homogenization of markets. In short, the MNCs with the worldwide resources at their command have spawned an integrated international economic system. To India's leaders it became clear that an insulated system would not receive the benefit of its external environment's nourishment.

Regionalization

A significant trend in the movement of nations has been the process of regionalization. From Europe to the Americas to Asia, the process is in motion. The creation of South Asian Association for Regional Cooperation (SAARC) in 1985 continues the process of regionalization in Asia. The seven members of SAARC are India, Pakistan, Bangladesh, Sri Lanka, Nepal, Bhutan, and the Republic of Maldive Island. The stimulus for the development of SAARC has come as much from the possible marginalization of less developed countries in a world of regional blocks as from the notable success of regional groups like the (Association of South East Asian Nations) (ASEAN). The motivation to achieve rapid economic development through the mechanism of collective self-reliance, visible in regionalization, appears to be only vaguely similar to the group formation in the 1970s in the context of the call for the New International Economic Order. That call was more ideological, hemispheral, and socialistic in nature. The present trend is much more pragmatic, proximal and market oriented.

While SAARC is still in an inchoate stage, a noteworthy feature of the organization is its asymmetry. India dwarfs other member states in terms of population, area, size, and diversification of the economy as well as having a fairly well-developed economic and marketing infrastructure. Unlike India, most of the economies are "monocultural." For instance, its GNP, which makes up roughly 81 percent of the combined figure for the member countries, is more than seven times the size of the next largest economy, Pakistan.[7]

Global Desocialization

With the general destruction of the citadels of socialism across the world, the movement toward market economy has been set in motion. While countries are still seeking their own unique approaches to the conceptualization and solidification of the concept of a market mechanism, several key requirements are generally accepted. These include the liberalization and deregulation of the economy and privatization of SOEs. These are the processes which have gathered momentum in India since the 1980s and particularly since 1985. Thus, the ties to the old Russian central planning model have become defunct (Thomas 1990). However, it should be clearly noted that deregulation and privatization are also at work in the developed countries, for instance the privatization of British Telephone system.

The Success of E P Industrialization and
The Failure of IS Industrialization

A factor of great impact on the Indian leaders has been the laudable success of the NICs. These countries have successfully followed an export orientation approach to industrialization (Todaro 1989). They have been able to develop the capability to compete even in sophisticated technologies at the international level. However, protection from external competition in an environment of IS industrialization had made India a high-cost economy. Its manufactures, which included capital goods, intermediate goods, and consumer goods were not able to compete in quality or price. Technological obsolescence, arising out of limited foreign collaboration and trying to compete with outdated technology, accentuated the problem.

The Changing Perception of MNCs

There has been a positive change in the perception of the MNCs across the world. Indian policymakers have gone through a similar revision of their views about the cost-benefits of MNCs' potential contribution to economic development (Agarwala 1989). Important to this change has been the rise of the Japanese MNCs and other Asian MNCs which did not bring with them the historical baggage of neocolonialism, and the United Nations involvement in the development of the Code of Conduct for MNCs. The MNC package delivered to the LDCs includes national need satisfaction in every element of the "augmented product." These include capital, technology, management, and effective worldwide marketing channels. In an interdependent world of trade and competition, these are critical ingredients in the success of EP strategy of industrialization. For India's policymakers, the changing perception of the role and legitimacy of the MNC has confirmed the validity of using them as the vehicle for the transfer of appropriate technology and the infusion of scarce capital. This is especially useful in the context of severe foreign exchange difficulties arising out of its external debt burden and balance of payment difficulties.

THE PRESSURE OF INTERNAL FORCES

Viewed in isolation, the success of the Indian strategy of development based on the concept of self-reliance and on the methodology of centralized planning is undeniable. Every single strategic sector of the economy is self-reliant. There is no foreign control or domination across the wide diversity of industrial activity and capital intensity ("Industrial Transformation in India" 1991). In each one of these areas, India possesses the capability to design, manufacture, and market. But once the isolationist perspective is removed and the assumption of insulated economy is dropped, the performance of India's development is seen to be far below its potential. Moreover, other Asian countries have outperformed India.

The mixed economy possesses two spheres of inefficiency, one in the public sector and the other in the private sector. This phenomenon manifests itself in India's inability to compete in the international market place. Inadequate infrastructure, various bottlenecks, misallocation of resources, imbalanced regional development, the presence of parallel economy, the urban-rural development gap, and the demand-supply gap are all largely consequences of the central planning approach. In turn, they collectively contribute to general inefficiency (see, e.g., "India" 1991). However, there are circumstances unique to the private sector and to the public sector.

The public sector has become a source of massive public waste because of the bureaucratic control. These SOEs have become the instruments for achieving social goals and political ends. Economic considerations have been regulated to a lesser role. Management effectiveness and market objectives are of little concern because there is little if any such accountability. The demands of the stakeholders are not present. The private sector suffers from its own malaise arising out of the licensing requirements coupled with the MRTP and other restrictions to growth. Thus, unlike the domestic U.S. market, where a large market has led to scale economies, the Indian market rewards inefficiency. Market protection and absence of competition have promoted such performance. Hence, the private sector, while dynamic in the sense of being enterprising, has generally preferred the safe haven provided by domestic protection to the unfamiliar and risky environment of foreign markets. Even when enormous government inducements for instance, export incentive schemes, duty drawback schemes, import replenishment schemes, and the like, were able to motivate a firm to overcome its chronic protectionist attitude, it often discovered that Indian manufactures were not internationally competitive.

INDIA—AWAY FROM AUTAKRY

As has been stated earlier, India has been moving toward a policy of liberalization since the 1980s—a process which has been set in motion in many parts of the world. However, the term itself has not been clearly defined in literature, possibly because preliberalization policies have varied across the globe (Gillespie and Alden 1990). These were dependent on political and economic philosophy based on cultural values and situational factors. In a general sense, economic liberalization can be referred to as a process of creating freedom from artificially established economic constraints of governments. Thus, a liberalized policy may itself suffer from a degree of restraint. The policy may deal with the domestic or external sector of a national economy. However, in general a preliberalization stage involves an autarkic orientation where the pursuit of import substitution industrialization is a significant element. There is also significant government participation in the economic development process at the macro and micro level as either planner and/or controller and/or owner and/or manager of the factors of production and marketing. Thus, liberalization often involves deregulation, privatization, decentralization, and deinsulation. In India's case all these processes are a part of the liberalization process.

As early as the 1960s India's policymakers became aware of the negative effects of the skewed incentive system which restrained economic growth and contributed to the decline of India's share in world manufacture exports

("Reforms Aim at Boosting Exports" 1990). India often failed to convert its comparative advantage into a sustainable competitive edge in the international marketplace. By necessity, a system of counterincentives, as stated earlier, had to be developed to improve the relative attractiveness of export markets. In a sense, the domestic market inefficiencies had to be subsidized. Gradually, imports became a key element in the export promotion policy. The strict import substitution-based industrialization gave way to an aggressive import-based export orientation. Import licensing has continued to be liberalized by adding new items to the Open General License and decanalizing.[8] Now almost half of India's exports belong to the nontraditional area, some of which are highly sophisticated products like computer software.

In the 1970s and 1980s the realization that the economic direction of the country required reassessment, and restructuring became even more pronounced. A revision of several factors, hitherto assumed to be critical to the traditional approach, has been set in motion with the pace of change increasing from 1985. Some of the salient points of these changes are described below.

The poor performance of public sector enterprises has opened up the issue of SOE privatization, even in the heavy/capital intensive industries, in order to bring in some management discipline and accountability. The private sector has already undergone some deregulation. There is increasing delicensing of industries. Investment limits for licensing requirements have also been increased. MRTP restrictions have been diluted to allow large firms the flexibility to expand in order to achieve scale economies. Broadbanding[9] has been widened to give management the opportunity to diversify. Similarly, changes have been instituted in the small-scale industries. Delicensing of 100 percent export-oriented units and those established in export processing zones have been given a strong push. Foreign collaboration and technology transfer have been given due encouragement to resolve the problem of technological obsolescence. Thus, strategies oriented towards decontrol, decentralization, delicensing, and deregulation, concepts somewhat alien to the spirit of self-reliance, are now evolving.

These reforms have already begun to change the structure of the Indian market. Competition has brought in a profit squeeze across the top 100 companies. The seller's market has now become a buyer's market. A consolidation of industries is in progress. Inefficient Indian firms, including some subsidiaries of MNCs, like Remington Rand, which have survived in the protected Indian environment, cannot expect to do so anymore (Ninan 1988)[10]. From the perspective of foreign firms, particularly the MNCs, however, opening the doors of an autarkic system provide numerous market and business opportunities.

OPPORTUNITIES IN INDIA FOR MNCs:
THE KEY QUESTIONS—WHERE AND HOW

While the liberalization process is still continuing, the insulation surrounding the Indian economy is only just beginning to crack. For instance, the reforms in the areas of import licensing, technology transfer, and foreign collaboration have yet to be followed by a liberalization of FERA, a key concern for multinationals. The basic tenet of FERA has remained intact as it pertains to the 40 percent foreign equity ceiling. However, its interpretation has become more liberal. This is particularly true in the case of vital technology and 100 percent export commitments. In 1989, the permission to sell 25 percent of the total production was granted to some foreign firms. Also, a fast track project approval scheme has been developed.

The 100 percent export route has been followed by several companies, including Linde Aktiengesellchaf (West Germany, petrochemicals), to enter India. Companies have also been allowed to enter India as a sole foreign venture (without a local partner), especially if the International Financial Corporation (IFC) invests in the project. Carrier Aircon (U.S.A., air conditioning), and Unicardan AG (West Germany) illustrate this approach. Texas Instruments and Citibank have used export processing zones (EPZ) to establish wholly owned software exporting units. Many other firms have followed with majority joint ventures in EPZs. For instance, Halliburton Services (U.S.A.) with 60 percent equity expects to provide oil field services locally. Companies have also been given permission to enter India by investing in existing companies. Pfaudler (U.S.A.) was allowed to buy a 40 percent stake in Gujarat Machinery (Raman and Balakrishna 1989; see also, *India Abroad* 1990). Still more dramatic is similar entry in the services area, for example: McCann Erickson (40% in Tara Sinha Advertising); Lazard Feres (20% in Merchant Bank).

The liberalization process is perhaps best symbolized by the following two examples: Pepsi Cola and Maruti-Suzuki.

Pepsi Cola

Pepsi Cola's joint venture, approved in 1988, took roughly six years for processing. It involves both a state partner (Punjab) and a private Indian firm (Voltas). The approximate equity breakdown is as follows: Pepsico 40 percent, Punjab Agro Industries 36 percent, Voltas 24 percent. The four components of the project are: (1) an agro research center; (2) a potato and grain processing unit; (3) a fruit and vegetable processing unit; and, (4) a soft drink concentrate unit. The stringent government-imposed conditions include requirements that: (1) exports must be 50 percent of total production cost; (2) foreign sales should include 80 percent Pepsi-made products plus 20 percent others; (3) export obligation must continue for a ten-year period during which no dividends or capital may be repatriated until the export obligation has been satisfied; (4) the foreign exchange inflow to outflow ratio is to be set at five to one; (5) the soft drink concentrate should be no greater than 25 percent of total turnover; (6) products for the domestic market may not have foreign brand names; and, (7) raw material imports are to conform to import policies, including duty payments (see "India Clears Pepsico" 1990; "Pepsico's Entry Into India" 1988). Pepsi has obviously taken a long-term "globalization approach" in its entry into India. On the one hand its concern is the massive middle class of at least 150 million people, and on the other its perspective is the global competition with archrival Coca Cola. A critical aspect of this venture is the development of competitive strategy based on global sourcing of ingredients with due weight being given to India as a R&D base.

Maruti-Suzuki

The joint venture—Maruti Udyog limited (MUL)—between an SOE, Maruti (60%) and Suzuki of Japan (40%), proved so successful that Suzuki increased its original equity participation (26%). Established in 1982 by an Act of Parliament for the manufacture of cars and vans, it produced 105,000 units out of an industry total of 166,742 in 1989-90. It not only succeeded in developing exports to Hungary, Australia, and France, but also in increasing the domestic content to the level of 87 percent to 91 percent using about 375 local vendors. The success has already encouraged General Motors to review its future prospects in India after a gap of about 35 years. Maruti's performance can be put in a better perspective when seen in the context of a previously stagnant Indian market. The market leader, the Ambassador car (a swadeshi product), has remained virtually the same since the mid 1950s ("Sterling Record" 1991; see also Kaufman 1988). The car is made by Hindustan Motors, with whom General Motors was originally affiliated. Again in this venture a "globalization" approach is visible, as was the case in the Pepsi venture, the focus being a national market (India) but in a global perspective.

Strategic Approaches to India's Opportunities

Considering the globalization—regionalization syndrome, discussed earlier, the approach to India's business prospects and its comparative advantage (market size, cheap labor, human capital, natural resources, diversified industrial structure marketing infrastructure, etc.) must be seen on a production base—market continuum. This requires a supranational perspective coupled with national strategies. Thus, the traditional *international* entry strategy approach, in terms of exporting-contracting-investing, seems to be inappropriate and outdated.[11] Now taking a multinational view, several strategic approaches can be identified.

As A Market In Itself

Sheer numbers make India a potentially attractive place to do business. The improving economic environment enhances that potential for MNCs. For example, a growing middle class of at least 150 million consumers has a strong propensity to consume durable and consumer goods. When combined with an increasing ability to purchase such goods, India becomes a target too lucrative to ignore.

As An Expanded Market: In The Context Of SAARC

The formation of SAARC widens the scope of opportunities. Important characteristics of this emerging organization include a region rich in resources (including jute, cotton, tea, fishery, iron, mica), and a population size of at least one billion, one-fifth of which can be a viable market for consumer durables and nondurables. There are endless possibilities for the identification and pursuit of multinational development projects. The member countries are proximal, which creates similar topographical and climatic considerations. Furthermore, the existence of a degree of socio-cultural homogeneity (with a common official language, English) creates some similarity in problem-solving attitudes and behaviors. Thus, there exists a potential for synergies and developing opportunities for networking in trade, joint marketing, cooperative production and regional purchasing. Moreover, local SAARC markets (like Bhutan and the Maldives) which were per se economically infeasible because of their small size, can now become viable segments for possible targeting (Siddiqi forthcoming). This approach is best exemplified by Intel (U.S.A.). The establishment of their liaison office, IntelAsia in Bangalore (India) allows the firm to sell its products in Pakistan, Bangladesh, and Sri Lanka.

Expanded Market: Context Of SAARC-ASEAN Interaction

Operating in the local/national and regional/SAARC markets, is only a limited dimension of business opportunities. The opportunity set expands significantly when an interregional (SAARC-ASEAN) perspective is taken. The prospects for SAARC-ASEAN trade arises because of varying regional comparative advantages arising from different national resource endowments and different routes to economic development.

Expanded Market: Context Of East Europe And USSR

India has been very closely involved in rupee trade with Eastern European countries and the U.S.S.R. Similar (but not identical) socialistic economic philosophies, and development problems, like the nonconvertability of local currencies, created bilateral relationships which have grown considerably. For MNCs a joint venture partner seen in this context may be invaluable, especially when the venture utilizes the established bilateral channels. Estee Lauder's venture with Modis of India, as well as Rank Xerox's venture, also with Modis, takes this approach (Raman and Balakrishna 1989).

In The Context Of The U.S. Market

The immense pool of qualified engineers and scientists in India is already being utilized by MNCs for the development of software, and the servicing of hardware through the establishment of service facilities and R&D centers. Texas Instruments, AT&T, Bell South, and Hewlet Packard are pursuing this strategy in the development of software (McQueen 1988).

In The Context Of Other Markets Not Mentioned

Given the critical role of global sourcing, the previous strategies could play a more extensive role, namely the interlinking of far-flung subsidiaries in a multinational firm via a research, service, or production base. R&D centers have been established by firms like Astra (Sweden, pharmaceuticals), Plessey (UK, telecommunications), and Honeywell-Bull. Biocon (Ireland) has converted its research laboratory into a production base. Interestingly, half its output is now sold in the Indian market (Raman and Balakrishna 1989).

Country of Origin Factor

The worldwide experience and resources of MNCs, place them in a unique competitive position to exploit the benefits of a large, diversified market (Moyer and Hollander 1989, p. 79). Local firms, while possessing location-specific advantage, rarely have the supranational perspective or the managerial experience to effectively exploit the benefits of regionalization like SAARC. However with the deinsulation of the economy, the outward orientation of Indian firms has evolved (Basu 1989), primarily through trade and less often through foreign direct investment. Indian firms have yet to develop successful worldwide brand names, partially because a positive country-of-origin image has yet to be established. However, the top Indian business houses have succeeded in establishing joint ventures, mostly in the ASEAN countries and in Africa.

For the individual MNCs—Japanese, American, European—a critical factor for market success would be the ability to utilize their home country advantage and to maintain patience and flexibility in their negotiations with a slow bureaucracy. The Japanese, as the biggest creditor country, have a head start with their willingness to fund megaprojects like those involving several SAARC members. They have shown great ingenuity in targeting industries. A case in point is the automotive market. The two-wheeler market is now one of the most dynamic sectors of the economy. Honda, Mazda, and Toyota are some of the companies that have helped make this mass market intensely competitive (Shekhar 1990).

CONCLUSION

India's gradual but relentless push toward liberalization is almost axiomatic. The twin deficits, the external debt, the need to become a participant in the global economic system, and the need to compete internationally for scarce funds (with the East European countries and others) are strong elements promoting this process. Though the movement toward an open market suggests the replacement of the inward-oriented concept of self-reliance with collective self-reliance (manifested in SAARC), India's general commitment to its "quasi socialism" cannot be denied. The government will plan, control, and define the strategic socioeconomic direction of the country. This should be clear from the content of the eighth Five Year Plan (1991-1996). The Approach Paper to it has been appropriately titled: "Towards Social Transformation" (Singh 1990).

However, from the MNC's strategic perspective, India's potential as a market, with a resourceful middle and upper class and/or diversified production base and/or R&D base, should be considered in the wider regional/ global context in the design of multinational marketing strategies. At the same time, a variety of factors must necessarily be considered as discounting variables in opportunity assessment. Poverty, pollution, population growth, the presence of a parallel economy, political instability, and social turmoil remain factors for long-term concern.

NOTES

1. India is known as the largest democracy. Therefore, the question is not one of political liberalization as is the case with the East European countries, the U.S.S.R. and China. We are concerned with liberalization in an economic sense.

2. Politically, India has played a leading role in the development of the non-aligned movement.

3. India's industrial policy was first announced in 1948, and recognized the role of foreign capital. It was revised in 1956 to reflect a socialistic pattern of development. Industries were categorized as those belonging to Schedule A for exclusive State activity, those in Schedule B being progressively State owned but private enterprises were to supplement State's activity, and those belonging outside these two Schedules where the private sector was free to operate. For details see *India 1985* (1986). Industrial policy revisions have also been made in the years 1980, 1982 and 1990.

4. Phased Manufacturing Program refers to the gradual increase in local content.

Canalization refers to those imports which belong to the sole domain of public sector.

5.   The swadeshi movement was born during the struggle for independence. It refers to the rejection of foreign products and their substitution by indigenous products.

6.   Personal interview with Union Carbide (New York) executives in 1974.

7.   However, the member states have some of the lowest per capita income: $150/Bhutan, $160/Bangladesh, $170/Nepal, $330/India, $350/Pakistan, $410/the Maldives, $420/Sri Lanka. This factor puts India below Pakistan, the Maldives, and Sri Lanka. The 1988 quantitative data is based upon *The Europe World Year Book* (1990).

8.   The private sector is not restricted from importing these items.

9.   Broadbanding allows firms the flexibility to switch between similar product lines.

10.   From a multinational strategy perspective, however, the presence of an inefficient Remington Rand in an insulated environment minimized the destabilization of Sperry Rand's (now Unisys) multinational integration.

11.   For the traditional approach, see Root (1987).

REFERENCES

Agarwala, P.N. 1989. "Changing Perceptions of MNCs." *Business World* (August 16-29), p. 20.

Basu, D. 1989. "Charging Out." *Business World* (August 16-29), pp. 54-59.

Chandra, B. 1990. "1947-1990, India's Journey to Economic Independence." *Telegraph* (August 15).

Dunning, J.H. 1988. "The Future of the Multinational Enterpris.," In *International Business Classics,* edited by J.C. Baker et al. Lexington, MA: Lexington Books.

The Europe World Year Book. 1990. Vols. I and II. London: Europe Publications.

Gillespie, K., and D. Alden. 1990. "Consumer Product Export Opportunities to Liberalizing LDCs: A Life-Cycle Approach." *Journal of International Business Studies* 20(1):93-112.

"India." 1991. *The Economist* (May 4).

India Abroad. 1990. October 26.

"India Clears Pepsico to Sell Soft Drinks; Venture to Spend $1 Billion Over Decade." 1990. *The Wall Street Journal* (May 24), p. A6.

India 1985. 1986. Compiled and edited by Research and Reference Division, Ministry of Information and Broadcasting, Publication Division, Government of India, New Delhi, May.

"Industrial Transformation in India Through 1980s." 1991. *India Economic News* (May).

Kaufman, M. 1988. "In India, A Living Legend Fills the Roads." *The Philadelphia Inquirer* (January 17), p. 2-A.

Kumar, N. 1990. *Multinational Enterprises in India.* New York: Routledge.

McQueen, C. 1988. "Liberal Economic Policies and Steady Growth Are Luring More American Companies to India." *Business America* 109(21):14-17.

Moyer, R., and S.C. Hollander. 1989. *Markets and Marketing in Developing Economies.* Homewood, IL: Irwin.

Ninan, T.N. 1988. "The Old Order Changeth." *India Today* (May 15), pp. 54-58.

"Pepsico's Entry Into India Has Lessons for Other MNCs." 1988. *Business Asia* 20(40):319-320.

Raman, A.P., and P. Balakrishna. 1989. "New Routes to an Old Market." *Economic Times* (January 16), p. 2.

"Reforms Aim at Boosting Exports." *Business Standard* (July 17).

Root, F.R. 1987. *Entry Strategies for International Markets.* Lexington, MA: Lexington Books.

Scalapino, R.A. 1989. *The Politics of Development.* Cambridge, MA: Harvard University Press.

Shekhar, S. 1990. "Japanese Auto Tieups Move Into The Fast Lane." *Business World* (November 21-December 4), pp. 41-45.

Siddiqi, M.M.S. forthcoming. "Business Outlook in the 1990s: India in the Context of South Asia." *The Mid-Atlantic Journal of Business.*

Singh, V.P. 1990. Prime Minister of India, *Inaugural Address,* Forty First Meeting of the National Development Council, June 18.

"Sterling Record of Joint Participation: Maruti Top Performer." 1991. *India Economic News* (April), p. 4.

Thomas, T. 1990. "India: Self-Reliance is an Outmoded Concept." *Economic Times* (September 27).

Todaro, M.P. 1989. *Economic Development in the Third World,* 4th ed. New York: Longmans.

THE POTENTIAL OF INTERNATIONAL
BUSINESS RESEARCH IN SPACE

Mike H. Ryan

INTRODUCTION

A global approach to business is often described as the requisite requirement
for future success. However, this terminology is already obsolete.
Technological developments have placed an entirely new territory within the
grasp of private enterprise. This new tract encompasses that area outside the
atmosphere and gravity of the planet Earth. Orbital space, the moon, Mars,
the asteroids, and all other planetary bodies are potential sites and sources for
new business opportunities. Many believe that the next major industrial
revolution will be based in space and that it will become the primary
competitive arena for twenty-first century.

Many nations are embracing the opportunities which they see in space
development. Nations such as Japan, Germany, Australia, and France are
rapidly increasing the gap between themselves and others who are unable to
use or unwilling to see the potential of space. The Japanese and Europeans
are developing new approaches for commercializing space research, reflecting
their commitment to the long-term benefit of space programs for their
respective industrial futures.

International Research in the Business Disciplines, Volume 1, pages 203-215.
Copyright © 1993 by JAI Press Inc.
All rights of reproduction in any form reserved.
ISBN: 1-55938-538-3

Certainly, the United States and the Soviet Union maintain respectable leads in many relevant aerospace technologies. However, in a highly competitive environment technological leadership may provide only a fleeting advantage.[1] As economic and political changes occur within the Soviet Union they too are beginning to foster a commercial counterpart in their traditional long-term view for space development. The addition of a long-term commercial approach marks an elemental change in the competitive infrastructure which has governed world space activities for the last two and one half decades.

> The current void in U.S. commercial space policy reflects not only a lack of imagination or attitude, but more importantly the absence of a long term vision for this nation's industrial future. While this nation has been debating industrial issues left over from the early part of this century other nations are preparing to establish industrial bases for the twenty-first (Ryan 1991a).

International competition will produce fundamental changes in commercial space activity. Here as in most other modern industrial areas, the long-term requirements do not allow for quick fixes or massive catch-up efforts. Therefore, those nations which actively pursue commercial space opportunities with diligence, vision, and *consistent* development policies will be likely to reap the benefits. Collectively, these expansive changes represent significant research challenges and opportunities for those interested in being on the cutting edge of management practice. It is incumbent upon those who study business to be as farsighted as those who engage in it.

SOME POSSIBLE RESEARCH OPPORTUNITIES

The identification and selection of research ideas is, at best, an arbitrary decision. The point is not to be all encompassing or even completely descriptive. The purpose is to demonstrate that there are a variety of potentially interesting research questions related to commercial space activities. Some of these are sufficiently unique as to pose fairly substantial barriers to study. A few have only limited application to other industries. Still, most space-based situations do have their terrestrial counterparts. What makes these question(s) interesting is that their application in a space environment forces a reexamination of all initial assumptions held.

Such activity always has the possibility of generating new insights. These new insights may in turn have application to areas not part of the original question. The creation and/or discovery of new knowledge is not necessarily linear. It is important to remember that in a weightless environment up and down are arbitrary distinctions. Generally, up and down represent choices of convenience and, hence, they are not governed by some immutable law. Perhaps contact with similar "management" situations will remind us that some of our "scientific" observations on business may be equally arbitrary.

General Management

For example, the following have all been described repeatedly as substantial barriers for firms which desire to engage in commercial space ventures:

1. lack of appropriate industrial infrastructure;
2. lack of stability in the setting of priorities and goals;
3. blurring the distinction between commercialization and privatization;
4. failure to recognize the demands of international competition;
5. unwillingness to separate government funding from the political process; and,
6. the lack of innovative organizational structures upon which private firms could build a long-term commitment to space-based businesses.

Each of these "issues" should foster any number of potentially imaginative research questions when applied to the actual conditions facing management decision makers.

Organizational and Human Behavior

The stories about astronauts declining to complete assignments when they felt overworked have made several good case studies. Soviet cosmonauts have become quite stubborn when they felt they were working too hard. Managing people working in orbit, from the ground, may never be the workable proposition of managing employees in another country. But the situation requires more study than it has received to date. Are the conditions under which people labor in space closer to that of submarine crews, oil platform workers, saturation divers, arctic explorers, or some combination of all the above? That information might be very useful for hiring, retention, or estimating the possible success of specific space ventures.

In like manner, totally different management practices may be needed to govern multifirm industrial platforms in space. Traditional barriers to product information, proprietary research, and manufacturing processes may not be workable in an environment where shared information may be a question of survival and not just competitive advantage. Maybe an entirely new class of professional manager will be required for multifirm, multinational, multijurisdictional space facilities. In such circumstances, should they act as simple fiduciaries, frontier marshals, U.N. peace-keeping forces, or some exotic combination yet unidentified? Who should train such people? How should they be trained? How do you ensure their integrity? The questions are virtually endless and the answers may have less in common with previous business experience than many might wish.

Finance

Space is just a place. A hundred miles more or less is all it takes to be in space. But from a financial point of view, it is far removed from the world's financial marketplace. How does one gage the financial risk of space-based business? Are traditional applications of financial risk factors appropriate to use for space activities?

As the time frame over which an investment is active moves further into the future the expected risk increases and therefore the necessary return to compensate for that risk must increase. Generally, the returns needed to encourage significant long term investment must compensate not only for the length of time involved but also for other, more certain, returns which have to be foregone. If there is no expected return during the initial phases of a project other concerns include the lack of flexibility. Lack of cash flow during the initial years does not allow offsetting of risk but investing in other unrelated activities. Consequently, the need to offset lost potential also figures into every long term investment decision. Further concerns include the potential obsolescence of any undertaking given new technology or changing priorities. Without some mechanism to reduce risk or increase the real return the prudent investment decision is not to undertake very long term activities (Ryan 1991b, p. 7).

What are the possibilities, given that space investment time frames must extend far into the future? Private firms are also functionally limited, given their general orientation away from long-term sustained risk. United States firms in particular have an additional burden due to generally shorter investment time frames as compared to their foreign competitors. If the intent is for American firms to become involved in space business at any realistic level, then investment and planning infrastructures must be encouraged to change to accommodate very long-term activities. Determining the best and most appropriate means to accomplish such an objective is a question of considerable importance to the private sector.

Risk Management

In highly competitive industries firms cannot afford to invest in projects whose potential for undermining their future survival is viewed as excessive. Excessive usually infers that top management has made a "bet the company" type of decision. History is replete with the remnants of firms which having bet against the odds, lost, and then disappeared. If winning does not carry as significant a consequence as losing, that is, dominant market position, huge returns, crushed competition and soon, then why take the risk at all, given other, less sanguine possibilities. Just how risky is space business, and are common measures of risk equal to the task of assessment?

A business can fail for any number of reasons. However, another business able to learn from that failure can move on. The only lasting failures are produced by systems in which no one is ever willing to take a risk. In order for a system to improve it must be able to change. Change entails risk at its most basic level. Therefore, all advancement requiring change produces risks of one sort or another. American managers need to recognize that avoiding risk is not the same as managing it. Far too many U.S. companies do not seem to know the difference. Might this explain the willingness of some American firms to manipulate their financial resources to enhance firm value rather than devoting a similar effort toward the production of new products and/or services? Could this also explain the apparent reluctance of private firms to engage in space ventures?

Strategy

Vacillation of any sort fosters prudence on the part of private firms. United States government activities to date have not had the consistency, either good or bad, which private firms deem necessary for prudent strategic action. The prudent strategist therefore uses great caution before tackling any space-based activities. This implies that the pursuit of other business(es) having less risk, makes good sense, and to a risk-adverse firm, an inherently superior strategy. The assumptions that one makes about strategic risk influence both business decisions and investment strategies (see Moore 1983).[2]

Pragmatically, it usually entails placing one's energy and money into activities and/or investments having a proven rate of return. Obtaining proven rates of return requires significant knowledge about the past, present, and future of an activity. Without such information there is only the supposition that one knows enough to be able to predict when and under what circumstances a profit is possible. Strategic choice is based on an understanding of previous decisions. The problem is that where space-related business is involved previous strategic decisions may not provide a sufficiently robust comparison. The quality of the strategy is adversely affected by the lack of good information. Solid business research has the potential to identify better strategies and the conditions under which comparisons might make sense. Either approach would be an improvement on the current situation facing many companies.

Research and Development

The most consistent theme which underlies discussion on the decline of American competitive ability has been the failure to remain technologically competitive (Dean 1987, p. 7). Therefore, the best reason for pursuing business in space may be that it provides a proven avenue for developing future technology. Assessments by various sources continue to supply evidence that investment in space technology has produced significant returns.[3] Dollar amounts for estimated returns for space have never been very specific. If they were, it might be easier to sell commercial space or at least to make evaluation of specific types of projects easier. Such assessments, based on solid research, could be of immense value to the public and private sector. Will the creation of new industries, jobs, techniques, and individual technologies tend to support the value-added nature of space investment? Could U.S. firms reduce long-term risks related to technological competitiveness by a sustained commitment to space development?

The best mechanisms to encourage this type of activity are still unclear. What is fairly clear is that technical development is generally viewed as the single most important source of economic growth and development (Tuma 1987). For example, Japanese and American policies concerning technological research and development differ sharply. Japanese industry places a much higher priority on R&D, and government R&D funding is targeted at areas of strategic commercial importance, such as software productivity and artificial intelligence. However, in the United States, most government R&D funding is devoted to military and space-related projects. Due in part to this imbalance between military and commercial R&D, the reserve of technical knowledge in the United States is being depleted. The resulting intense competition from the Japanese in industries such as electronics and automobiles indicates that the Japanese approach to R&D has paid off while the U.S. approach has not.

Such results also point out the inadequacy of the long-standing assumption that the benefits of U.S. government spending for military R&D and basic scientific research automatically would spill over to the civilian side of the economy and enhance the competitiveness of U.S. commercial industries. Thus suggesting that many U.S. firms could improve their competitive ability by acquiring foreign technical information (Alic 1988). A comparison based on such a question might be very interesting indeed.

Business and Public Policy

Most commercial ventures do not happen unless projects can be justified on fairly exacting criteria. Generally, future projects must have the potential for generating sufficient revenue. The key is to reduce, if not wholly eliminate, any risks associated with alternative investments, fluctuating market conditions, or government funding. Government funding may reduce a variety of risks under some conditions. All parties have an interest in legislation which supports long-term efforts in the form of R&D credits, other assorted tax incentives, free trade zones or whatever. Which approaches are likely to be best and under what conditions should public policy be used to stimulate commercial space activity?

Japanese and European firms have long benefitted from such support, but federal funding in the United States generally carries secondary criteria often having little to do with the project at hand. The strength of a private firm should be in producing goods and services, not in playing politics. Here, one of the most interesting questions is what is the real question that ought to be addressed by public policymakers.

Some method for private sector resource sharing is virtually mandatory for space business. The resources necessary even for relatively small projects have financial, organizational, governmental, or technological requirements so great as to become distinct and separate barriers.[4] These barriers are so huge that even the largest firms would have difficulty in overcoming them. Without resource sharing, even to the extent of eliminating many of the provisions of American antitrust legislation, large-scale commercial space activity will remain unlikely. Responding to similar resource and cooperative limitations, many U.S. firms have sought out partners abroad. Are there alternate approaches that might be preferable? And if so, why and under what conditions?

International Management

Even international cooperation has its problems when discussing commercial space applications (see Bourely 1990; Christol 1990). For example, concerns about national security have long plagued the commercial launch market. Anxiety on the part of government agencies at the prospect of any potential transfer of Western technology has effectively eliminated a number of projects. Predatory pricing concerns have led to limits on contracts between U.S. firms and potential foreign suppliers of space services. Whether such actions are justified is a policy question beyond the scope of this discussion. However, the business implications of such policies are pretty clear. Going abroad as a mechanism for reducing the resources required for space activity is not a panacea. What might U.S. firms do to improve resource efficiency as they develop options for business in space? (see, e.g., Soete 1987). What mechanisms would produce the "best" international results?

A seldom mentioned, but serious, potential problem is that of the *have* versus the *have not* nations. The world economic system is a function of many economies. They are certainly not uniform either in terms of their performance or capability. It is not reasonable to expect them to stand by and passively accept space development if resources and opportunities are not somehow shared (see, e.g., Fagerberg 1978). Such sentiments are not always viewed as consistent with the goals of the Western economic powers or the assumptions of "free" enterprise. Many questions need to be addressed as to the conditions under which business in space will be conducted. Some of the most critical and sensitive issues are so philosophical in content that their true importance might be lost on pragmatic business people. Yet, the philosophy which will ultimately provide the foundation of business activity in space is perhaps one of the great unresolved international policy issues of the late twentieth century.

GENERAL INSIGHTS FROM OTHER FIELDS

Patterns of trade and industrial development mark the passage of time as readily as the years. The process of industrial transformation is ongoing although somewhat haphazard. There are nations boldly striding into the twenty-first century while others struggle desperately out of sixteenth-century economies. The problems inherent in private sector participation in space ventures have their counterparts in virtually every industrial effort of the last several centuries. Contemporary critics of commercial space ventures suggest that limited opportunities and lack of necessary infrastructure are the primary reasons for the lack of commercial success (see Egan 1989). The issue is usually presented as a matter of timing. Commercial space is described as too immature an industry to be profitable. Therefore, it is too soon to expect projects to be self-supporting. The question is whether or not this is really the case. Projects having the potential to be self-supporting have met unexpected resistance. Why? Part of the answer is in the perception that space-based business contains comparatively greater risks than terrestrial-based business. This may not be an accurate assessment. The consequences of erroneous assumptions, particularly for the United States, is a critical impediment to the development of viable space businesses.

Other nations and their respective firms, both public and private, are not quite as willing to ignore the potential of space (see Harr and Kohli 1990). Suggestions that the private sector limit its activities until the government builds the necessary infrastructure is generally seen as an abdication of responsibility. If free enterprise is to remain the key to American business then the private sector itself must take the necessary steps to promote that approach in space. Space-based businesses will require even greater diligence than that given the more traditional international marketplace (see Magaziner and Patinkin 1989).[5] And, ultimately, the competitive environment may prove to be far tougher.

The primary international policymakers for space are not always those having the most favorable attitudes towards the Western idea of a free market. Consequently, great care must be exercised in order to insure favorable application of legal principles outside the earth's traditional boundaries. Additionally, the number of nations developing space business capability is increasing rapidly. Of these, many do not view the role of government vis-à-vis business in quite the same context as the United States. This distinction could prove critical as laws and regulations evolve to govern space development. International law is a matter of agreement among nations not private companies. Having an environment conducive to business is imperative. Those nations having an interest in space will generally make the rules governing it. If U.S. firms miss the boat by virtue of their disinterest, then the real problems associated with doing business anywhere will be exacerbated in space. By not playing the game now, private companies could be forced to use someone else's rules at a later date. Prudent long-term strategy suggests that it is better to be part of the process from the first.[6]

The idea that U.S. firms (or any other nations's) can delay for any significant period is inadequate given the developing space-business environment. Waiting for the government is likely to be an exercise in futility. For example, the space station design changed (and may change yet again) so frequently that even our international space partners, Japan and Europe, are very concerned. And, no design to date seems particularly suitable for commercial activity. If other governments cannot get a firm commitment from the U.S. government, why should a private company expect to do so? Even if such a commitment were forthcoming, could it be counted on, given the funding situation in Congress, changing executive priorities, or the inherent difficulties associated with the federal bureaucracy? Would any reasonable businessperson bet their company on such a relationship? This is not a rhetorical question, given the importance that many government agencies play in encouraging and/or discouraging commercial space efforts.

There are the obvious limitations imposed by an inadequate commercial transportation system. However, apart from getting there, space operations may actually pose no greater problems than many Earth-based activities. Given the state of world affairs, space-based business should entail fewer risks than those experienced by many firms on a daily basis. The perception of business risk may be greater than its reality. Vacillating policies as to the role private companies can expect to play in space is partly to blame. United States government space policy stems from several sources. Not all of these are comfortable with the prospect of independent activity in space. Some concerns are legitimate, others less so. The difficulty is that a consensus relating to private firms in space has never really existed. Thus, private firms are counseled to wait until either the business potential of space is proven, or the government supplies guarantees which remove most of the risks (see Macauley 1989; Struthers 1989). Unfortunately for U.S. firms, other nations' companies do not see the value in waiting for someone else to act.

Realistically, the notion that American companies delay involvement until some future date is an abandonment of space as a competitive arena (see Lewis and Lewis 1987). Delay can be afforded only by organizations whose competitive position permits such flexibility.

Even the most casual observer of American business would have noticed that life has gotten tougher for U.S. manufacturing firms over the past decade. Foreign competition has increasingly endangered the profitability—and even the survival—of many American firms. ... In order for a manufacturing firm to be competitive today, it must be able to withstand competition from around the globe (Sean 1987, p. 3).

Currently, no U.S. firm can claim a level of preeminence in space so as to preclude strong competitors from abroad. Furthermore, such conditions are not going to be established by firms which choose not to compete. If U.S. firms believe that there is business potential in space-related activities, then they must move more aggressively to develop that capacity. To make such activity easier to manage, significant research questions ought to be addressed as soon as practical. The industrial powerhouses of the twenty-first century will be those having the wisdom to see the opportunity that space offers and the courage to seize the initiative (see Goodrich 1989).

What might U.S. firms do to improve both their efficiency and effectiveness as they develop options for business in space? To improve, one should examine those places and institutions where specific efforts have resulted in industrial successes. To that end, Japanese and European industrial consortiums are particularly instructive. Japan has long operated mechanisms suitable for the formation of long-term projects. Their approach has proven successful in industrial environments as varied as consumer electronics and automobiles. Aerospace technology, with attention to commercial space, is viewed as one of the most important industrial targets presently available. Consequently, Japanese space efforts are directed more clearly at the long-term business potential of space with well over one hundred firms involved. What makes their approach interesting is the extent to which these firms work together for their mutual benefit. As an added incentive, the government not only provides support but its blessings for extensive cooperative efforts, particularly in situations where resources are limited or redundant activity makes little sense (see Rothwell 1986).

Europe is promoting its own response to Japanese cooperative business activities. While commercial space cooperation is not nearly so homogeneous, there have been some interesting European innovations aimed at promoting commercial activity. One such project is EUREKA, a French-conceived program, organized on the premise that industrial leadership is fueled by high-technology R&D. If such projects continue to prompt an overall improvement in the number and quality of industrial products, commercial space is a likely next target. At present, American firms would appear to be operating in a much more limited fashion than their competition. At the very least, U.S. firms must take the initiative and move to create comparable industrial organization forms. Studies which focus on the pattern and structure of such organizations could be of immense usefulness in determining which organizational mechanisms would produce the best results. Without cooperative options similar to those developing in Europe or already in place in Japan and the Soviet Union, U.S. firms will have difficulty competing at the necessary level of intensity.[7] Furthermore, a united effort may be what is ultimately required to arouse Congress sufficiently to respond to the increasing number of commercial space issues having international components.

CONCLUDING OBSERVATIONS

Many of the remaining factors inhibiting U.S. firms are problematic. For example, issues of ownership, property rights, patents, currency, cost sharing, legal authority, jurisdictional questions, and repatriation of profits are continuing international obstacles which might inhibit even the most farsighted firms. Interested governments must agree on a mechanism for private sector participation in space which provides the means for their companies to do business without undo complications. It is the existence of practical business problems which effectively limit private sector participation in commercial space activity. Consequently, all private firms have a vested interest in resolving these problems to the extent that they might wish to participate in business in space at some future date (see Papp and McIntyre 1987; Goldman 1988). United States firms have a more specific charge to action. For, although American companies face similar difficulties as their foreign counterparts in a number of areas, they have yet to develop a common means for promoting integrated solutions to the factors inhibiting commercial space development. Until such a mechanism evolves or is created, individual U.S. firms will remain at a competitive disadvantage. Thus, many firms will not pursue commercial space opportunities because the risks remain too high, the returns too low, and the resources exceed what they can make available. The rewards of commercial space efforts will then go to other nations and their companies who have found various means of dealing with the practical problems of business in space. The importance of continued research in all of these areas should be very clear.

NOTES

1. As an example of what some suggest should be considered with a single competitor, for example, Japan, see Davidson (1984) and Prestowitz (1988).

2. The understanding that risk is all pervasive is critical. Caution or rational assessments of associated risk may reduce some risks (generally known) but not always. Businessmen have a tendency to either assume that the real risks are known or regulate risks to low-probability events. A true understanding of the nature of risk suggests that these approaches may produce greater risk rather than less.

3.   Over 30,000 secondary applications of aerospace technology have emerged during NASA's existence. On a dollar-for-dollar basis the investment in space technology has more than paid for itself in new products alone (see Haggerty 1987).

4.   For the most complete current discussion on the factors related to R&D cooperation, see Murphy (1991).

5.   One of the enduring characteristics of international business is its unyielding level of competition. Industrial nations seeking the value-added industries of the twenty-first century already view business in space as perhaps the most significant competitive arena to develop.

6.   For a more complete discussion/description of the potential problems and issues facing business, see Reynolds and Merges (1989).

7.   One possibility would be the creation of a U.S. Space Corporation. An overview of the issues and factors involved is described in Ryan (1991a).

REFERENCES

Alic, J.A. 1988. "The Rise and Fall of R&D." *Mechanical Engineering* 110(4):28-33.

Bourely, M. 1990. "The Legal Hazards of Transatlantic Cooperation in Space." *Space Policy* 6(4):323-331.

Christol, C.Q. 1990. "Outer Space Exploitability: International Law and Developing Nations." *Space Policy* 6(2):146-160.

Davidson, W.H. 1984. *The Amazing Race: Winning the Technorivalry with Japan.* New York: Wiley & Sons.

Dean, J.W., Jr. 1987. *Deciding to Innovate: How Firms Justify Advanced Technology.* Cambridge, MA: Ballinger.

Egan, J.J. 1989. "Conducting Business and Scientific Experiments in Space." Pp. 135-142 in *Space: National Programs and International Cooperation,* edited by W.C. Thompson and S.W. Guerrier. Boulder, CO: Westview Press.

Goldman, N.C. 1988. *American Space Law: International and Domestic.* (Ames: Iowa State University Press.

Goodrich, J.N. 1989. *The Commercialization of Outer Space.* New York: Quorum Books.

Haggerty, J.J. 1987. *Spinoffs 1987.* Washington, DC: NASA, Office of Commercial Programs, Technology Utilization Division, August.

Harr, M., and R. Kohli. 1990. *Commercial Utilization of Space: An International Comparison of Framework Conditions.* Columbus, OH: Battelle Press.

Lewis, J.S., and R.A. Lewis. 1987. *Space Resources: Breaking the Bonds of Earth.* New York: Columbia University Press.

Macauley, M.K. 1989. "Rethinking Space Policy: The Need to Unearth the Economics of Space." Pp. 131-143 in *Space Policy Reconsidered,* edited by R. Byerly, Jr. Boulder, CO: Westview Press.

Magaziner, I., and M. Patinkin. 1989. *The Silent War.* New York: Random House.

Moore, P.G. 1983. *The Business of Risk.* Cambridge: Cambridge University Press.

Murphy, W.J. 1991. *R&D Cooperation Among Marketplace Competitors.* New York: Quorum Books.

Papp, D.S., and J.R. McIntyre, eds. *International Space Policy.* New York: Quorum Books.

Prestowitz, C.V., Jr. 1988. *Trading Places: How We Allowed Japan to Take the Lead.* New York: Basic Books.

Reynolds, G.H., and R.P. Merges. 1989. *Outer Space: Problems of Law and Policy.* Boulder, CO: Westview Press.

Rothwell, R. 1986. "Public Innovation Policy: To Have or to Have Not?" *R & D Management* (UK) 16(1):25-36.

Ryan, M.H. 1991a. "Getting Out of the Quagmire: American Space Policy and Private Enterprise." *Space Commerce* 1(2):183-194.

Ryan, M.H. 1991b. "A Practical Perspective on Space Enterprise." In *Proceedings of the 10th International Space Development Conference,* edited by R.C. Blackledge, C.L. Redfield, and S.B. Seida. San Diego, CA: Univelt Inc.

Soete, L. 1987. "The Impact of Technological Innovation on International Trade Patterns: The Evidence Reconsidered." *Research Policy* (Netherlands) 16(2-4):101-130.

Struthers, J. 1989. "Encouraging a U.S.Commercial Space Industry." Pp. 145-154 in *Space Policy Reconsidered,* edited by R. Byerly, Jr. Boulder, CO: Westview Press.

Tuma, E.H. 1987. "Technology Transfer and Economic Development: Lessons of History." *Journal of Developing Areas* 21(4):403-427.

J A I P R E S S

New Approaches to Employee Management

Edited by **David M. Saunders,** *Faculty of Management, McGill University*

Volume 1, Fairness in Employee Selection
1992, 228 pp. $73.25
ISBN 11-55938-595-2

CONTENTS: Editorial Statement. Preface, *David M. Saunders.* **Fairness and Ethical Considerations in Employee Selection,** *Ricahrd Arvey.* **Beyond Differential Prediction: Fairness in Selection,** *Neil Schmitt and Stephen W. Gilliland.* **Employment Testing and Public Policy: The Case of Integrity Tets,** *Paul R. Sacketet.* **Reconciling Economic and Social Objectives in Personnel Selection: Impact of Alternative Decision Rules,** *Wayne F. Cascio. Career Paths of Successful Executives: Do they Differ by Sex?, Laurie Larwood.* **What Predicts Employer Propensity to Gather Protected Group Information from Job Applicants,** *David M. Saunders, Joanne D. Leck and Lyne Marcil.* **Applicant Reactions to Protected Group Membership Inquiries During the Recruitment Process,** *Alan M. Saks.* **Response Alternatives to Discriminatory Inquiries,** *Joann Keyton and Jeffrey K. Springston.* **Breaking the Barriers: Women, Knowledge and Equality in the University,** *Sarah Westphal and Colleen Sheppard.* **Race, Sex, and Higher Education: Employment Equity on Campus,** *Rainer Knopff.*

JAI PRESS INC.

55 Old Post Road - No. 2   P.O. Box 1678
Greenwich, Connecticut 06836-1678
Tel: (203) 661-7602   Fax: (203)661-0792

Research in Organizational Behavior
An Annual Series of Analytical Essays and Critical Reviews

Edited by **L.L. Cummings,** *Carlson School of Management, University of Minnesota* and **Barry M. Staw,** *School of Business Administation, University of California, Berkeley*

Volume 15, 1993, 408 pp. $73.25
ISBN 1-55938-522-7

CONTENTS: Preface, *L.L. Cummings and Barry M. Staw.* **The Contracts of Individuals and Organizations,** *Denise M. Rousseau and Judi McLean Parks.* **Socialization Amidst Diversity: The Impact of Demograpics on Work Team Oldtimers and Newcomers,** *Susan E. Jackson, Veronica K.Stone, and Eden B. Alvarez.* **The 'Learning Bureaucracy': New United Motor Manfacturing, Inc.,** *Paul S. Adler.* **The Making of Organizational Opportunities: An Interpretive Pathway to Organizational Change,** *Jane E. Dutton.* **Organizational Impression Management as a Reciprocal Influence Process: The Neglected Role of the Organizational Audience,** *Linda E. Ginzel, Roderick M. Kramer, and Robert L. Sutton.* **A Goal Hierarchy Model of Personality, Motivation, and Leadership,** *Russell Cropanzano, Keith James, and Maryalice Citera.* **Economic and Behavioral Perspectives on Safety,** *Alfred Marcus, Mary L. Nichols, and Gregory E. McAvoy.* **Cross-Level Analysis of Organizations: Social Resource Management Model,** *P. Christopher Earley and Jack Britain.*

Also Available:
Volumes 1-14 (1978-1992) $73.25 each

JAI PRESS INC.
55 Old Post Road - No. 2   P.O. Box 1678
Greenwich, Connecticut 06836-1678
Tel: (203) 661-7602   Fax: (203)661-0792

Management Laureates:
A Collection of Autobiographical Essays

Arthur G. Bedeian, *Department of Management, Louisiana State University*

REVIEW: "The collection of autobiographical essays is a creative project. No other publication in management has asked leading contributors to reflect on their experiences and the factors and forces that influenced their professional and personal development. Each essay is accompanied by a photograph and complete bibliography of each individual's work. The thirty-four autobiographies represent the editor's selection of "management laureates," those who have achieved distinction in research and publication, teaching, and consulting. These laureates are holders of distinguished professorships—almost all are Fellows of the Academy of Management, some have been presidents of the Academy of Management, and others have distinguished themselves professionally. It would be difficult, if not impossible, to read one of our scholarly journals without finding at least one of these individuals cited.

The laureates come from different disciplines and have made contributions in a variety of management related topics: leadership, motivation, human resource management, strategic management, production/operations management and systems theory. The editor suggests that those chosen represent only a sample of distinguished individuals in management. No criteria are provided for how these particular individuals were selected, but careful reading will reveal that those selected are indeed distinguished contributors to the management discipline.

The essays of these laureates will be interesting to a wide range of readers—students, academicians, and practitioners. Through the essays we get to know both the people and ideas which have influenced the course of management teaching and practice. As these individuals speak of their intellectual legacy, they are simultaneously helping to develop the researchers, teachers, and practitioners of tomorrow. Each of us can better understand the contributions of these laureates by knowing something about them as people. Most of what we know of these individuals has been gathered from the flyleaf of a book, a note at the end of an article, or the sterilized linear format of a *Who's Who. Management Laureates* provides the opportunities for in-depth, introspective revelations about individuals who are among the contemporary leaders in the management discipline."

—THE EXECUTIVE
Daniel A. Wren
University of Oklahoma

Future volumes will be available annually and may be ordered on a standing order basis.

JAI PRESS

Research in Personnel and Human Resources Management

Edited by **Gerald R. Ferris,** *Institute of Labor and Industrial Relations, University of Illinois* and **Kendrith M. Rowland,** *Department of Business Administration, University of Illinois*

Volume 10, 1992, 389 pp. $63.50
ISBN 1-55938-427-1

Also Available:

JAI PRESS INC.

55 Old Post Road - No. 2   P.O. Box 1678
Greenwich, Connecticut 06836-1678
Tel: (203) 661-7602   Fax: (203)661-0792